New Language Learning and Teaching Environments

Series Editor
Hayo Reinders
Department of Education
Department of Languages
Anaheim University
King Mongkut's University of Technology Thonburi
Anaheim
Bangkok, New Zealand

New Language Learning and Teaching Environments is an exciting new book series edited by Hayo Reinders, dedicated to recent developments in learner-centred approaches and the impact of technology on learning and teaching inside and outside the language classroom. The series aims to:

- Publish cutting-edge research into current developments and innovation in language learning and teaching practice.
- Publish applied accounts of the ways in which these developments impact on current and future language education.
- Encourage dissemination and cross-fertilisation of policies and practice relating to learner-centred pedagogies for language learning and teaching in new learning environments.
- Disseminate research and best practice in out-of-class and informal language learning.

The series is a multidisciplinary forum for the very latest developments in language education, taking a pedagogic approach with a clear focus on the learner, and with clear implications for both researchers and language practitioners. It is the first such series to provide an outlet for researchers to publish their work, and the first stop for teachers interested in this area.

Sin Wang Chong • Hayo Reinders
Editors

Innovation in Language Learning and Teaching

The Case of England, Northern Ireland, Scotland, and Wales

Editors
Sin Wang Chong
University of St Andrews
St Andrews, UK

Hayo Reinders
Anaheim University
Anaheim, CA, USA

ISSN 2946-2932 ISSN 2946-2940 (electronic)
New Language Learning and Teaching Environments
ISBN 978-3-031-66240-9 ISBN 978-3-031-66241-6 (eBook)
https://doi.org/10.1007/978-3-031-66241-6

© The Editor(s) (if applicable) and The Author(s), under exclusive licence to Springer Nature Switzerland AG 2024

This work is subject to copyright. All rights are solely and exclusively licensed by the Publisher, whether the whole or part of the material is concerned, specifically the rights of translation, reprinting, reuse of illustrations, recitation, broadcasting, reproduction on microfilms or in any other physical way, and transmission or information storage and retrieval, electronic adaptation, computer software, or by similar or dissimilar methodology now known or hereafter developed.
The use of general descriptive names, registered names, trademarks, service marks, etc. in this publication does not imply, even in the absence of a specific statement, that such names are exempt from the relevant protective laws and regulations and therefore free for general use.
The publisher, the authors and the editors are safe to assume that the advice and information in this book are believed to be true and accurate at the date of publication. Neither the publisher nor the authors or the editors give a warranty, expressed or implied, with respect to the material contained herein or for any errors or omissions that may have been made. The publisher remains neutral with regard to jurisdictional claims in published maps and institutional affiliations.

Cover illustration : stellalevi/Getty Images.

This Palgrave Macmillan imprint is published by the registered company Springer Nature Switzerland AG.
The registered company address is: Gewerbestrasse 11, 6330 Cham, Switzerland

If disposing of this product, please recycle the paper.

Praise for *Innovation in Language Learning and Teaching*

"This book showcases the diversity of innovative practice across various language education sectors throughout the UK. It illustrates how pursuit of innovation is always purposeful, resourceful, and strategic. Against a backdrop of critical debate around the status of language education in the UK, the voices here collectively communicate a richly affirmative message and offer valuable local insights that have wider resonance across the field."
—Professor Ema Ushioda, *University of Warwick, England*

"In the age of Large Language Models (LLMs) and geopolitical upheaval, the art of language teaching faces a period of potential disruption. Yet, societal change and technological innovations have influenced how we teach language for millennia. From the expansion of the earliest empires, through the invention of the modern printing press, the mass displacement of the Huguenots, to the proliferation of word processing software, linguists and language teachers have always innovated in response to these changes.

This book offers insights into such innovations at all levels; from the classroom to government policies on language teaching across the four nations of the United Kingdom. Fresh perspectives on teaching methods, assessment, and collaborative provision are offered in what makes essential reading for the 21st century language teacher in the UK."
—Dr. Gabriel John Roberts, *Cardiff Metropolitan University, Wales*

"How is language education being innovated across the United Kingdom's four nations? This key question is empirically explored in the contributions to this collection, brought together in a 'conceptual framework of innovation in language education'. The core chapters represent diverse perspectives on innovation in modern foreign language and English language teaching across a wide range of institutional contexts, at classroom, module, curriculum, teacher education, and policy levels in England, Northern Ireland, Scotland, and Wales. Offering valuable insights to practitioners, policymakers, teacher educators, and education and applied linguistics researchers, this volume crucially emphasisesthe importance of dialogue and equitable partnership between these different groups."
—Dr. Viola Wiegand, *University of Stirling, Scotland*

"This volume represents a comprehensive and timely investigation of Language Education which brings to light the innovative spirit of linguists across the UK. Chong and Reinders' volume will be a great companion for those of us with interests in managing innovations in our own language education contexts: full of useful conceptual and practical learning opportunities and examples of excellence in innovation drawn from the four nations. Engagement with each of the chapters in this volume will inspire you to continue to meet the challenges the UK language education community faces with renewed enthusiasm and determination."

—Dr. Leanne Henderson, *Queen's University Belfast, Northern Ireland*

Contents

Part I Introduction   1

Innovation in Language Education in the United Kingdom:
Voices from the Four Nations   3
Sin Wang Chong and Hayo Reinders

Part II England   17

Introducing Flipped Learning to a Pre-Sessional English
for Academic Purposes Course in a Research-Intensive
University in England   19
Ben Nazer

Sustainable Language Programme Design and Management
at a Widening Participation University   41
Becky Muradás-Taylor and Rachel Wicaksono

Through the Lens of Culture: The Transformative Value
of a Content and Language Intercultural Learning Approach
in England   63
Ruth Koro

Part III Northern Ireland 99

The Evaluation of the Young Persons' Stepping-Stone Programme: A Pilot ESOL 16+ Course for Newcomers in Northern Ireland 101
Declan Flanagan, Susan Logue, and Christina Sevdali

Content and Language Integrated Learning: A Comparative Study in Northern Ireland 131
Sarah O'Neill

Part IV Scotland 155

Developing a Rationale for Teaching Local Languages to Young Language Learners: A Case Study of Teaching and Learning Chinese Language and Culture in a Scottish Primary School 157
David Roxburgh

Student Perceptions of the Effectiveness of Technology Enhanced Learning in Blended Learning Contexts During the COVID-19 Pandemic 179
Fiona Nimmo

Assessing Doctorateness in the Professional Doctorate Portfolio for Language Practitioners: From Publishability to Impact 205
Mark Carver

To Test or Not to Test? Assessing the English Proficiency of International Applicants to a Scottish University with Reference to Educational Background 225
Eoin Jordan

Part V Wales   257

Teaching Teaching: Challenges and Opportunities in the MFL Classroom   259
Christiane Günther and Greg Herman

Explicit Teaching of English Morphology and Etymology: Innovative Solutions to Developing Children's Word Decoding and Comprehension Skills in Wales   283
Ellen Bristow

Language Education for People Seeking Asylum in Wales: A Nation of Sanctuary Approach   307
Mike Chick and Barrie Llewelyn

Part VI Conclusion   329

Innovating Language Education in Partnership: The Less-Treaded Path   331
Sin Wang Chong and Hayo Reinders

Index   337

Notes on Contributors

Ellen Bristow is a researcher and tutor in Linguistics and academic writing at Cardiff and Cardiff Metropolitan Universities. Her research focuses on the development of children's metalinguistic skills and confidence in school classrooms. Ellen has previously worked as literacy teacher and Education Research Policy Assistant for the Welsh Government.

Mark Carver is Director of Postgraduate Research at the International Education and Lifelong Learning Institute at the University of St Andrews in Scotland, where he runs the Professional Doctorate programme in TESOL. Mark's research interests are in teacher professional learning, assessment and feedback, programme evaluation, and innovative qualitative methods.

Mike Chick has worked in language teaching for over twenty-five years. At the University of South Wales, he is a TESOL teacher education lecturer and is the University Refugee Champion. His research interests surround language education for migrants in Wales and he is currently researching social justice and language education.

Sin Wang Chong is Director of Research and Director of Impact and Innovation at the International Education and Lifelong Learning Institute, University of St Andrews, UK. Concurrently, he is Honorary Research Professor, Head of Evidence Synthesis, and Chair of Research

Ethics at the National Institute of Teaching in England. He founded and co-directs TESOLgraphics (tesolgraphics.com) to facilitate research-practice partnership.

Declan Flanagan is an English language practitioner with over twenty years of experience in various contexts (EFL ESOL, and EAL) and is currently a senior lecturer in EAP at Queen's University Belfast. He is also an education coordinator for Looked After Children (LAC) and unaccompanied minors within the Belfast: Health and Social Care Trust (HSC). Declan is a sociolinguist who studies the social and cultural factors influencing linguistic communication, particularly English language education provision. His current research focuses on the role of English language education in divided societies, intergroup relations, and equality/equity in education throughout Ireland. Declan has recently become the coordinator of the NATECLA (Island of Ireland) branch and IATEFL ESOL-SIG and the NATECLA Language Issues Journal editor.

Christiane Günther is Senior Lecturer in German in the Department of Modern Languages, Translation, and Interpreting at Swansea University teaching language and interpreting modules at both undergraduate and postgraduate level. Christiane was the lead of the development of the teaching pathway and coordinates the Introduction to Language Teaching module. Christiane is also a trainer for the Goethe-Institut in London and offers upskilling courses for primary and secondary school German language teachers.

Greg Herman is Senior Lecturer in French in the Department of Modern Languages, Translation and Interpreting at Swansea University. After completing his PhD (University of Aberdeen, 2013) he undertook a PGCE with the University of Cumbria, before taking up post at Swansea University. With an interest in pedagogy and second language acquisition, he played a key role in the design of the teaching pathway which is now embedded in the department's Modern Languages degree programme, and has contributed to outreach and widening participation.

Eoin Jordan is the Director of the International Education Institute at University of St Andrews. He leads the development of English language requirements for degree programmes across the university, and his research interests include: English as a Lingua Franca; World Englishes; peer assessment; educational technologies; vocabulary acquisition and assessment.

Ruth Koro taught Modern Languages in secondary schools in England, before joining the school of Education at the University of Nottingham. Her research focuses on approaches integrating language and culture, curriculum design to develop learners' intercultural understanding, and beginning teachers' readiness and capacity to promote intercultural understanding in their classrooms.

Barrie Llewelyn is Senior Lecturer in Creative Writing at the University of South Wales. Her research interest focuses on writing for wellbeing. She facilitates 'Speak to Me' a project that brings together local English speakers with English learners in creative workshops.

Susan Logue completed her PhD at Ulster University with a study which investigated the impact of biological, psychological, and environmental factors on newcomer children's language proficiency. Since then, Susan has completed research projects focusing on refugee and immigrant populations and their language ability as well as health sciences research.

Becky Muradás-Taylor is Associate Professor of Languages and Linguistics and Deputy Head for Programme Design in the School of Languages, Cultures and Societies at the University of Leeds. She was previously Associate Head: Curriculum Development in the School of Education, Language and Psychology at York St John University.

Ben Nazer is an associate lecturer who teaches, coordinates, and works on materials development and course design for pre-sessional courses at the UCL Centre for Languages and International Education. He has a Master's degree in Applied Linguistics and TESOL, a Postgraduate certificate in Higher Education, and is HEA Fellow.

Fiona Nimmo is a programme coordinator at the University of Strathclyde, a senior fellow of the Higher Education Academy, and a BALEAP assessor. Fiona designs and delivers on a range of cross-Faculty Academic Practice and TESOL/Teacher Education courses. She has a keen interest in professional development and holds a BEd, an MEd TESOL, and an MSc in Higher Education. Fiona is currently working towards a Doctorate in Education.

Sarah O'Neill is a qualified languages teacher and PhD research student in Modern Language Education Policy at Queen's University Belfast. Her PhD is entitled: Developing CLIL-informed Policy and Practice in Language Education. Her research investigates the policy traction of Content and Language Integrated Learning (CLIL) within the UK and Ireland.

Hayo Reinders is TESOL Professor and Director of Research at Anaheim University, USA and Professor of Applied Linguistics at KMUTT in Thailand. He founded the Institute for Teacher Leadership (www.teacherleadership.ac) to empower teachers and learners with research and leadership skills.

David Roxburgh is Senior Teaching Fellow with extensive experience of the Scottish primary curriculum. His research and scholarship focuses on the promotion of Mandarin Chinese, particularly its cultural base. More broadly, his interests relate to L3 frameworks, models and pedagogies as under-researched themes within Scotland's '1+2 policy' base, UK and other international contexts.

Christina Sevdali is a senior lecturer in linguistics at Ulster University. She works on historical linguistics and multilingualism. She also works on projects on language learning and support in primary and post-primary schools. She has published her research in Syntax, Natural language and linguistic theory and Glossa among others.

Rachel Wicaksono is Professor of TESOL and Applied Linguistics, and Head of the School of Education, Language and Psychology, at York St John University. She is Higher Education Academy National Teaching Fellow and member of the British Association for Applied Linguistics Executive Committee.

List of Figures

Innovation in Language Education in the United Kingdom: Voices from the Four Nations

Fig. 1	A conceptual framework of innovation in language education	8

Sustainable Language Programme Design and Management at a Widening Participation University

Fig. 1	Below average tariff universities offering languages, adapted from Muradás-Taylor and Taylor (2024)	44

The Evaluation of the Young Persons' Stepping-Stone Programme: A Pilot ESOL 16+ Course for Newcomers in Northern Ireland

Fig. 1	The Project phases of the Young Persons' Stepping-Stone Project	105
Fig. 2	16+ESOL routes to learning resources: Glasgow Clyde College (Ma & Richardson, 2019)	107
Fig. 3	Chart showing language complexity scores for Language Assessment 1 and Language Assessment 2	112
Fig. 4	Boxplot showing language proficiency scores (MLU Score) for Language Assessment 1 and Language Assessment 2	113

Fig. 5	Chart showing well-being scores from the Outcomes Star Assessment at the beginning and end of the project	115
Fig. 6	Boxplot showing the mean Outcomes Star well-being scores at the beginning (Assessment 1) and end of the project (Assessment 2)	116
Fig. 7	Chart showing the scores for prosocial behaviour at assessments 1 and 2	117
Fig. 8	Boxplot showing the mean prosocial behaviour scores at the beginning (Prosocial Assessment 1) and end of the project (Prosocial Assessment 2)	118
Fig. 9	Chart showing the scores for emotional problems at assessments 1 and 2	119
Fig. 10	Boxplot showing the mean emotional problems scores at the beginning (Assessment 1) and end of the project (Assessment 2)	120
Fig. 11	Chart showing the interaction between prosocial behaviour and language proficiency	121
Fig. 12	Chart showing the interaction between emotional problems and language proficiency	122

Content and Language Integrated Learning: A Comparative Study in Northern Ireland

Fig. 1	Proportion of pupils in agreement by school (pre-test)	140

Developing a Rationale for Teaching Local Languages to Young Language Learners: A Case Study of Teaching and Learning Chinese Language and Culture in a Scottish Primary School

Fig. 1	Representation of the transdisciplinary framework (Douglas Fir Group, 2016, p. 25)	164
Fig. 2	I understand why I am learning CLC (by total, $N = 374$)	166
Fig. 3	I would like to continue learning CLC in secondary school (by total, $N = 374$)	168
Fig. 4	Traditional vs. innovative pedagogies promoting CLC (Roxburgh, 2021)	169

List of Figures   xvii

Student Perceptions of the Effectiveness of Technology Enhanced Learning in Blended Learning Contexts During the COVID-19 Pandemic

Fig. 1   Prisma Statement. (Adapted from Page M. J., McKenzie J. E., Bossuyt P.M., Boutron I., Hoffmann T. C., Mulrow C. D., et al. (2021). The PRISMA 2020 statement: an updated guideline for reporting systematic reviews. *British Medical Journal, 372*:71)   184

To Test or Not to Test? Assessing the English Proficiency of International Applicants to a Scottish University with Reference to Educational Background

Fig. 1   (a) Sample language profile (Retrieved from https://www.st-andrews.ac.uk/subjects/entry/language-requirements/profiles/7-d/); (b) Sample language profile (Retrieved from https://www.st-andrews.ac.uk/subjects/entry/language-requirements/profiles/7-s/)   239

Fig. 2   List of language profiles with associated CEFR thresholds (Retrieved from https://www.st-andrews.ac.uk/subjects/entry/language-requirements/profiles/reference-tables/)   240

Fig. 3   Timeline of English language entry requirement developments (pre-2019 to 2024)   250

Explicit Teaching of English Morphology and Etymology: Innovative Solutions to Developing Children's Word Decoding and Comprehension Skills in Wales

Fig. 1   Morphology-based descriptions of learning in the LLC AoLE   287

Fig. 2   Etymology-based descriptions of learning in the LLC AoLE   288

Innovating Language Education in Partnership: The Less-Treaded Path

Fig. 1   An innovation ecosystem for language education   334

List of Tables

Introducing Flipped Learning to a Pre-Sessional English for Academic Purposes Course in a Research-Intensive University in England

Table 1	Typical weekly timetable for a face-to-face student pre-pandemic	26
Table 2	Typical 'flipped learning' day for a Chinese student	28

Through the Lens of Culture: The Transformative Value of a Content and Language Intercultural Learning Approach in England

Table 1	Framework for transformative intercultural CLIL pedagogy	76
Table 2	Pre- and post-test students' first responses on the benefits of language learning ($N = 60$)	83

The Evaluation of the Young Persons' Stepping-Stone Programme: A Pilot ESOL 16+ Course for Newcomers in Northern Ireland

Table 1	Examples of expressive grammatical forms from Language Assessment 1 (pre-intervention) and Language Assessment 2 (post-intervention)	113

Table 2	Impact of prosocial well-being from the fitted model on accuracy of MLU	122
Table 3	Impact of emotional problems from fitted model on accuracy of MLU	122

Content and Language Integrated Learning: A Comparative Study in Northern Ireland

Table 1	Counts and frequencies of pupils completing a matched pre-/post-questionnaire by school type, gender, FSME and type of approach	139

Developing a Rationale for Teaching Local Languages to Young Language Learners: A Case Study of Teaching and Learning Chinese Language and Culture in a Scottish Primary School

Table 1	Categorisation of pupils' open-ended responses to reasons for learning CLC (by total, $N = 374$)	167

Student Perceptions of the Effectiveness of Technology Enhanced Learning in Blended Learning Contexts During the COVID-19 Pandemic

Table 1	PICOSS table	182
Table 2	SCOPUS	182
Table 3	ERIC	183
Table 4	Descriptive data	187

Assessing Doctorateness in the Professional Doctorate Portfolio for Language Practitioners: From Publishability to Impact

Table 1	Expansion of the concept of doctorateness to incorporate professional values relevant to DProf TESOL	211
Table 2	Key guiding values for innovations	219

To Test or Not to Test? Assessing the English Proficiency of International Applicants to a Scottish University with Reference to Educational Background

Table 1 CEFR scale for language profiles with IELTS alignment   238

Explicit Teaching of English Morphology and Etymology: Innovative Solutions to Developing Children's Word Decoding and Comprehension Skills in Wales

Table 1 Morphological analysis of high/low frequency words in the GCSE word corpus   294

Table 2 Etymologies of high/low frequency words in the GCSE word corpus   300

Part I

Introduction

Innovation in Language Education in the United Kingdom: Voices from the Four Nations

Sin Wang Chong and Hayo Reinders

1 Language Education Provision in the United Kingdom

Despite being a largely Anglophone country, the population of the United Kingdom is increasingly diverse in terms of its cultural, ethnic, and linguistic backgrounds. According to the 2021 census, 81.7% of regular residents in England and Wales were "White", of which 74.4% were "English, Welsh, Scottish, Northern Irish or British". People who identified themselves as "White" decreased from 86.0% 10 years ago, with those belonging to the "English, Welsh, Scottish, Northern Irish or British" category diminishing from 80.5% in 2011 and 87.5% in 2001

S. W. Chong (✉)
University of St Andrews, St Andrews, UK
e-mail: swc5@st-andrews.ac.uk

H. Reinders
Anaheim University, Anaheim, CA, USA

© The Author(s), under exclusive license to Springer Nature Switzerland AG 2024
S. W. Chong, H. Reinders (eds.), *Innovation in Language Learning and Teaching*, New Language Learning and Teaching Environments, https://doi.org/10.1007/978-3-031-66241-6_1

(Office for National Statistics, 2022). There are similar trends in Scotland and in Northern Ireland. In Scotland, the 2011 census[1] noted the decrease of the "White" ethnic group from 98.0% in 2001 to 96.0% in 2011, while people identifying as "Asian", most notably "Pakistani" and "Chinese", almost doubled from 2001 to 2011 (Scotland's Census, 2023). In Northern Ireland, the 2021 census revealed that the percentage of ethnic minorities doubled when compared with figures in 2011 and quadrupled when viewed against the 2001 data (Northern Ireland Statistics and Research Agency, 2023). In terms of languages that are spoken in the United Kingdom, the above census data show that there are more than 600 languages spoken in the four nations, which is six times more than in 1979. Minority languages most commonly spoken in England and Wales are Polish, Romanian, Punjabi, Urdu, and Portuguese (Office for National Statistics, 2022). Minority languages used in Scotland are Scots, Gaelic, Polish, Urdu, and Punjabi (Scotland's Census, 2023) and those in Northern Ireland are Polish, Lithuanian, Irish, Romanian, and Portuguese (Northern Ireland Statistics and Research Agency, 2023).

There are many reasons contributing to the diversification of the languages in use in the United Kingdom. Education policies play a major part. In England, for example, although its scope of implementation is contestable, the 2014 Primary National Curriculum made language learning compulsory in primary schools at Key Stage 2 (age 7–11) (Department for Education, 2013). In Scotland, a notable illustration is the "1+2 Languages" policy introduced in 2020–2021 that aims to teach all pupils aged 5 and above a modern language from Primary 1 and a second modern language from Primary 5 (Scottish Government, 2017). The Welsh Government published their Welsh language strategy action plan for 2023–2024, where they acknowledge the importance of "creating bilingual citizens" (Welsh Government, 2023). Across the Irish Sea, the "Languages for the Future" strategy for Northern Ireland outlines the need for cultivating language capacity for multilingual and multicultural communication (Department of Education, 2012). In addition to government-led language education initiatives, more people immigrate to

---

[1] Ethnicity data of Census 2022 are not yet published at the time of writing.

the United Kingdom for work, study, family reunion, and humanitarian reasons. In 2023, the number of entry clearance visas granted was 20% higher than that in 2022, with more work and study visas granted than in 2019 (UK Government, 2024). With more migrants residing in the United Kingdom, there is also a concomitant need for adult language provision, or ESOL (English for Speakers of Other Languages), for asylum seekers, refugees, and migrants, much of which is run by locally run charitable organisations.

Being the third most popular country for international students in the world, the United Kingdom hosts an increasing number of international university students (UNESCO Institute for Statistics, 2021). The number of sponsored study visas granted in 2023 was 70% greater than in 2019, with 90% of them for higher education (UK Government, 2024). International students in higher education made up a large proportion of the total student population in 2021–2022; most notably, nearly half (45%) of the postgraduate student population in the United Kingdom are international students (HESA, 2023). With such an enormous number of international university students studying in the four countries, the provision of language support is crucial to ensure they have a positive learning experience. Accordingly, universities in the United Kingdom offer pre-sessional English for Academic Purposes courses for international students, with some offered in-house and others outsourced to a provider. In addition to pre-sessional language courses, it is common for UK universities to offer in-sessional support, which can take the form of one-off workshops, seminars, or one-on-one consultations. Staff working in in-sessional support collaborate with academic staff in departments and schools, as well as in the libraries, student support services units, and so on, to develop language support strategies specific to the needs of all students. Support mostly focuses on academic writing, but also other areas such as discipline-specific language support. Some universities have a dedicated self-access language learning centre that hosts a wide range of online resources (e.g. books, videos, language exam preparation resources), where students can learn English based on their interests and needs on their own.

2 Opportunities and Challenges

In recent years, there have been heated debates and controversial claims about the value of language education in the United Kingdom. The benefits for language learning in schools and universities are regularly featured in the media and include developing a person's "cultural sensitivity, international awareness and a global mindset" (*The Guardian*, 2014). Moreover, learning an additional language proves to be conducive to an individual's employability and social mobility because there are more jobs that require employees to travel around the world (CBI/Pearson, 2019). English, which has traditionally been viewed as the world's lingua franca, is no longer the only dominating language used in the international economy (The British Academy, Born Global, 2014).

However, this positive viewpoint is only part of the picture. In July 2023, the UK government announced plans to impose a limit on the number of students universities can recruit for the so-called rip-off degrees, that is, programmes that have high dropout rates or programmes that have a low employment success rate of graduates. At the time of writing, several universities including the University of Aberdeen in Scotland and the University of Kent in England have announced plans to shut down or phase out their modern languages programmes, and Birkbeck, University of London, has made a statement about an institutional restructure that includes merging several departments, including the departments of English and Language, Cultures and Applied Linguistics, despite hosting some of the most prestigious language degrees in the countries. In school education, there is a lack of resources allocated to training modern languages teachers and for learners to access foreign language learning opportunities, especially in socio-economically disadvantaged areas (Tinsley & Board, 2017).

Nevertheless, the picture is not all gloomy. Despite the lack of government/institutional support and resources, linguists, teachers, the third sector, and many who are involved in language education are working hard to find innovative solutions to ensure that the United Kingdom continues to offer world-class language learning experiences to local and international students. A recent example is the establishment of *The*

Languages Gateway, which aims to "help increase language-learning across the UK by facilitating access to existing opportunities and information, by increasing awareness of them, and by fostering links between different sectors" (The Languages Gateway, 2024). This project, which is co-developed by the British Academy, the Arts and Humanities Research Council, the association of School and College Leaders, the British Council, and Universities UK, is a quintessential example to illustrate partnerships among teachers, academics, government officials, and funders to curate resources and events about learning of languages that are available in the United Kingdom. There are also professional associations and learned societies in the four nations that advocate for excellence in language learning and teaching such as the Association for Language Learning Northern Association of Teachers of English to Speakers of Other Languages, Scottish Association for Teaching English as a Foreign Language, the British Association for Applied Linguistics, Linguistics Association of Great Britain, University Council for Languages, and the British Association of Lecturers in English for Academic Purposes, to name but a few. Innovation and advocacy of excellence needs to be supported by robust research evidence and cultivation of a scholarship culture where language teachers and teacher educators have a space for documenting, experimenting, and reflecting on their own pedagogical practices. Some of these professional communities are provided by university centres that have an explicit focus on involving language education practitioners in research, such as the Centre for Excellence in Language Teaching at the University of Leeds, which publishes its own journal, *The Language Scholar*, for English for Academic Purposes professionals. The Northern Ireland Centre for Information on Language Teaching and Research conducts its own research on language learning policies in the United Kingdom and Ireland, and provides resources and training opportunities for teaching modern foreign languages, working directly with language teachers. Such initiatives are evidence of continued excellence in language education in the four nations and are illustrations of the focus of this collection of chapters.

3 Conceptualising Innovation in Language Education

The collection of reports and reflections in this book is a testimony of the wealth of enthusiasm, expertise, and knowledge in language education in the four nations. While editing this book, we were constantly encouraged by the narratives from language teachers and researchers about their inventive practices, and were most impressed by their determination and creativity in bringing about change and improvement in spite of the current challenges. Reading the chapters in this book has prompted us to rethink the meaning of "innovation" and its multifaceted nature. It has also given us insight into the variables contributing to the likelihood of success of different projects and programmes. Based on the collective wisdom offered by the contributors to this book, we put forward a conceptual framework for understanding innovation in language education (Fig. 1). We hope readers will find this framework not only relevant to the United Kingdom but also other contexts. While the framework may not be exhaustive, we aim to distil our thoughts on instigating, implementing, and evaluating innovation in language education. In what

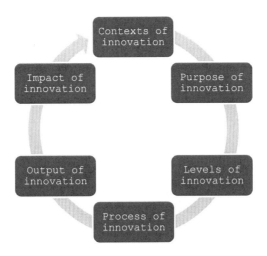

Fig. 1 A conceptual framework of innovation in language education

follows, we will unpack each element in the framework while pointing to chapters in this book when appropriate.

Contexts of Innovation

There is no one-size-fits-all approach to innovation; one innovation may gain traction in one context but have limited success in another. It is vital that language teachers and researchers who embark on an innovative project first consider the contexts where the innovation will be implemented. We would like to emphasise the plurality of the notion of "contexts", as we and our projects are all situated in various environments simultaneously. Ecological Systems Theory posits that there are at least four levels of context: *micro* (contexts an individual is directly involved in), *meso* (contexts an individual is indirectly involved in), *macro* (contexts an individual is not involved in but is influenced by), and *chrono* (the past, present, and future of contextual changes) (Chong et al., 2023).

For the purpose of illustration, consider the case of Beatrice, who is a Spanish teacher in a secondary school in England. Beatrice teaches three classes of pupils (micro-context), following the scheme of work of the language curriculum at their school (meso-context). At the same time, what is covered in the scheme of work is by and large influenced by the government's policy to make learning a foreign language compulsory at schools (macro-context); Beatrice and her colleagues also have more frequent discussions on the increasing use of artificial intelligence in learning Spanish (chrono-context). Adopting an ecological perspective on innovation in language education is crucial because, by considering the multiple contexts in which one is situated, we can recgonise the affordances and constraints in each context, and consider how an innovative idea can maximise its benefits for learners and teachers while operating within the confines of institutional, societal, or cultural limitations. An ecological view also entails innovators becoming aware that people are shaped by the environments they are in; at the same time, people, who are agentic beings, (re-)create the environments around them.

"Contexts" are both spatial/material and relational. Returning to our example in the previous paragraph about the Spanish teacher, Beatrice, her awareness of her surroundings is not limited to the physical environments she is in or the resources at her disposal (e.g. funding support, availability of teaching materials) but also includes the people who she interacts with, including her pupils, her colleagues, her line manager, the school principal, officials from the Department for Education, and the wider societal discourse about the values for learning Spanish, as well as the cultures and values they represent. The relational aspect of "contexts" is crucial because it influences who may be willing to be involved in the innovative endeavour and its ultimate impact and sustainability.

Purpose of Innovation

Successful innovation is not about innovating for its own sake or reinventing the wheel. We acknowledge that the term "innovation" is sometimes misused by policymakers or school leaders to promote their own political and educational agenda, which, more often than not, is initiated from the top down. *Innovation is about identifying opportunities and creative and context-specific solutions for real-world problems or improvements on current practices.* There is an array of purposes for designing and implementing an innovation for language education, which we broadly categorise as *proactive, reactive,* and *shared. Proactive* purposes are those that relate to the improvement of current practices, such as improving students' proficiency in the target language. For example, evidence from a meta-analysis may show the benefits of peer feedback for L2 writing skills in quasi-experimental settings. A group of teachers may come across this evidence and attempt to implement peer feedback in intact classes. Some innovations may be a *reaction* to certain requirements or problems; an unexpected influx of refugees may prompt the immediate provision of additional language support. In an ideal world, the purpose for exploring an innovative practice is *shared* among all parties concerned such as students, teachers, schools, and policymakers, but we acknowledge that this is rarely the case. In our experience, purposes that are proactive and shared are far more likely to lead to successful and sustainable innovation and impact.

There are a number of additional caveats when discussing innovation. For example, although innovation involves change, not every change is an innovation. Similarly, although every innovation offers something "new", the nature of that novelty is subjective, and context-dependent. For example, the use of mobile devices to learn languages may not be considered groundbreaking in the United Kingdom but it may be perceived as innovative in other countries where access to technology is emerging. And on the role of technology, it will be clear to everyone who has lived through the pandemic that such technology-supported changes as "emergency remote language teaching" do not necessarily involve and are certainly not equivalent to pedagogical improvement; the role of technology, although often a driver of innovation, is ambiguous. The key consideration is not the object of change (the intended "product") but how that change is implemented (the "process"). Does it affect practices in a sustainable manner, for example, ensuring that changes are not short term and reversed when the project is "over"? Does it enhance stakeholders' (teachers/learners/administrators) skills and wellbeing or does it draw resources away from everyday practices? Does it enhance effectiveness (pedagogical outcomes), or only efficiency (reducing costs)?

Process of Innovation

Reviewing the chapters of the book, we identify four pathways to designing and implementing an innovation: *practitioner-led*, *researcher-led*, *manager/policy-led*, and *partnership*. The "practitioner-led" and "partnership" pathways are considered more bottom-up, informal, and sustainable while the "researcher-led" and "manager/policy-led" tracks are more top-down, formal, and, often, short-lived.

Practitioner-led innovation begins with a group of teachers who are intrinsically motivated to improve their own teaching practice or students' performance, or a small team of colleagues who are interested in deepening their understanding of a particular aspect of teaching (e.g. use of formative assessment). They use their own time to engage in activities such as starting a journal club to know more about what research has to say about effective language teaching. They then share their understanding and decide on a topic that they would like to experiment with. Depending on their level of commitment, these teachers may co-design a lesson based on the topic of interest and observe each other's lessons. They may also collect students' views about their experiences. If the lessons are successful, they may invite other colleagues to observe their class and discuss scaling up the innovation with their line manager.

Innovation in the form of partnership involves multiple parties working collaboratively to achieve a shared goal. This can sometimes be confused with "researcher-led" or "manager/policy-led" innovation. Different from the latter two, partnership in innovation is exemplified through an equal level of commitment, involvement, and leadership of different parties in the process of innovation. While a "researcher-led" innovation may be a project led by a team of academics who enter a school to collect data about how an innovative practice is implemented and its usefulness, partnership in innovation involves projects that are co-designed and enacted by both teachers and researchers. Obviously, teachers and researchers play different roles in the project, but they complement each other in terms of expertise and experience. A case in point is that teachers will lead on the design of the innovative pedagogy while the researchers will be in charge of designing an intervention and observation study to collect empirical data to inform the next iteration of practice. Partnership in innovation also differs from "manager-/policy-led" innovation, which is one that is advocated by school managers or government officials in policy documents but the impetus for such innovation may not be shared by teachers.

Levels of Innovation

The contributions in this book shed important light on the various levels of innovation, including classroom, module, curriculum, teacher education, and policy. *Classroom-level innovation* concerns pedagogies and instructional approaches. Some pedagogical innovations documented in this book include translanguaging (Chap. 5), content language integrated learning (CLIL) (Chap. 6), teaching languages to young learners (Chap. 7), and the use of technology in a language classroom (Chap. 8). At a *module level*, we see examples of innovative pedagogical practices that are employed consistently throughout a course, such as the use of flipped learning in an English for Academic Purposes module in England (Chap. 2) and multiple ways that modern foreign languages courses can be designed (Chap. 11). At a *curriculum level*, innovation refers to cycles of programme (re-)design, implementation, and evaluation. Through analysing programme and module enrollment data, Muradás-Taylor and Wicaksono (Chap. 3) reflect on their journey to revamp the language programme provision at a widening participation university that successfully improved student intake and experience. Innovation can also be about *teacher education* that aims to improve the quality of initial teacher education and continuous professional development of language teachers (East, 2022). We see examples such as the development and critical reflection of a portfolio-based online professional doctorate at a research-intensive Scottish university for English language teachers (Chap. 9) and the introduction of a creative and participatory pedagogy in ESOL teacher education, one that focuses on learners' everyday needs and concerns (Chap. 13). At a *university policy level*, we are pleased to include a chapter on the development of procedures and guidance for assessing English language proficiency levels of international students using a holistic, transparent, and inclusive approach at a Scottish university (Chap. 10).

Output and Impact of Innovation

The last two dimensions in our framework are the output and impact of an innovation. Output and impact are intertwined but are not synonymous. Output concerns the product of the innovation, the tangible aspect of the innovation process such as an adapted CLIL pedagogical approach (Chaps. 5 and 6), a revamped module using flipped learning principles and practices (Chap. 2), merging of language programmes (Chap. 3), a new professional doctorate programme for language teachers (Chap. 9), or a new set of criteria for assessing English language proficiency levels of international students (Chap. 10). On the other hand, the impact of an innovation is more difficult to capture. It can relate to observable outcomes, such as improvements in language proficiency, increased student intake numbers, or number of staff engaged in professional development. Some impact may be less visible, such as improvement in learners' attitudes, or teachers' reported wellbeing.

It is important to recognise also that not all aspects of impact relate to the *product* of the innovation (e.g. increased retention rates as a result of the implementation of a new support programme). Equally, participating in the process of conceiving of and implementing an innovation can have its own benefits, such as better working relationships with colleagues, a deeper understanding of the organisation, or the development of new skills. The most sustainable projects are those that not only achieve their intended outcomes, but lead to greater agency of all stakeholders as a result.

4 Conclusion

As discussed at the outset of this chapter, the state-of-play in language education in the United Kingdom presents unique opportunities and challenges to learners, teachers, policymakers, and researchers. The contributions to this book are therefore timely, as true innovation is needed now more than ever. With a collection of 12 reflective accounts of the impetus, process, and evaluation of innovations at the classroom, module, programme, teacher education, and policy levels, we hope that this book serves as a beacon of hope and a source of inspiration for teachers, teacher educators, policymakers, and researchers in the four nations who are involved in language education. We are pleased that this book provides a comprehensive view on the innovation that is currently taking place in the four nations, with three England-based contributions, two contributions from Northern Ireland, four chapters from Scotland, and three chapters from Wale. These chapters capture innovative practices in a wide array of contexts including primary education, secondary education, higher education, and adult education. Despite the differences in the political and socio-economic situations of the four nations, one overarching theme from these chapters is the unwavering determination of language educators to constantly improve the quality of language instruction and their fervent belief that language learning benefits individuals, and society as a whole.

We invite you to be inspired and encouraged by the adventures of our contributors and pay it forward in your own contexts.

References

CBI/Pearson. (2019). *Education and learning for the modern world.* CBI/Pearson Education and Skills Survey Report 2019. https://www.cbi.org.uk/media/3841/12546_tess_2019.pdf

Chong, S. W., Isaacs, T., & McKinley, J. (2023). Ecological systems theory and second language research. *Language Teaching, 56*, 333–348. https://doi.org/10.1017/s0261444822000283

Department for Education. (2013). National curriculum in England: Primary curriculum. https://www.gov.uk/government/publications/national-curriculum-in-england-primary-curriculum

Department of Education. (2012). Languages for the future: Northern Ireland languages strategy. https://www.education-ni.gov.uk/publications/languages-future-northern-ireland-languages-strategy-final-report

East, M. (2022). *Mediating innovation through language teacher education.* Cambridge University Press.

Higher Education Student Data. (2023). Where do HE students come from? https://www.hesa.ac.uk/data-and-analysis/students/where-from

Northern Ireland Statistics and Research Agency. (2023). *Census 2021.* https://www.nisra.gov.uk/statistics/census/2021-census#:~:text=Information%20on%20Census%202021%20in,in%20Northern%20Ireland%20was%20768%2C810

Office for National Statistics. (2022). Census 2021. https://www.ons.gov.uk/census

Scotland's Census. (2023). *Census 2021 results.* https://www.scotlandscensus.gov.uk/search-the-census#/

Scottish Government. (2017). 1+2 languages: A continuing policy. https://www.gov.scot/publications/1-2-languages-continuing-policy/

The British Academy. (2014). Born Global. https://www.thebritishacademy.ac.uk/projects/born-global/

The Guardian. (2014). Learning languages is key to UK's success in the global economy. https://www.theguardian.com/education/0014/jun/19/learning-language-key-to-economic-success

The Languages Gateway. (2024). The languages gateway. https://www.thelanguagesgateway.uk/

Tinsley, T., & Board, K. (2017). Language trends 2016/17: Language teaching in primary and secondary schools in England. https://www.britishcouncil.org/sites/default/files/language_trends_survey_2017_0.pdf

UK Government. (2024). Immigration system statistics, year ending December 2023. https://www.gov.uk/government/statistics/immigration-system-statistics-year-ending-december-2023

UNESCO Institute for Statistics. (2021). Global flow of tertiary-level students. https://uis.unesco.org/en/uis-student-flow

Welsh Government. (2023). *Cymraeg 2050: Welsh language strategy action plan 2023 to 2024*. https://www.gov.wales/cymraeg-2050-welsh-language-strategy-action-plan-2023-2024-html#:~:text=2023%20to%202024%20will%20be,synthetic%20Welsh%20and%20bilingual%20voices

Part II

England

Introducing Flipped Learning to a Pre-Sessional English for Academic Purposes Course in a Research-Intensive University in England

Ben Nazer

1   Introduction

The COVID-19 pandemic caused disruption to UK universities as the first lockdown in March 2020 forced many to adapt their courses for online delivery. Initial approaches to managing this could best be described (in many cases) as 'emergency online teaching' (Hodges et al., 2020). However, O'dea and Stern (2022) argue that universities adapted quickly, and that this disruption accelerated interest in digital pedagogies. I was part of a team that developed materials for a pre-sessional English for Academic Purposes (EAP) course at a traditional UK university as it was adapted for online delivery. Part of the process of adapting the course was to introduce a flipped learning approach. In the pages that follow,

B. Nazer (✉)
University College London, London, UK
e-mail: b.nazer@ucl.ac.uk

flipped learning is introduced with some information about the particular context for its introduction. This is explored further through a literature review exploring the potential benefits of flipped learning as well as the impetus for introducing the approach in our context.

Following that is a personal reflection of what worked and what did not as we iterated the development of our course. At the end of each summer, we collected student and teacher feedback, ran focus groups, and responded to external examiner reports. Through reflecting on these strands of feedback, we were able to improve our delivery model. This chapter focuses on responses to the summer 2020, 2021, and 2022 courses. It is important to stress that these are personal reflections. Reporting on all the information collected, and all the changes made to improve the course each year, is outside the scope of a single chapter. Rather, this is a selective focus on specific areas of concern relevant to the flipped learning approach.

2 What Is Flipped Learning?

According to Birgili et al. (2021), the origins of flipped learning lie in the work of John Bergmann and Aeron Sams who initially used the term "flipped classroom" to refer to their work in United States schools. Bergmann and Sams (2014, p. xi) themselves suggest that flipped learning in their context came from the realisation that asking students to watch video lectures directly explaining key concepts allowed them to focus on "group work and individualized attention" in class. The Flipped Learning Network, described as a "non-profit online community" (Flipped Learning Network, 2016), released an official definition in 2014:

> Flipped Learning is a pedagogical approach in which direct instruction moves from the group learning space to the individual learning space, and the resulting group space is transformed into a dynamic, interactive learning environment where the educator guides students as they apply concepts and engage creatively in the subject matter. (Flipped Learning Network, 2014)

It is useful, in considering this definition, to consider exactly what the authors mean by 'direct instruction'. Unfortunately, as noted in Heward and Twyman (2021), this term is contested and there are multiple definitions. Cronje (2020) makes a helpful distinction between direct instruction and learning-by-doing. There are situations (e.g. where there is a simple established procedure to reach a solution) where students are best simply provided with information—directly instructed—and learning-by-doing would be a waste of time. While flipped learning is sometimes associated with passively watching videos, the definition above suggests it can apply to any organisational approach where tasks which require less interactive engagement are completed before class to prioritise learning-by-doing in class.

This idea of learning-by-doing and the "dynamic, interactive learning environment" (Flipped Learning Network, 2014) is closely linked to the concept of active learning. Active learning is described by Talbert and Mor-Avi (2019) as based on active participation and the completion of tasks, as compared to passively receiving information or taking notes. There has been considerable research interest in active learning, and studies show the effectiveness of active learning models (Freeman et al., 2014; Nguyen et al., 2021). Active learning, then, suggests a way of thinking about what to do in class time using a flipped approach. However, Li et al. (2021) note that, while the link between flipped learning and active learning is often referred to, many flipped learning studies are vague on their theoretical underpinnings. Despite the official definition, the loosely described nature of flipped learning in practice could in part explain its popularity, as it can be pragmatically employed in different ways.

Jenkins et al. (2017) offer a way to pin down the potentially loose nature of flipped learning by suggesting that we view flipped learning design as a common-sense pedagogical strategy that supports active and engaged learning. While Bergmann and Sams (2014, pp. 24–25) make rather bold claims that flipped learning is a "transformational method" and a "grass roots movement", I feel that a significantly more modest view is appropriate. Rather than thinking of flipped learning as a unified method that offers a framework for managing classes and developing learning materials, it is simply an organising strategy. Encouraging students to complete work independently can then support active learning in class. Put in these terms, flipped learning is less of an innovation or groundbreaking approach, and more a way of thinking about how and when to stage activities. Learning more suited to direct instruction or individual learning does not waste class time, but supports tasks which are more suited to active learning and learning-by-doing, such that the latter can be more successful when classmates are available.

3 Information About the Specific Context: Pre-Sessional EAP in the United Kingdom

Pre-sessional courses are widespread in universities across the United Kingdom and are typically short student-funded courses taken in the summer to prepare international students for academic study in their chosen discipline (Pearson, 2020). According to Universities UK (2022), England is very well represented as the destination for 82% of international students across the four nations in 2020–2021, compared to around 6% for Northern Ireland and Wales combined, with Scotland accounting for around 12% of the market. However, these contexts are similar in the sense that pre-sessional courses are widely seen as a way of increasing access to degree programmes for students whose language requirements are below the requested IELTS level. This allows universities to accept and attract more international students who typically pay higher fees (Pearson, 2020). Our institution, typical also to Thorpe et al.'s (2017) discussion, allows international students to attain a provisional offer for study on their postgraduate or undergraduate degree programme if they are short of the usual language requirement. As such, pre-sessional courses have both academic and gatekeeping purposes. Students must pass the course to demonstrate they have sufficient language skills to study in an institution where English is the medium of instruction. This is relevant to the introduction of flipped learning as our pre-sessional course is short and intense with students who are highly motivated by the need to pass.

The nature of the course also impacts the kinds of teaching and learning activities that are appropriate. As discussed in Tomlinson and Masuhara (2017), language learning is gradual and implicit, such that declarative knowledge about language does not necessarily lead to acquisition; much language learning is learning-by-doing. On a longer course, materials can be designed to encourage implicit learning of complex systems. However, the intense nature of a pre-sessional means that courses often rely more on the explicit teaching of concepts. For example, learning what an argument is in academic writing, and how it can be expressed as a series of claims (Wingate, 2012), is knowledge that can be learned, can be relatively easily memorised, and can improve a student's essay writing. The need for such concepts to be conveyed for students through direct instruction is an example of where pre-sessional courses may be particularly suited to a flipped learning approach.

4   Exploring the Case for a Flipped Learning Approach

In this section I consider studies relevant to introducing flipped learning to an EAP course. As alluded to above, and in Charles and Pecorari (2016), EAP draws from a range of pedagogical approaches, as well as being related to English Language Teaching (ELT). As such, flipped learning studies of interest include those in general academic contexts, especially higher education, as well as in language learning-specific contexts.

Taking a broad approach to better understanding the contexts and purposes of flipped learning research, Birgili et al. (2021) reviewed over 300 research and conceptual articles published between 2012 and 2018. The authors make a strong claim that their content analyses of studies related to the flipped learning approach "prove" that it is effective in a range of contexts, with a positive effect on student outcomes (Birgili et al., 2021, p. 382). However, other meta-analyses make more modest claims. Cheng et al. (2019, p. 813), for example, did note a positive impact, but described this as "trivial to small under a random-effects model". The authors speculate that with such a small impact, it may not be appropriate to invest time and energy in switching to a flipped learning instructional strategy.

Similarly, Låg and Sæle's (2019) meta-analysis of 272 studies found that flipped learning benefits student outcomes; however, they also noted that the overall effect was very small. The authors did note, encouragingly for EAP, that the effect was larger when considering language learning courses, and they speculate that such courses could, in fact, be particularly suitable for flipped learning. Looking specifically at flipped learning for language study, Vitta and Al-Hoorie (2020) found that such approaches can be effective in terms of student outcomes. However, a key finding mirrored in Låg and Sæle (2019) and Cheng et al. (2019) is that the three meta-analyses showed a great deal of heterogeneity, suggesting that there are a range of factors that can influence the success of flipped learning and results may be more about the execution than the method.

As Vitta and Al-Hoorie (2020) note, the important question is less whether flipped learning is effective, as it clearly can be, and more how to make it work in specific contexts. As Låg and Sæle (2019) suggest, we might expect the strategy to work if it involves other examples of good practice. The importance of student-to-student social interaction is also relevant. Foldnes (2016) compared two strategies for flipped learning. One strategy employed individual study and guided tuition, with no specific support for group work. The second strategy added a cooperative learning element "where active learning is implemented through cooperative teamwork" (Foldnes, 2016, p. 43). Perhaps unsurprisingly, Foldnes (2016) found that adding a cooperative element to flipped learning had a significant impact on outcomes.

This echoes a point already made: it seems reasonable to argue that a flipped learning approach can benefit students if it helps to prioritise class time towards active learning. Major (2020) argues that collaborative work similar to the model Foldnes (2016) described is an effective way to achieve active learning in higher education. While a distinction can be made between cooperative learning and collaborative learning (Davidson & Major, 2014), the essential aspect is to encourage students to work in a variety of patterns, including small groups. As with findings on active learning, cooperative and collaborative learning activities are widely accepted as being effective in many contexts, including higher education (Kyndt et al., 2013; Major, 2020).

Bredow et al.'s (2021) meta-analysis focusing specifically on higher education contexts aims to provide some clarity to the question of whether to introduce a flipped learning approach. Comparing this to 'lecture-based' learning, they find that there are some advantages. However, their comments on the heterogeneity of outcomes are similar to those already discussed. In a section titled "The case for Flipped Learning" Bredow et al.'s (2021) discussion is based on similar concepts to Cronje's (2020) distinction between direct instruction and learning-by-doing. Bredow et al. (2021) agree with points already made that one of the key benefits of flipped learning is the prioritisation of active learning. A further point that Bredow et al. (2021) make is that students will be better able to discuss material in class if it is not new to them, that is, if it has been learned through direct instruction in the individual learning space.

Similar claims can be found in smaller-scale studies, including those focused on ELT. For example, Kerr's (2020) research on the potential benefits of flipped learning in such contexts notes that providing independent study materials can give learners more control over how they access materials. Making these available online can make accessibility tools, such as screen readers, available for those who need them. In addition, learning materials are self-paced, which means that students can vary how long they spend on different activities. If students are struggling to understand audio or video content, they have the freedom to "listen or view as often as needed" (Kerr, 2020, p. 6). This can help students feel more prepared for class. Cunningham (2016), also writing about language learners in an academic context, describes such materials as both asynchronous and non-transient; students can return to materials from earlier in the course if they feel they need to, aiding understanding of course material.

5 Our Impetus for Introducing the Flipped Learning Approach

While the move to online delivery accelerated the need to reconfigure the course, this was only one aspect of the impetus for change. To understand the impetus, it is helpful to briefly describe the course as it was taught beforehand. Prior to 2020, in-person lessons were delivered with the support of printed course books. A typical student's day would involve attending three hours of classes in the morning and completing homework or independently preparing for assessments in the afternoon. Aside from tutorial support, those three hours a day of class time made up the bulk of the students' learning activities, with students deciding how to organise their own time outside of class. A wide range of activities were completed in lessons based around reading, writing, speaking, listening, and research skills (Table 1). Lessons included elements of direct instruction, as well as tasks that required individual attention, such as reading a text or listening to a lecture. Most lessons also included individual production tasks, such as writing or creating slides for a presentation.

Thinking about the range of different activities that were completed in these lessons, I personally found merit in Laurillard's (2012) ideas for a framework of different ways of learning to guide how we could organise and order the tasks. This framework discusses the importance of providing a balance of six types of learning. They are learning through: "acquisition", "inquiry", "practice", "production", "discussion", and "collaboration" (Laurillard, 2012, p. 96). What is clear from the framework is that some kinds of learning activity can be meaningfully completed individually, while others require the presence of a teacher and classmates. In the pre-pandemic example above, all essential lesson tasks were completed in

Table 1 Typical weekly timetable for a face-to-face student pre-pandemic

	Monday	Tuesday	Wednesday	Thursday	Friday
Morning	Reading and writing	Speaking and listening	Reading and writing	Research skills	Speaking and listening
Afternoon	Unguided self-study and homework from 2PM to 5PM.				

lesson time, which was not necessarily the most productive way to organise learning activities.

As such, the impetus for flipped learning followed naturally from the discussion in previous sections. Introducing flipped learning provided the opportunity to use students' self-guided independent study time more efficiently and ensure this was productive. At the same time, we also reduced the need for class teachers to provide direct instruction, hopefully leading to a more dynamic classroom environment. The decision to guide students' independent study time allowed the materials development team to think about what activities were more naturally suited to independent individual activity, and what kinds of instructional activities were more collaborative and would benefit from discussion and dialogue.

The need to deliver the pre-sessional online also brought these motivations to the foreground partly due to concerns, also discussed in MacDiarmid and Rolinska (2021), for the potential for "screen fatigue". One concern was that three-hour classes would be too much for teachers and students unused to spending so much time online. With the majority of our students studying in East Asia, we were also aware that standard UK working hours for teachers would be late in the evening for many students. This in turn led to the realisation that such students could complete a significant amount of study before attending a late afternoon class. The model of flipped learning we developed attempted to leverage these influences to develop the best possible student learning experience under such circumstances.

6 Introducing the Flipped Learning Approach to Our First Online Pre-Sessional

This section describes key changes made to the pre-sessional course in order to move it to a fully online mode of delivery. As a member of the pre-sessional team, I was not responsible for making these decisions, but was made aware of the motivations and purposes.

It was decided that a typical student day should start with two hours of guided independent study. Activities from previous years' courses were carefully checked to see which could be brought into the individual learning space to make up the flipped learning materials. These included the direct instruction of simple concepts, such as an introduction to the concepts of skimming and scanning, or the basic rules for writing a citation. They also included any pre-reading of academic articles and listening to content lectures, as well as the completion of individual research and so on.

To provide sufficient communicative learning opportunities, and in line with Laurillard's (2012) commentary on the importance of peer learning and collaboration, the team introduced a two-hour "study group". Students were asked to meet before class to clarify their understanding of independent study materials through discussion and collaboration. This was an opportunity for students to provide peer feedback on one another's work, and plan for the lesson with the teacher. In line with Jenkins et al.'s (2017) view that the flipped learning strategy needs both a higher-level pedagogy and a pedagogical philosophy, the goal was to create an "engaged community of learners". It was felt that study groups should keep the same group for the duration of the course to allow students to develop a sense of a mutually supportive community of peers.

The four hours spent individually and then in groups was intended to support class time with the teacher, with classes intended to be as active and communicative as possible. As such, a typical student in China might have the following daily schedule (Table 2):

Table 2 Typical 'flipped learning' day for a Chinese student

Morning (between 9AM and 1PM) • 2-hour independent study	Engage with independent study materials, for example, complete reading tasks and an accompanying worksheet
Afternoon (between 1PM and 4PM) • 2-hour study group	Arrange to meet with the assigned study group to discuss answers to independent study tasks and potentially collaborate on group tasks
Evening (between 4PM and 9.30PM) • 2-hour seminar	Two study groups combine to attend a seminar led by the teacher

A sixteen-student class (the maximum) consisted of four study groups. By teaching two study groups, or eight students in a seminar, the teachers only needed to prepare for one seminar a day, and with a relatively small group.

A principled approach to organising supportive study groups is not a new idea (see, for example, Beichner et al. (2007, pp. 7–10) for a useful discussion on this). However, study groups appeared to be a useful addition to the basic flipped strategy that ensured students got maximum benefit from the kind of cooperative approach that Foldnes (2016) found made a significant difference.

7   What Worked, and What Didn't: Reflections

Reflecting on the 2020 Pre-Sessional

As outlined in the introduction, the pre-sessional team have a formalised information gathering and reflective cycle where a wide range of sources are gathered and scrutinised to help us iterate upon and improve our course delivery. This involves student and teacher surveys, short reflective reports from the permanent pre-sessional team, and an external examiners report. After the 2020 pre-sessional we received very positive student and teacher feedback, with many students commenting on the success of the study group, and the bonds they formed with one another. Students were similarly positive about their experience engaging with online materials in their own time.

However, on reflection, it was clear that the self-study materials were not particularly interactive, consisting for the most part of word documents, as these had been adapted quickly to suit the new reality. Feedback from teachers suggested they wanted more varied activities to use in seminars. In particular, some commented that seminars could become an exercise in providing answers to the independent and group study tasks rather than engagement in meaningful teaching. Wilson (2020), in discussing resistance to flipped approaches, argues that there may be an expectation in university environments that teachers perform the act of teaching in certain ways. We have a body of regular pre-sessional teachers with significant expertise in delivering lessons, and we may not have fully considered reactions to the idea that "Flipped Learning suppresses *teacher* in the mode of lecturer" (Wilson, 2020, p. 5).

Two achievable goals for the 2021 pre-sessional, then, were to develop independent study materials that were fully interactive and to vary the range of activities teachers completed in seminars in a way that acknowledged their expertise. We decided to reduce the seminar time down to 90 minutes, and increase independent study time to 3 hours.

To support us in meeting the goals, we engaged with literature on blended learning design, such as Kerres and Witt (2003), and papers on flipped learning, such as Lee et al. (2017). One key area where we needed extra support and training was issues around accessibility. We had internal accessibility experts test our interactive learning tasks, and provide us advice. As MacDiarmid and Rolinska (2021) mention, we were advised to streamline instructions to keep everything as clear as possible and provided (generous) approximate timings for all independent study activities to ensure that students knew how long things should take.

The team also used Laurillard et al.'s (2013) Learning Design Support Environment to assist in the planning of six-hour units of material in such a way as to provide a range of learning activities. The Learning Designer (UCL Knowledge Lab, 2018) is a planning tool that enables the materials developer to see how much time is being spent on different kinds of learning to achieve an appropriate balance. The tool allows for the construction of lesson plan summaries as part of a deliberate learning design process. We didn't simply recreate previous courses for an online environment, but redesigned and aligned all independent study, study group, and seminar tasks to meet our goals for a productive online learning experience. While we did include some 'talking heads' instructional videos, the bulk of our independent learning materials were developed using the h5p Moodle plugin, allowing for interactive activities, such as short quizzes and matching activities, as well as embedded media and reading tasks.

Reflecting on the 2021 Pre-Sessional

As noted above, while the 2020 pre-sessional primarily involved adapting materials for online delivery, the 2021 pre-sessional was almost completely redesigned for the online format. As with the 2020 pre-sessional, mechanisms to gather feedback from students demonstrated a very high level of satisfaction with the course overall.

In comparing team reflections, one thing that was discussed was that there were still challenges with the development of effective study group dynamics. A small, but significant, number of teachers reported that they found one of their study groups was noticeably performing worse than the others in terms of preparing for seminars and producing work on time. We agreed to set two small goals in relation to this. We wanted to consider ways to make group interactions more positive, and we wanted to ensure that the independent study activities were as clear as possible. One possible reason for a lack of engagement in study group could, after all, be that some students had not managed to complete enough of the independent student activities to be ready to discuss content.

We turned to literature such as Opdecam and Everaert (2018) and Aggarwal and O'Brien (2008), to consider the possibility that successful group work may be being disrupted by 'social loafing'. This is where a member of the group takes a back seat and is content for others to produce more in collaborative work. We do not have graded group assignments, and we complete significant amounts of peer-to-peer feedback within study groups, so appear to avoid some of the concerns outlined in Opdecam and Everaert (2018). However, one simple approach was to write into the study group documents suggestions for role distribution, such as scribe or grammar expert, as mentioned in Seyoum and Molla (2022).

The second point, that a lack of engagement with independent study materials could be spilling into study group, echoes a theoretical pitfall discussed earlier and in Vitta and Al-Hoorie (2020). Students who are struggling with the course content, perhaps because they have a lower proficiency in English, could be at risk of engaging less effectively with the course overall. A potential weakness of the flipped strategy is that poor engagement at the start of a unit cycle could be hard to recover from. In response, we further streamlined instructions, and tried to look for opportunities to simplify language instruction, as well as reducing the number of tasks for students to complete daily. A simple example of this was the amount of reading material students were introduced to in a single lesson. In the 2021 pre-sessional students were introduced to four key texts in the first or second independent study session. For 2022, we decided to only introduce a single key text in a unit of study.

These changes were all made with a view to returning to fully in-person teaching for 2022. While they needed streamlining, the independent study materials developed in 2021 were considered a successful intervention, and guiding students' independent learning time is a feature of our pre-sessional that will remain in the future. As such, elements of a flipped approach to course design had been successfully embedded into our course. However, one weakness of the online model was that teachers could not monitor study group time, partly because of the differences in time zones, with students in East Asia completing tasks in the early hours of the morning compared to the United Kingdom. With the plan for 2022 being to return to in-person teaching, it was decided to maintain three hours of independent study, but bring study group into class time, with a three-hour lesson consisting of ninety minutes of student-centred study group discussion and ninety minutes of teacher-facilitated discussion.

Reflecting on the 2022 Pre-Sessional

Before the 2022 course, a series of COVID-19 restrictions in various countries led to disruption to the travel plans of many of our students. It was decided only a few months before the course started to offer two modes of study to our students. For those who were unable to attend in person, online classes were offered. As this was not the intended design for the course, it was decided that these would be three-hour classes with a thirty-minute break as originally planned. Teachers were assigned either an online or face-to-face class, based on their preference.

As with the previous pre-sessional courses, we found that students indicated a very high degree of satisfaction with the course overall. However, one thing that we continued to struggle with was the successful management of study groups. In 2022, teachers were asked to provide clear assistance (where necessary) on group roles, and then monitor study groups, but resist leading them. Some teachers who monitored study groups found it helpful to manage the discussion and ensure a closer alignment with the lesson goals. Some teachers were concerned that students didn't use this time effectively.

Another concern was that, while we streamlined our independent study materials every year, a persistent aspect of feedback was that these materials were still a significant workload burden. As alluded to in the 2021 reflection, and seen in, for example, both Brewer and Movahedazarhouligh (2018) and Arslan (2020), student concerns about workload are common with a flipped learning approach. Students were only introduced to a single text in each unit of study. However, they might have been expected to read the article, as well as receive input on, for example, summary writing and paraphrasing, and then write a short summary. For some students, this took longer than the three hours we had allocated.

One way to reconcile these concerns is a change that we believe is highly appropriate to the flipped learning approach. To provide a single focus for independent study, while at the same time providing a structured and role-based approach to class discussion, we introduced Academic Reading Circles (Seburn, 2016) to the 2023 pre-sessional. The principle is that, where a student needs to become familiar with a key text, three hours of independent study consists primarily of reading the article following a reading guide (with comprehension questions) to aid in their understanding. They then prepare for a group discussion to be completed in class time. The allocation of roles in an Academic Reading Circle is much more clearly defined in Seburn's (2016) work than we previously provided for and mitigates against social loafing. We have also been encouraged by personal reports on the successful implementation of Academic Reading Circles in other pre-sessional courses, engaging with reports from Cowley-Haselden (2020) and Marinkova and Leslie (2021).

Closely related to this are questions about the balance of learning through collaboration and discussion compared to learning through inquiry, practice, and production (referring to Laurillard's 2012 framework). As already discussed, an ELT course may skew towards collaboration and discussion as any meaningful classroom tasks that require language use can help with implicit language learning. In 2020, we put aside around one third of a unit's allocated learning time for these methods with a two-hour study group. Later, ninety minutes, or around one quarter of a day's study, was assigned to this. However, it is possible that for our pre-sessional, with the limited time available for students to benefit from such implicit learning, this was a generous allowance. We have gone from putting aside ninety minutes in every six-hour unit of study to returning to a more basic, but flexible, approach of having three hours of independent study followed by three hours of lesson time. The latter is organised by the teacher, and still contains a significant amount of collaborative work and discussion. Lessons follow active learning principles, aim for a dynamic environment, and at times make use of Academic Reading Circles. However, this time is more flexible, with the requirement for extended study group discussion removed from our delivery model, as it was not always entirely necessary for our learning outcomes.

8   Discussion

Our experiences with introducing flipped learning to a short and intense course of study have been positive. While many institutions are discussing a 'return to normal', changes we made in response to COVID-19 have become embedded into our course. While at no point did we get everything right, the materials development team demonstrated an ability to create engaging and interactive independent study materials that students found useful. The ability to plan six-hour units of study to prioritise active learning principles in lesson time improved engagement with the materials and the quality of lesson time itself. Even so, despite the significant enthusiasm (and even hype) for flipped learning, in line with Jenkins et al. (2017), I have argued that it is less of a model, or even an approach, and more of an organisational strategy.

A common concern for introducing flipped learning approaches is student workload, and this has to be carefully managed. Another concern, noted in, for example, Wilson (2020), is the workload for teachers. As pre-sessional courses are often prepared by a core team, and then delivered by a larger team of returning teachers, it was possible to ensure students across multiple classes studied the same materials. In a large university department, cognisant of parity of student experience and other concerns, it made sense to develop materials in this way. Indeed, our independent study materials would not have been as well developed, engaging, or comprehensive if a full-time team of writers had not been available. However, this suggests that our experiences of introducing flipped learning are most relevant to this model of rolling out a single course to many classes. As such, it is difficult to recommend that individual teachers engage in flipped learning to such an extent, unless, perhaps, they are expected to have opportunities to iterate and expand on their materials year on year, or have sufficient time available to plan for planning and preparation.

It is also important to mention the kind of knowledge and expertise required from the materials development team to achieve relatively modest goals. Koehler and Mishra's (2009) framework describing knowledge required to teach with technology has understandably received a lot of interest. The combination of technological, pedagogical, and content knowledge (abbreviated as TPACK) is not necessarily easily developed. In order to provide fully interactive online learning materials, the development team needed a sound understanding of pedagogical concepts. We also needed content-specific knowledge for EAP, such as understanding the university context, and the ability to make decisions about which theoretical frameworks we use to inform EAP specific materials. The technological knowledge required to create interactive materials has been significant and involves working across multiple platforms, such as SharePoint and Moodle, as well as writing html code and developing h5p interactive tasks.

Putting these things together, it is hard to fully recommend flipped learning approaches to a wide range of teaching contexts. While it might be possible for an individual teacher to 'flip' some activities piece-meal, or work to ensure, for example, that planning and preparation tasks are completed before class to prioritise active learning in class, our experience suggests the approach tends to work best at the syllabus design level. It is also clear that while some do view flipped learning as an innovation, the process of iterating our course over multiple cycles has been invaluable in deciding the most suitable ways to introduce flipped learning to our context. Not every team, or teacher, has the opportunity to gather as much feedback as we were able to, has time for reflection, or even iterates the same or similar course material. However, what we can say is that the process of iteration has been at least as important as the initial introduction of a new approach in helping us develop a course that meets the needs of our students.

References

Aggarwal, P., & O'Brien, C. L. (2008). Social loafing on group projects: Structural antecedents and effect on student satisfaction. *Journal of Marketing Education, 30*(3), 255–264.

Arslan, A. (2020). A systematic review on flipped learning in teaching English as a foreign or second language. *Journal of Language and Linguistic Studies, 16*(2), Article 2. https://doi.org/10.17263/jlls.759300

Beichner, R. J., Saul, J. M., Abbott, D. S., Morse, J. J., Deardorff, D., Allain, R. J., Bonham, S. W., Dancy, M. H., & Risley, J. S. (2007). The student-centered activities for large enrollment undergraduate programs (SCALE-UP) project. *Research-Based Reform of University Physics, 1*(1), 2–39.

Bergmann, J., & Sams, A. (2014). *Flipped learning: Gateway to student engagement*. International Society for Technology in Education.

Birgili, B., Seggie, F. N., & Oğuz, E. (2021). The trends and outcomes of flipped learning research between 2012 and 2018: A descriptive content analysis. *Journal of Computers in Education, 8*(3), 365–394. https://doi.org/10.1007/s40692-021-00183-y

Bredow, C. A., Roehling, P. V., Knorp, A. J., & Sweet, A. M. (2021). To flip or not to flip? A meta-analysis of the efficacy of flipped learning in higher education. *Review of Educational Research, 91*(6), 878–918. https://doi.org/10.3102/00346543211019122

Brewer, R., & Movahedazarhouligh, S. (2018). Successful stories and conflicts: A literature review on the effectiveness of flipped learning in higher education.

Journal of Computer Assisted Learning, 34(4), 409–416. https://doi.org/10.1111/jcal.12250

Charles, M., & Pecorari, D. (2016). *Introducing English for academic purposes.* Routledge.

Cheng, L., Ritzhaupt, A. D., & Antonenko, P. (2019). Effects of the flipped classroom instructional strategy on students' learning outcomes: A meta-analysis. *Educational Technology Research and Development, 67*(4), 793–824.

Cowley-Haselden, S. (2020). Building knowledge to ease troublesomeness: Affording theory knowledgeability through academic reading circles. *Journal of University Teaching & Learning Practice, 17*(2) https://doi.org/10.53761/1.17.2.8

Cronje, J. (2020). Towards a new definition of blended learning. *Electronic Journal of E-Learning, 18*(2), Article 2. https://doi.org/10.34190/EJEL.20.18.2.001

Cunningham, U. (2016). Language pedagogy and non-transience in the flipped classroom. *Journal of Open, Flexible and Distance Learning, 20*(1), 44–58.

Davidson, N., & Major, C. H. (2014). Boundary crossings: Cooperative learning, collaborative learning, and problem-based learning. *Journal on Excellence in College Teaching, 25.*

Flipped Learning Network. (2014, March 12). Definition of flipped learning. *Flipped Learning Network Hub.* https://flippedlearning.org/definition-of-flipped-learning/

Flipped Learning Network. (2016, November 24). Who we are. *Flipped Learning Network Hub.* https://flippedlearning.org/who-we-are/

Foldnes, N. (2016). The flipped classroom and cooperative learning: Evidence from a randomised experiment. *Active Learning in Higher Education, 17*(1), 39–49. https://doi.org/10.1177/1469787415616726

Freeman, S., Eddy, S. L., McDonough, M., Smith, M. K., Okoroafor, N., Jordt, H., & Wenderoth, M. P. (2014). Active learning increases student performance in science, engineering, and mathematics. *Proceedings of the National Academy of Sciences, 111*(23), 8410–8415. https://doi.org/10.1073/pnas.1319030111

Heward, W. L., & Twyman, J. S. (2021). Teach more in less time: Introduction to the special section on direct instruction. *Behavior Analysis in Practice, 14*(3), 763–765. https://doi.org/10.1007/s40617-021-00639-8

Hodges, C., Moore, S., Lockee, B., Trust, T., & Bond, A. (2020, March 27). *The difference between emergency remote teaching and online learning.* EDUCAUSE Review. https://er.educause.edu/articles/2020/3/the-difference-between-emergency-remote-teaching-and-online-learning

Jenkins, M., Bokosmaty, R., Brown, M., Browne, C., Gao, Q., Hanson, J., & Kupatadze, K. (2017). Enhancing the design and analysis of flipped learning strategies. *Teaching & Learning Inquiry, 5*(1), 65–77.

Kerr, P. (2020). *Flipped learning.* Cambridge University Press. https://www.cambridge.org/ph/files/9115/9438/9974/CambridgePapers_in_ELT-Flipped_Learning_minipaper_ONLINE.pdf?

Kerres, M., & Witt, C. D. (2003). A didactical framework for the design of blended learning arrangements. *Journal of Educational Media, 28*(2–3), 101–113. https://doi.org/10.1080/1358165032000165653

Koehler, M., & Mishra, P. (2009). What is technological pedagogical content knowledge (TPACK)? *Contemporary Issues in Technology and Teacher Education, 9*(1), 60–70.

Kyndt, E., Raes, E., Lismont, B., Timmers, F., Cascallar, E., & Dochy, F. (2013). A meta-analysis of the effects of face-to-face cooperative learning. Do recent studies falsify or verify earlier findings? *Educational Research Review, 10*, 133–149. https://doi.org/10.1016/j.edurev.2013.02.002

Låg, T., & Sæle, R. G. (2019). Does the flipped classroom improve student learning and satisfaction? A systematic review and meta-analysis. *AERA Open, 5*(3), 1–17.

Laurillard, D. (2012). *Teaching as a design science: Building pedagogical patterns for learning and technology.* Routledge.

Laurillard, D., Charlton, P., Craft, B., Dimakopoulos, D., Ljubojevic, D., Magoulas, G., Masterman, E., Pujadas, R., Whitley, E. A., & Whittlestone, K. (2013). A constructionist learning environment for teachers to model learning designs: Modelling learning designs. *Journal of Computer Assisted Learning, 29*(1), 15–30. https://doi.org/10.1111/j.1365-2729.2011.00458.x

Lee, J., Lim, C., & Kim, H. (2017). Development of an instructional design model for flipped learning in higher education. *Educational Technology Research and Development, 65*(2), 427–453. https://doi.org/10.1007/s11423-016-9502-1

Li, R., Lund, A., & Nordsteien, A. (2021). The link between flipped and active learning: A scoping review. *Teaching in Higher Education*, 1–35. https://doi.org/10.1080/13562517.2021.1943655

Macdiarmid, C., & Rolinska, A. (2021). Harnessing online course development skills: A crisis- prompted but carefully planned EAP course. *Journal of*

Perspectives in Applied Academic Practice, 9(2), 159–168. https://doi.org/10.14297/jpaap.v9i2.490

Major, C. (2020). Collaborative learning: A tried and true active learning method for the college classroom. *New Directions for Teaching and Learning, 2020*(164), 19–28. https://doi.org/10.1002/tl.20420

Marinkova, M., & Leslie, A. (2021). Research, Keele University. *Journal of Academic Development and Education Special Edition (Becoming Well Read)*. https://doi.org/10.21252/ce5b-ka44

Nguyen, K. A., Borrego, M., Finelli, C. J., DeMonbrun, M., Crockett, C., Tharayil, S., Shekhar, P., Waters, C., & Rosenberg, R. (2021). Instructor strategies to aid implementation of active learning: A systematic literature review. *International Journal of STEM Education, 8*(1), 9. https://doi.org/10.1186/s40594-021-00270-7

O'Dea, X. (Christine), & Stern, J. (2022). Virtually the same?: Online higher education in the post Covid-19 era. *British Journal of Educational Technology, 53*(3): 437–442. https://doi.org/10.1111/bjet.13211

Opdecam, E., & Everaert, P. (2018). Seven disagreements about cooperative learning. *Accounting Education, 27*(3), 223–233.

Pearson, W. S. (2020). The effectiveness of pre-sessional EAP programmes in UK higher education: A review of the evidence. *Review of Education, 8*(2), 420–447. https://doi.org/10.1002/rev3.3191

Seburn, T. (2016). *Academic reading circles*. The Round.

Seyoum, Y., & Molla, S. (2022). Teachers' and students' roles in promoting cooperative learning at Haramaya, Dire Dawa, and Jigjiga Universities, Ethiopia. *Education Research International, 2022*, 1–11. https://doi.org/10.1155/2022/7334592

Talbert, R., & Mor-Avi, A. (2019). A space for learning: An analysis of research on active learning spaces. *Heliyon, 5*(12), e02967. https://doi.org/10.1016/j.heliyon.2019.e02967

Thorpe, A., Snell, M., Davey-Evans, S., & Talman, R. (2017). Improving the academic performance of non-native English-speaking students: The contribution of pre-sessional English language programmes. *Higher Education Quarterly, 71*(1), 5–32. https://doi.org/10.1111/hequ.12109

Tomlinson, B., & Masuhara, H. (2017). *The complete guide to the theory and practice of materials development for language learning*. John Wiley & Sons, Incorporated. http://ebookcentral.proquest.com/lib/ucl/detail.action?docID=4875227

UCL Knowledge Lab. (2018, February 9). *Learning designer.* https://www.ucl.ac.uk/learning-designer/

Universities UK. (2022, June 20). *International facts and figures 2022.* https://www.universitiesuk.ac.uk/universities-uk-international/insights-and-publications/uuki-publications/international-facts-and-figures-2022

Vitta, J. P., & Al-Hoorie, A. H. (2020). The flipped classroom in second language learning: A meta-analysis. *Language Teaching Research, 136216882098140.* https://doi.org/10.1177/1362168820981403

Wilson, K. (2020). What does it mean to *do* teaching? A qualitative study of resistance to Flipped Learning in a higher education context. *Teaching in Higher Education, 1–14.* https://doi.org/10.1080/13562517.2020.1822312

Wingate, U. (2012). 'Argument!' helping students understand what essay writing is about. *Journal of English for Academic Purposes, 11*(2), 145–154.

Sustainable Language Programme Design and Management at a Widening Participation University

Becky Muradás-Taylor and Rachel Wicaksono

1   Introduction

We present innovations in programme design at York St John University, a small widening participation university. These innovations transformed our language degree provision: what was complex, financially unsustainable, and at risk of closure, is now a model for sustainable programme design, with one in thirteen undergraduate students joining the university to study a language in 2021. This contrasts markedly with other lower tariff universities, the majority of which do not, or no longer, offer languages to degree level. In this chapter, we reflect on our approach—in our roles as Head of School and previous Subject Director—to designing

B. Muradás-Taylor (✉)
University of Leeds, Leeds, UK
e-mail: B.Muradas-Taylor@leeds.ac.uk

R. Wicaksono
York St John University, York, UK

and managing a language programme at a low-tariff widening participation university.

International, National and Local Context

Levels of enrolment on language degree programmes are of concern in majority English-speaking countries such as the UK, USA and Australia (Brown & Caruso, 2016, p. 453). Language learning in these countries is often referred to as being in crisis (Brown & Caruso, 2016, p. 453; Lanvers et al., 2021, pp. 2–3) resulting in a lack of linguistic and cultural knowledge. English speakers 'face competition on their home labour markets with everyone else in the world, while having no real access to those labour markets in which another language remains required' (Van Parijs, 2004, p. 130)—estimated to cost the UK, for example, 3.5% of GDP in lost export trade (Foreman-Peck & Wang, 2014).

The crisis in language education is perhaps not surprising, given the status of English as a global language. Learners of English can expect 'high return of investment, high motivation […] opportunities to practice [and] strong education policy and support for learning' (Lanvers et al., 2021, p. 4). In contrast, language learners in majority English-speaking countries are 'surrounded by a culture of an English monolingual mindset' where it is believed that 'English is enough' (Lanvers et al., 2021, p. 4). This belief is underpinned by a wide range of assumptions, referred to by Hall, Smith and Wicaksono (2017, pp. 4–14) as 'dead end' thinking about what language 'is' and what it does; including beliefs such as, 'people who speak two languages are confused' and 'a nation has, or should have, one language'. Further examples of this, typically, monolingual mindset include the ideas that formal language learning 'doesn't work', children learn languages better than adults, technology will make language learning redundant (Foster, 2019, pp. 265–266), and that the version of a language used by its so-called native speakers is the only legitimate target variety (Wicaksono, 2012; Wicaksono, 2020). These are beliefs which, particularly when they are reinforced by teaching methods and assessment design in schools, can cause young people to hold 'negative views about their current and future language learning ability' (Lanvers & Chambers, 2019, pp. 434–435).

In England, where, we suspect, these beliefs are held particularly strongly, the percentage of young people who entered for a language GCSE, the national exam taken at age 16, fell from 76% in 2002 to 40% in 2011 (Tinsley & Doležal, 2018, p. 3), grew slightly to 49% by 2014 (Tinsley & Doležal, 2018, p. 3) and has remained roughly steady since (Collen, 2022, p. 22). This is despite the government's ambition for 75% of young people to take a language GCSE by 2022 and 90% by 2025 (Department for Education, 2019). The number of young people who study a language A level, the national exam taken at age 18, fell from 40,000 in 1996 to 27,000 in 2005 (Tinsley & Doležal, 2018, p. 4), remaining low since (Collen, 2020, p. 5). The resulting fall in the number of undergraduate language students has led to the closure of many university language departments and programmes, with 105 universities offering languages degrees in the year 2000 (Boffey, 2013) but only 64 in 2019 (Polisca et al., 2019, p. 9).

International, national and local factors are at play here. Whereas a language GCSE in England has not been compulsory since 2004, Wales has a policy of 'bilingualism + 1' with Welsh compulsory from age 3–16 (Jones, 2016, p. 1) and Scotland has committed to the European Union's '1+ 2 model' of teaching two languages in addition to English (Lanvers et al., 2018, p. 779). In Germany, despite concern about 'foreign language monolingualism' (Lanvers & Chambers, 2019, p. 430), many schools teach languages other than English, even teaching geography and/or history, for example, in a language other than German or English (Lanvers & Chambers, 2019, p. 433). And while the numbers of entries to language GCSEs or their international equivalents have declined in England, Scotland, Wales, Northern Ireland and New Zealand, they have not declined in Ireland or Australia (Churchward, 2019). How successful countries have been rising to the challenge of teaching languages other than English seems to vary. Issues particular to England include a poor transition from primary to secondary school (Collen, 2020, p. 9), and low grades in languages GCSEs that dissuade young people from taking them or schools from offering them (Lanvers, 2017, p. 52). Areas of the country with high social deprivation, especially urban areas in the North of England, are the most likely not to offer languages (Tinsley & Doležal, 2018, p. 5); in Middlesbrough, in the North East, only 29% of young people took a language GCSE in 2017 (Tinsley & Doležal, 2018, p. 3).

The Universities and Colleges Admissions Service (UCAS), the UK admissions service for higher education, collects data on university admissions. A recent analysis of UCAS data, by one of the authors of this chapter, showed that English universities with above average entry tariffs, and students from more-privileged socioeconomic backgrounds, generally offer languages to degree level, whereas universities with below average entry tariffs, and students from less-privileged socioeconomic backgrounds, generally do not (Muradás-Taylor, 2023). At the other extreme, most universities with an entry tariff higher than 145 offer a range of five or more languages to degree level (Muradás-Taylor, 2023).

A follow-up study (Muradás-Taylor & Taylor, 2024) showed that there are large areas of the North, East and South West of England that are further than a commutable distance of 60 km from a university offering language degrees at below average entry tariff. This excludes people from studying languages at university, since we know that students from less-privileged socioeconomic backgrounds, some ethnic minority backgrounds, and students from the North of England, are more likely to commute (Donnelly & Gamsu, 2018). Figure 1, adapted from Muradás-Taylor and Taylor (2024) illustrates these cold spots, with the number of

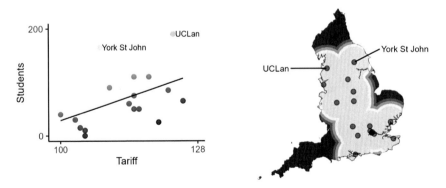

Fig. 1 Below average tariff universities offering languages, adapted from Muradás-Taylor and Taylor (2024)

students accepting places to study languages at below average tariff universities in 2020, and their location, also shown.

As a widening participation university, with, in 2019, an average entry tariff of 108 UCAS points (Guardian, 2022) and 40% of students from the least privileged socioeconomic backgrounds (POLAR quintiles 1 and 2, Office for Students, 2022a), York St John is unusual in offering languages to degree level. As can be seen from Fig. 1, it is situated in a key strategic position geographically, with cold spots to the north and south, and has a large number of language students for its tariff, exceeded only by UCLan. Languages are thriving at York St John, due to the impact of the programme design which we describe in this chapter.

Curriculum/Programme Design

While much has been written on curriculum design, little directly addresses the key issue at the heart of the language education crisis: declining student numbers and unsustainable courses. Most research into university curriculum design focuses on a particular goal or aspect of the curriculum, for example: retention (Bovill et al., 2011) or decolonisation (Schucan Bird & Pitman, 2020) (although see O'Neill, 2015, for a book-length guide to designing programmes at university). Books on designing 'language' programmes (Dubin & Olshtain, 1986; Macalister & Nation, 2011; Markee, 1997; Mickan & Wallace, 2020; Nation & Macalister, 2010)—which, despite their titles, focus on English language teaching, not the teaching of other languages—do not need to consider how to attract students, given the global demand for English learning. The same is true of schools, the focus of much research on curriculum design. For example, a recent special issue of the *Curriculum Journal* explores 'macro-level' issues, such as the interaction between national curricula and policy-making, 'meso-level' issues, such as content selection and continuing professional development for teachers, and 'micro-level' issues, such as classroom interaction between teacher and students (Priestley & Philippou, 2019) but not how to attract students, given that the setting is compulsory education.

Perhaps the most relevant concept from curriculum design research is 'environment analysis' (also called 'situation analysis' or 'constraints analysis', Nation & Macalister, 2010, pp. 17–18), that is, asking questions about the students, the teachers and the situation such as time, space and materials—especially if 'students' is re-framed to consider young people that are not currently applying to study languages at university, but might if the right programmes were available. We also notice synergies between our approach and 'Design Thinking', 'a human-centered approach to innovation and problem-solving, characterized by trial and error and the integration of people from multiple disciplines taking part in the planning and decision-making process' (Brown, 2008, cited in Crites & Rye, 2020, p. 2). Design Thinking starts with 'a deep understanding of the needs, motivations and realities of the users or stakeholders', where 'having explicit knowledge of users' needs is more important than having access to numerical data and demographics' (Crites & Rye, 2020, pp. 2–3). We will return to the similarities and differences between our approach and Design Thinking in the discussion.

According to Liddicoat (2020, p. 116), there is a 'small body' of research on 'strategies adopted by universities or departments to address declining participation'; he gives Brown and Caruso (2016) as an example. They describe a major overhaul in curriculum design at the University of Western Australia, where 150 undergraduate degrees were replaced with five: Bachelor of Arts, Commerce, Design, Philosophy and Science (Brown & Caruso, 2016, p. 462). Students on the new programmes must take some 'broadening units' outside of the faculty, and students from all faculties, including the Faculty of Arts, can choose a language as a broadening unit. This led to 'much higher' enrolment in language units (Brown & Caruso, 2016, p. 464). While having more students study languages as part of their degree is an excellent outcome, it is not clear that this change had an impact on the number of students specialising in languages, which is the focus of the current chapter.

Of perhaps most relevance to questions of language degree programme design and management are the two joint reports by the University Council of Modern Languages (UCML)—now University Council For Languages (UCFL)—and the British Academy (British Academy & UCML, 2022; UCML & British Academy, 2021). These analyse changes in the number of students studying languages. The first report (UCML & British Academy, 2021, p. 4) stated that programmes consisting of a single language (e.g. French) or two languages (e.g. French and Spanish) have been particularly affected by falls in student numbers, declining by 22% between 2012 and 2018. In contrast, they said that joint honours programmes, where languages are studied in combination with other subjects, have not declined overall, and the numbers of students studying languages with politics, linguistics, TESOL and translation have increased. UCML and British Academy (2021, p. 5) also looked at the numbers of students studying each language, reporting that French, German, Italian, Portuguese, Russian and Spanish have fallen, Japanese and Korean have risen, and Arabic has remained steady. Based on these two findings, they recommended that language departments should 're-examine their course offerings with a view to both expanding the range of courses in combination with other […] subjects [and] a greater range of non-European languages' (UCML and British Academy, 2021, p. 4). Note however that their most recent report, analysing the period 2012 to 2021, shows that the trend for joint honours programmes to show less decline is only observed in Russell Group universities; in other universities, student numbers have fallen irrespective of programme type (British Academy & UCML, 2022, p. 13).

Also of relevance to language programme design is Liddicoat (2020), a survey of what university websites in UK and Australia say about their language programmes. He compares the languages offered; the amount of contact time per week; whether ab initio (from beginners) and continuing (e.g. post A level) starting points are offered; whether ab initio students and continuing students are on 'converging' programmes—and if so whether they merge in the second or third year of the programme—or 'sequential' programmes, graduating on different levels; whether beginners language teaching is assigned to teaching fellows and language teaching in later years or literature/area studies content assigned to teaching and research academics; and whether study abroad is compulsory. He concludes that differences between programmes are 'the result of ad hoc decisions' (Liddicoat, 2020, p. 133), adding that 'pedagogy often does not appear to be the basis on which decisions are made […] it is possible for similar, linguistically close languages, such as Italian and Spanish, to receive very different time allocations within the same university' (Liddicoat, 2020, p. 129).

2 Programme Design and Management

In this section we describe (1) the language programmes at York St John as they were in 2017, when the first author became Subject Director for languages and the second author was Head of School; (2) the changes we made between 2017 and 2021; (3) the positive impact of these changes and (4) those aspects that were not successful or are still in progress.

Where We Were

That York St John offered languages to degree level was unusual given that most widening participation universities—those with below average entry tariffs and high proportions of students from POLAR quintiles 1 and 2—do not. Not only that, but five languages were offered to degree level—British Sign Language (BSL), French, German, Japanese and Spanish; especially unusual given that a range of five or more languages is normally only seen in universities with the very highest entry tariffs. This achievement was the result of innovation by the previous management who validated joint honours language degrees using modules from the institution-wide languages programme. The languages were offered in combination with business management, education studies, English language and English literature, with Spanish also offered with tourism management and BSL also offered with children, young people and families (CYPF). Later, French, German, Japanese and Spanish were launched in combination with TESOL and dual languages (language X and/with language Y) programmes were added.

By 2017, the number of different language programmes had grown to 37. However, only 52 first years entered in total, making the average programme size 1.4 students. German was of particular concern, with only two first years joining that year across ten different programmes. In 2018, York St John went through a university-wide restructure, and the language programmes were identified as being financially unsustainable due to their high staff costs as a proportion of fee income. At that stage, Japanese had one programme recruiting large numbers of students—TESOL and Japanese—plus five other programmes with low or no recruitment. With the introduction of the dual languages programmes, numbers on BSL had grown to 9 from 4 the previous year, French had grown from 7 to 8 and Spanish had grown from 9 to 17. However, these students were spread across multiple programmes: six different programmes for BSL, eight for French and nine for Spanish. The large number of small programmes was causing an unsustainable administrative burden. This affected timetabling, module choices, marketing, quality assurance, academic leads and the languages and linguistics administration team, as described below.

The timetabling challenge was immense, compounded by language modules also being offered as electives on most other programmes: effectively, no language module could clash with any module on any other programme. The language modules followed a ladder model (referred to as 'sequential' in Liddicoat, 2020): beginners, continuation, intermediate 1, intermediate 2, advanced 1 and 2 and proficiency. First years were allocated to an appropriate starting level, with complete beginners, those post-GCSE and those post-A level starting on different levels. First-year post A-level students were taught together with third years who had progressed from beginners, compounding the timetabling challenge.

The large number of programmes impacted the module choice process. At York St John, students are enrolled automatically on core modules, and choose their options online. Centrally located professional services colleagues generate 'module diets' from the modules detailed in the programme specification and these are signed off by academics. In 2017, when we had 37 different programmes available to first-year students, a combination of staff changes and the sheer size of the task meant that these were signed off without proper scrutiny. As a result, every single student was initially given an incorrect module diet—being offered modules that were not running and not being offered modules that were, requiring huge resource to rectify.

Module choices were also an issue with study abroad. York St John was unusual in having three-year programmes where the second year was study abroad. The credits gained while studying abroad counted towards the degree classification, unlike most, if not all, English universities where the year abroad is in addition to three years. Because of this, it was necessary to: (1) match students carefully with host institutions to ensure that appropriate modules were available; (2) approve the module choices of each student; and (3) offer additional independent study modules for students to redeem credits after their return to the UK if insufficient credits had been obtained at the host university.

Other teams around the university who were unnecessarily burdened included the marketing team, who were unable to keep up with the maintenance of 37 different online programme descriptions; the quality assurance team, who were responsible for updating any module or programme amendment across multiple programme specifications; and academic leads and the languages and linguistics administration team, who were the first port of call for queries from students, professional services colleagues and academics.

Most importantly, the issues described above impacted negatively on the student experience in the following ways. Module choice issues meant that students had to change modules at short notice. The second year abroad put students under considerable pressure—not only were they studying alongside students from other universities who had already completed two years of their degree before going abroad, but they were also studying for credits. And some students considered the ladder model for languages unfair, feeling that they could have achieved a higher mark—and therefore degree classification—if they had been allowed to take a lower language level in the final year than they were assigned to.

What We Did

In order to save languages from closure, we needed to design new programmes that were both attractive and sustainable. We focussed on languages not taught in schools, closing first our German programmes, and, the following year, our French and Spanish programmes. We continued to offer BSL and Japanese and launched Korean as a new language. Although only a small number of universities offer Korean to degree level, we anticipated demand as prospective students were mentioning Korean at open days and in their personal statements. We did not require any previous study of any language, although many prospective students told us they were studying BSL, Japanese or Korean as self-study or outside of school.

We closed all programmes with business management, CYPF, English language, English literature, and tourism management, replacing the 37 programmes that were offered in 2017 with five: British Sign Language, Deaf Studies and Linguistics; Japanese, Intercultural Communication and Linguistics; Japanese, TESOL and Linguistics; Korean, Intercultural Communication and Linguistics; and Korean, TESOL and Linguistics. These all have tripartite titles: a language (either BSL, Japanese or Korean), one of deaf studies (for BSL) or TESOL or intercultural communication (for Japanese/Korean), and linguistics. The deaf studies/intercultural communication/TESOL strand of each programme was designed to be relevant to students' future careers. These strands were developed through a combination of adapting existing modules on our English language and linguistics (ELL) programme and writing new ones. Despite their tripartite content, the programmes are administered as single, not joint, honours, all within the languages and linguistics subject area.

We replaced the old ladder model of beginners to proficiency language modules. First-year students now take either a module for complete beginners or a module for students entering with prior knowledge. These two groups come together in second and final year for content-based language learning: Japanese and Korean are taught through topics such as education, transport, food, minoritised people, CV writing, and academic writing, and BSL students cover topics such as education, employment, recreation and health. Unlike the old programmes, which had study abroad as the second year of a three-year programme, the new Japanese and Korean programmes have study abroad as the third year of a four-year programme, in line with other UK universities.

Lastly, we recruited new staff who were able to teach both language and linguistics or applied linguistics, with a PhD and a track record of research. We also recruited two graduate teaching assistants (known as academic associates) to work towards a PhD while teaching BSL or Korean.

What Worked

The changes we made led to an increased intake of first-year undergraduate students from 52 in 2017 to 165 in 2021. To put this in context, only 2165 first years joined the University in 2021 (HESA, 2023), meaning that one in thirteen undergraduates joined in a language programme. This meant more than £1,000,000 in additional income from first-year undergraduate students alone in 2021 compared to 2017, allowing for the recruitment of five new members of research-active academic staff and two academic associates. The new programmes attract underrepresented students to university: 32% have declared a disability and 29% are mature students, both unusually high for York St John and the sector. They also have wide geographic reach, with 60% of students coming from outside Yorkshire and the North East, compared to only 32% on other programmes in the university.

The changes resulted in a drastically reduced administrative burden, making the programmes more sustainable. The language modules are straightforward to timetable, no longer impacting on other programmes in the university. The module diets are simple to generate and there are no more issues with incorrect module diets. Because modules taken while studying abroad no longer count towards the degree classification, the work involved in matching students with host institutions and approving students' module choices is reduced, and independent study modules for students returning with insufficient credits are no longer needed. With 5 programmes, rather than 37, the resource involved in marketing and quality assurance, and the burden on academic leads and the languages and linguistics administration team are all reduced.

The changes also improved the student experience, since programmes run smoothly: module diets are signed off in time, and timetables run clash-free. Study abroad has, of course, been affected by different issues through the pandemic, but we have removed the stress of studying alongside students who have had more years of study before going abroad and of study abroad grades counting towards the degree classification. And we no longer have complaints that the ladder model impacts on the degree classification.

What Did Not Work

At the time of our curriculum review, the University was in a period of upheaval, undergoing restructures and offering enhanced redundancy packages to staff as part of a voluntary severance process. Because of the closure of the French, German and Spanish programmes, some colleagues had no choice but to accept 'voluntary' severance and leave the university. While the increased student recruitment on the new programmes was able to save languages overall from closure, the closures had enormous personal impact on those members of staff. Secondly, we had to close our institution-wide languages programme (previously, all language modules on the degree programmes, and other languages, were open to both students on other programmes and the public). Lastly, our high recruitment numbers may have solved one problem and created another. While recruitment to the Japanese and Korean programmes is high, retention is an issue, with a concerning number of students not continuing into the second year of their programme.

3   Discussion

Despite the international picture of decline in the learning of languages other than English, and the national context—with below average tariff universities like York St John the least likely to offer languages to degree level—we succeeded in redesigning our language degree programmes in a way that both grew student numbers and was financially sustainable. In this section, we compare our approach to the research on curriculum design described in the introduction, exploring what is innovative about what we did.

There are overlaps between our approach and 'design thinking' described in Crites and Rye (2020, p. 2) as 'a human-centered approach to innovation and problem-solving, characterized by trial and error and the integration of people from multiple disciplines taking part in the planning and decision-making process'. Our approach was driven by a desire to solve the problems we were facing, including low recruitment and complex and resource-intensive programmes. It was characterised by trial and error, making changes iteratively over the period 2017 to 2021. And 'people from multiple disciplines' were involved, including professional services colleagues in the finance, IT, marketing, quality assurance and timetabling teams.

However, we disagree that 'having explicit knowledge of users' needs is more important than having access to numerical data and demographics' (Crites & Rye, 2020, pp. 2–3). We argue that it is precisely through data—specifically, programme and module enrolment data—that we gained a deep understanding of students' needs and preferences. Our approach to this data may be unusual in that we used it to inform the design of new programmes to replace programmes that we closed. For example, we originally offered Japanese with TESOL, which recruited strongly, and with business management/education studies/English language/English literature, all with very low recruitment. We designed a Japanese, intercultural communication and linguistics programme—intended for students who wanted to work in Japan or in a role related to Japan, but did not want to teach English—which recruited more students than all the smaller programmes combined.

We notice that nowhere in the literature is a discussion of a sustainable number of programmes to offer per language. This absence may point to a widespread assumption that if there is a healthy number of students studying a language, it does not matter if they are spread across a number of different joint honours programmes. But once we recognised the administrative burden, and knock-on effect on the students, of multiple small programmes, we decided to take a different approach. Instead of adding joint honours combinations until a sufficient number of language students have been recruited, we asked how many programmes we could sustain per language. For Japanese and Korean, we found we could sustain two decent-sized programmes—one with TESOL and linguistics and the other with intercultural communication and linguistics. For BSL, we found, after some trial and error, that we could only sustain one programme: BSL, deaf studies and linguistics.

UCML and British Academy (2021, p. 4) recommend that 'language departments re-examine their course offerings with a view to […] expanding the range of courses in combination with other […] subjects'. This is based on their analysis that joint honours language programmes are not experiencing the same decline in student numbers as single honours, at least in Russell Group universities (British Academy & UCML, 2022, p. 13). What this advice does not take into account, however, is the negative side to joint honours language programmes which we have set out in detail in this chapter: the drain on resource in terms of timetabling, module diets, marketing, and quality assurance, and the resulting negative impact on students when these processes do not work smoothly. Our innovative solution to these competing demands is to design programmes that look like joint honours from the perspective of the students but are administered as single honours, within one subject area.

We view this as the best of both worlds: catering for students' preference for studying a language with another subject, but sustainable to administer. Most importantly, we were able to design whole programmes, rather than combining two 'half' programmes as is usual for joint honours. This was possible because we had recruited new lecturers with a doctoral-level qualification to teach both language and (applied) linguistics. This contrasts to the practice described by Liddicoat (2020) of having beginners language teaching assigned to teaching fellows and language teaching in later years assigned to teaching and research academics. We designed the modules taken alongside the language to be relevant to students' future careers: 'key concepts for TESOL', 'TESOL theories and methods' and 'TESOL decisions, dilemmas and design' for those students planning to teach English; 'language and society', 'intercultural communication' and 'language, identities and cultures' for those students wanting to work internationally or cross-culturally in a non-teaching role; and, for those students wanting to work with d/Deaf people, modules on 'deaf history', 'deaf cultures', 'deaf social theory', 'linguistic diversity in schools', and phonetics—with the latter two relevant to future careers in education or speech and language therapy.

UCML and British Academy (2021, p. 4) recommended that universities offer more non-European languages. We had notable success with Korean, which we were motivated to start offering because many applicants to our Japanese programmes were mentioning an interest in Korean at open days and in personal statements. While Korean is only offered to degree level at a small number of universities in the UK, the number of students studying it trebled from 2012 to 2018 (UCML & British Academy, 2021, p. 5), and it has also gained popularity in the USA, due to the 'increasing visibility of South Korea on the international stage […] and increasing involvement of the Korean government in the teaching of Korean internationally' (Byon, 2008). Launching Korean was only viable, however, because of the changes to programme design that we had made, in particular the tripartite programmes administered as single honours and the removal of the ladder model, so that students in multiple years were no longer timetabled together. Adding Korean to our old programme design (Korean and business management/English language/English literature/education studies plus all combinations of dual languages) would not have been possible due to the complexity of timetabling and module diets. Streamlining our programme design to just one or two programmes per language was therefore an important prerequisite to the launch of Korean, meaning that we could add a new language without causing an unsustainable administrative burden and resulting negative student experience.

We noted above that most research on curriculum design does not address the question of how to attract students, given that the majority of work has been carried out on compulsory education, English language teaching, or university courses where this is not an issue. We suggested that when considering students as part of an 'environment analysis' (Nation & Macalister, 2010, pp. 17–18), this could be re-framed to consider people who are not currently applying to study languages at university, but might if the right programmes were available. This is vital in the context of languages at widening participation universities, where programmes are closing due to low demand. Rather than assuming that prospective students do not want to study languages, our approach was to design programmes that they wanted to study. Key to this was offering languages not taught in schools. Due to the status of English as a global language and the myths around language and language learning described in the introduction, young people in majority English-speaking countries can hold 'negative views about their current and future language learning ability' (Lanvers & Chambers, 2019, pp. 434–435). By offering languages not taught in schools, we mitigate against this, reaching students who have been self-studying due to an interest or personal connection with the language or culture. Offering languages not taught in schools also means that the disparities in access to formal language study—with schools in less-privileged areas of the North of England less likely to offer languages, especially in Middlesbrough where York St John has several feeder schools (Tinsley & Doležal, 2018)—do not prevent students accessing university language programmes. We suggest, therefore, that when UCML and British Academy (2021, p. 4) recommend that universities offer more non-European languages, the key consideration here is to offer languages that young people want to study, rather than whether languages are European or not.

Summary and Next Steps

As we stated above, according to Liddicoat (2020, p. 116) there is a 'small body' of research on 'strategies adopted by universities or departments to address declining participation'. However, in the example he gives, Brown and Caruso (2016), the changes resulted in more students taking languages as a 'broadening unit' as part of their degree, rather than more students taking language degrees. As far as we are aware, we are the first to describe changes to programme design and management that led to a dramatic increase in the number of students taking a language degree and financially sustainable programmes. This success is particularly notable because York St John is a low tariff university with a large proportion of students from the least privileged socioeconomic backgrounds—the type of university which is unusual in offering languages to degree level.

The above comparison with previous research has allowed us to reflect on what is innovative about our approach and articulate the key points as follows:

1. Recognise the administrative burden of offering multiple small programmes, and the impact on students when processes such as timetabling do not work smoothly, and only offer as many programmes per language as can be sustained by the number of students—for us this was one for BSL and two each for Japanese/Korean—designing programmes to replace small programmes that are being withdrawn;

2. Design tailor-made programmes that are administered as single honours but appear to students to be joint honours, with the modules taken alongside the language relevant to students' future careers—for us these were TESOL, intercultural communication, working with d/Deaf people—recruiting additional staff to teach both a language and a related subject in which they hold a PhD;
3. Rather than assuming that students applying to low tariff universities do not want to study languages, design programmes that meet their needs and preferences by analysing programme and module enrolment data, as well as what prospective students mention at open days and in personal statements. For us this meant focussing on languages not taught in schools, mitigating against disparities in access to formal language study at school level and reaching students who had been self-studying due to an interest or personal connection with the language or culture.

More concisely, we summarise our approach as follows: recognising the administrative burden and financially unsustainability of offering multiple small programmes, analyse programme and module enrolment data to understand students' preferences, then design one, or two, tailor-made programmes per language.

Now that the programmes are in a financially sustainable position with a design that can easily be rolled out to other languages, the intention is to once again broaden the range of languages offered. In addition, a new nine-week not-for-credit BSL course was launched in 2022 (https://www.yorksj.ac.uk/courses/professional-and-short-courses/languages/introduction-to-british-sign-language/), offering a model for not-for-credit language teaching that could be expanded out to other languages.

We now need to turn our attention to retention. Universities where fewer than 80% of students progress to the second year of their programme may be subject to sanctions—such as monetary penalties, suspension or deregistration—by the Office for Students (OfS), the independent body who regulates the higher education sector (Jack, 2022). While continuation rates on our languages programmes are safely above the OfS threshold of 80% (Office for Students, 2022b), they are cause for concern. Our first years face a double transition—the transition into higher education, and the transition from language as hobby to language as a subject of formal study. Moreover, as language learners in a majority English-speaking country, they are surrounded by unhelpful beliefs and assumptions about language and language learning that can affect confidence. With this in mind, we are currently reviewing our assessment strategy in order to support students and improve retention.

4 Conclusion

Given the decline in language enrolments nationally, and to a large extent internationally, plus the fact that access to language study is unequal, with students from less-privileged backgrounds less able to access formal language study, it is imperative that we design programmes that are attractive to potential students and financially sustainable. While much has been written on curriculum design, little focus has been given to this question, probably because most curriculum design focuses on contexts where student demand is not an issue. In order to attract sufficient students, the previous approach at York St John, and, we suspect, elsewhere, was to offer multiple small joint honours programmes. However, the resulting administrative complexity meant that this approach was not sustainable. Here we present an alternative approach—one, or two, tailor-made programmes per language—which resulted in increased recruitment and sustainable programmes. Future research needs to explore the extent to which this might be applicable to other universities in the sector.

References

Boffey, D. (2013). Language teaching crisis as 40% of university departments face closure. *The Guardian*. https://www.theguardian.com/education/2013/aug/17/language-teaching-crisis-universities-closure

Bovill, C., Bulley, C. J., & Morss, K. (2011). Engaging and empowering first-year students through curriculum design: Perspectives from the literature. *Teaching in Higher Education, 16*(2), 197–209.

British Academy & UCML. (2022). *Languages Learning in Higher Education: Granular Trends.* https://www.thebritishacademy.ac.uk/publications/languages-learning-higher-education-granular-trends/

Brown, J., & Caruso, M. (2016). Access granted: Modern languages and issues of accessibility at university – A case study from Australia. *Language Learning in Higher Education, 6*(2), 453–471.

Byon, A. D. (2008). Korean as a foreign language in the USA: The instructional settings. *Language Culture and Curriculum, 21*(3), 244–255.

Churchward, D. (2019). *Recent trends in modern foreign language exams entries in Anglophone countries.* Ofqual. https://assets.publishing.service.gov.uk/government/uploads/system/uploads/attachment_data/file/844128/Recent_trends_in_modern_foreign_language_exam_entries_in_anglophone_countries_-_FINAL65573.pdf

Collen, I. (2020). Language trends 2020: Language teaching in primary and secondary schools in England. *The British Council.* https://www.britishcouncil.org/sites/default/files/language_trends_2020_0.pdf

Collen, I. (2022). Language Trends 2022: Language teaching in primary and secondary schools in England. *The British Council.* https://www.britishcouncil.org/sites/default/files/language_trends_report_2022.pdf

Crites, K., & Rye, E. (2020). Innovating language curriculum design through design thinking: A case study of a blended learning course at a Colombian university. *System, 94*, 102334.

Department for Education. (2019). *Guidance English Baccalaureate (EBacc).* https://www.gov.uk/government/publications/english-baccalaureate-ebacc/english-baccalaureate-ebacc

Donnelly, M., & Gamsu, S. (2018). *Home and away: Social, ethnic and spatial inequalities in student mobility.* The Sutton Trust.

Dubin, F., & Olshtain, E. (1986). *Course design: Developing programmes and materials for language learning.* Cambridge University Press.

Foreman-Peck, J., & Wang, Y. (2014). *The costs to the UK of language deficiencies as a barrier to UK engagement in exporting: A report to UK trade and investment.* https://assets.publishing.service.gov.uk/government/uploads/system/uploads/attachment_data/file/309899/Costs_to_UK_of_language_deficiencies_as_barrier_to_UK_engagement_in_exporting.pdf

Foster, I. (2019). The future of language learning. *Language, Culture and Curriculum, 32*(3), 261–269.

Guardian. (2022). *The best UK universities 2022 – Rankings*. https://www.theguardian.com/education/ng-interactive/2021/sep/11/the-best-uk-universities-2022-rankings

Hall, C. J., Smith, P. H., & Wicaksono, R. (2017). *Mapping applied linguistics: An introduction for students and practitioners* (2nd ed.). Routledge.

HESA. (2023). *Where do HE students study?* https://www.hesa.ac.uk/data-and-analysis/students/where-study

Jack, P. (2022). Many universities could face sanctions for missing OfS thresholds. *Times Higher Education*. https://www.timeshighereducation.com/news/many-universities-could-face-sanctions-missing-ofs-thresholds

Jones, M. (2016). *Research briefing: Welsh-medium education and Welsh as a subject*. https://senedd.wales/media/1d3glvbm/16-048-english-web.pdf

Lanvers, U. (2017). Elitism in language learning in the UK. In D. Rivers & K. Zotzmann (Eds.), *Isms in language education* (pp. 50–73). De Gruyter Mouton. https://doi.org/10.1515/9781501503085-004

Lanvers, U., & Chambers, G. (2019). In the shadow of global English? Comparing language learner motivation in Germany and the United Kingdom. *The Palgrave Handbook of Motivation for Language Learning*, 429–448.

Lanvers, U., Doughty, H., & Thompson, A. (2018). Brexit as linguistic symptom of Britain retreating into its shell? Brexit-induced politicisation of language learning. *The Modern Language Journal, 102*(4), 775–796. https://doi.org/10.1111/modl.12515

Lanvers, U., Thompson, A. S., & East, M. (2021). Introduction: Is language learning in Anglophone countries in crisis? In U. Lanvers, A. S. Thompson, & M. East (Eds.), *Language learning in Anglophone countries: Challenges, practices, ways forward* (pp. 1–15). Springer International Publishing. https://doi.org/10.1007/978-3-030-56654-8_1

Liddicoat, A. J. (2020). The position of languages in the university curriculum: Australia and the UK. In J. Fornasiero, S. M. A. Reed, R. Amery, et al. (Eds.), *Intersections in language planning and policy* (pp. 115–135). Springer. https://doi.org/10.1007/978-3-030-50925-5_8

Macalister, J., & Nation, I. S. P. (Eds.). (2011). *Case studies in language curriculum design: Concepts and approaches in action around the world*. Routledge.

Markee, N. (1997). *Managing curricular innovation*. Cambridge University Press.

Mickan, P., & Wallace, I. (Eds.). (2020). *The Routledge handbook of language education curriculum design*. Routledge.

Muradás-Taylor, B. (2023). Undergraduate language programmes in England: A widening participation crisis. *Arts and Humanities in Higher Education, 22*(3), 322–342.
Muradás-Taylor, B., & Taylor, P. (2024). 'Cold spots' in language degree provision in England. *The Language Learning Journal, 52*(1), 92–103.
Nation, I. S. P., & Macalister, J. (2010). *Language curriculum design.* Routledge.
O'Neill, G. (2015). *Curriculum design in higher education: Theory to practice.* https://researchrepository.ucd.ie/entities/publication/a3ebfbe2-5fd9-4c43-8793-6861a49a0055/details
Office for Students. (2022a). *Access and participation data dashboard.* https://www.officeforstudents.org.uk/data-and-analysis/access-and-participation-data-dashboard/
Office for Students. (2022b). *Student outcomes data dashboard.* https://www.officeforstudents.org.uk/data-and-analysis/student-outcomes-data-Dashboard/data-dashboard/
Polisca, E., Wright, V., Álvarez, I., & Montoro, C. (2019). Language provision in UK MFL departments 2019 survey. *University Council of Modern Languages.* https://university-council-modern-languages.org/wp-content/uploads/2019/12/LanguageProvisionMFLsSurvey2019.pdf
Priestley, M., & Philippou, S. (2019). Debate and critique in curriculum studies: New directions. *The Curriculum Journal, 30*(4), 347–351.
Schucan Bird, K., & Pitman, L. (2020). How diverse is your reading list? Exploring issues of representation and decolonisation in the UK. *Higher Education, 79*(5), 903–920.
Tinsley, T., & Doležal, N. (2018). Language trends 2018: Language teaching in primary and secondary schools in England. Survey report. *The British Council.* https://www.britishcouncil.org/sites/default/files/language_trends_2018_report.pdf
UCML & British Academy. (2021). *Report on Granular Trends in Modern Languages in UCAS Admissions Data, 2012–2018.* https://university-council-modern-languages.org/2021/07/05/ucml-and-british-academy-ucas-report/
Van Parijs, P. (2004). Europe's linguistic challenge. *European Journal of Sociology, 45*(1), 113–154.
Wicaksono, R. (2012). Raising students' awareness of the construction of communicative (in)competence in international classrooms. In J. Ryan (Ed.), *Cross cultural teaching and learning for home and international students: Internationalisation of pedagogy and curriculum in higher education.* Routledge.
Wicaksono, R. (2020). Native and non-native speakers of English in TESOL. In C. J. Hall & R. Wicaksono (Eds.), *Ontologies of English: Conceptualising the language for learning, teaching, and assessment.* Cambridge University Press.

Through the Lens of Culture: The Transformative Value of a Content and Language Intercultural Learning Approach in England

Ruth Koro

1 Introduction

The need to develop intercultural understanding is not a new imperative in a globalised world: it has long been present in business, albeit framed by instrumental arguments. Societies and classrooms are increasingly linguistically and culturally diverse, leading to a democratisation of intercultural encounters (Hennebry, 2014). Often seen as a challenge, this could, and should, be seen as a significant opportunity for language teachers (Markey et al., 2021) to educate the 'whole' learner (Kim, 2020, p. 520) and equip them with the dynamic skills they will need to interact effectively within—and between—diverse communities.

Of course, it is not just language teachers' responsibility to equip learners with the necessary intercultural skills (Lasagabaster, 2017), but by its

R. Koro (✉)
University of Nottingham, Nottingham, UK
e-mail: Ruth.Koro@nottingham.ac.uk

very nature, language teaching can play a pivotal role in achieving this. This is because language and culture are intrinsically connected—in order to communicate effectively, we use both language and culture to understand our own and others' perspectives (Sudhoff, 2010). This has led many to argue that an exploration of culture is essential to enable the meaningful, contextualised and effective acquisition of another language (Nechifor & Borca, 2020; Saniei, 2012).

This interrelationship between language and culture and the imperatives presented by globalisation have influenced language education policy and practice in many countries (Huber & Reynolds, 2014), with intercultural understanding becoming a key tenet in many curricula around the world. Consequently, in the language classroom (and beyond), there is a need for teachers to adopt pedagogical approaches which enable learners to become culturally aware (cultural awareness), develop their ability to understand different cultural perspectives (cultural understanding), and mediate effectively between their own and others' culture (intercultural understanding). Indeed, this is now seen as a 'social and political' responsibility by some (Byram & Wagner, 2018, p. 141).

Integrative approaches such as Content and Language Integrated Learning (CLIL), which centres on the '4Cs' of Content, Cognition, Communication and Culture (Coyle et al., 2010) seem to present opportunities to embed linguistic and cultural goals and to offer more stimulating content (Hunt, 2011) and a more engaging experience for language learners (Coonan, 2007). While 'not a panacea' (Dobson, 2020, p. 513), CLIL has therefore become a prominent feature of language policy and practice in Europe and beyond.

However, in the unique context of England, which I will explore further below, intercultural goals have failed to become embedded in policy or practice (Hennebry, 2014), as have innovative pedagogies such as CLIL—its uses remaining isolated and experimental in nature (Bower, 2020). This is particularly odd given the perennial issues of learner motivation—especially in the secondary classroom (Graham et al., 2016). While the case could therefore easily be made that innovation on these two fronts (intercultural goals and CLIL pedagogy) may be worth exploring, much of the focus for language education in discourse, policy and practice remains on narrow linguistic goals, and the rationale for language learning is almost exclusively expressed in instrumentalist terms, further feeding the problem surrounding motivation and engagement which have been prevailing in the national context (Coffey, 2018).

Given this unique and complex context, my argument is twofold: what may work best is an innovative pedagogical approach such as CLIL, but also an innovative take on CLIL, one which makes intercultural understanding its main goal. By reconceptualising the CLIL paradigm and exploring **content through the lens of culture**, intercultural exploration, interaction, communication and collaboration can frame and redefine the experience for learners and contribute to addressing the perennial—and as yet unsolved—issues of motivation for language learning in England's secondary schools.

In this chapter, I will begin by exploring the context of language learning in England, focusing on the place of intercultural learning in policy and practice. I will also discuss why approaches such as CLIL have remained marginal in the English context despite the potential benefits, before proposing a reconceptualised CLIL model to foster learners' intercultural attitudinal attributes, along with a framework to enable teachers to implement this in practice. This will be illustrated by the findings from an intervention study carried out in secondary language classrooms in England. It is hoped that the discussions in this chapter will make the case for the transformative value of the intercultural CLIL classroom, and that the proposed framework and findings from the study will provide useful takeaways for other teachers seeking to transmit the broader goals of language education and to make their learners' experience a more intercultural, enriching and holistic one.

2 Language Learning in England: Context, Policy and Practice

For many years, the lack of language skills in England has been of concern (Fielding, 2020), impacting the country's capacity on the global economic stage, and its readiness to face societal change and global challenges. Commenting on the issue, an All-Party Parliamentary Group on Modern Languages declared that 'the UK is in a languages crisis' (2019, p. 2). To add to this perduring challenge, the context of Brexit had contributed to heighten negative attitudes towards language learning in society (Scally et al., 2021) and to making 'issues of multilingualism and multiculturalism […] politically contentious' (Bowler, 2020, p. 14).

Cause or consequence of this longstanding crisis, the decline in language learning, is well-documented and often attributed to the move in 2004 to make language study non-compulsory beyond Key Stage 3 (KS3, ages 11–14; Wingate, 2018). As a result, in contrast to many EU countries, where nearly half (49%) of learners study more than two languages (Eurostat, 2022), in England, the proportion of pupils taking a GCSE examination at the end of Key Stage 4 (ages 14–16) fell from 86% to 46% between 1998 and 2021 (Long & Danechi, 2022).

While learners' motivation is prevalent as a root cause in debates (Dobson, 2018; Parrish & Lanvers, 2019), the issue is complex and often relates to the impact of popular and policy discourse on the curriculum and classroom practices. The following contributing factors are those most often mentioned in the literature:

Context

- the monolingual context and perceived status of English as a Lingua Franca (Lanvers, 2020)
- the benefits of language study being expressed in purely instrumentalist terms (Fielding, 2020) which fail to reflect learners' real sources of motivation (Coffey, 2018)
- Boys, disadvantaged and lower-attaining pupils all less likely to have positive views towards language learning and to pursue learning beyond compulsory stages (Broady, 2020; Lanvers, 2020; Peiser & Jones, 2013)

Policy

- The ineffectiveness of the prevalent pedagogical approaches centred on teacher-led instruction and on a narrow focus on linguistic goals, and on a 'cognitivist approach' in the curriculum and related assessment frameworks (Grüber & Hopwood, 2022, p. 257)

- the well-documented difficulty for pupils to achieve high grades in language examinations, when compared to other subjects (Lanvers et al., 2018)
- a drop in creative and innovative approaches to language teaching from primary to secondary level, (Graham et al., 2016), often related to curriculum and assessment pressures (Parrish, 2020)

Practice

- the little time (and money) afforded to language learning in schools (Grüber & Hopwood, 2022)
- a lack of consistency and quality in primary language teaching (Cardim-Dias & Zodgekar, 2022) and a lack of continuity and communication in the planning and delivery of transition between primary and secondary language learning (Fielding, 2020)
- frequent misinterpretation of or a complete lack of awareness about language learning theories among teachers (Wingate & Andon, 2018)
- a lack of intercultural and cognitively challenging content available to beginner learners (Porter et al., 2022)

While a range of recent policy initiatives have aimed to counter this trend, they have to date yielded little success (Hagger-Vaughan, 2020).

This set of challenges make the language learning context of England a complex one and contribute to the demotivation of learners, the decline of languages in schools, and the scarcity of innovative and engaging teaching practices in the classroom.

3 Intercultural Understanding in the Language Curriculum: The English Exception

From 2010, amid a new political landscape, a significant and rapid reform of the whole curriculum took place, taking a more traditionalist view of the purpose of education, and articulated around academic achievement, accountability and performativity (Lupton & Thomson, 2015). Despite promising declarations that 'learning a foreign language is a liberation from insularity and provides an opening to other cultures' (DfE, 2013, p. 172), the new language curriculum documents show little alignment to global policy trends highlighting the importance of intercultural goals (Grüber & Hopwood, 2022), and the focus remains on linguistic competence (Byram & Wagner, 2018).

A Modern Foreign Languages Pedagogy Review (Bauckham, 2016) and Curriculum Research Review (OCRR; Ofsted, 2021) were commissioned by the government and led to further reform of assessment frameworks (DfE, 2023). Both the Pedagogy and Research Reviews aim to share guiding principles for what is viewed as good pedagogical practice, and present vocabulary, phonics and grammar as the 'pillars of progression in the curriculum' to take learners from 'novice to expert' (Ofsted, 2021, Pillars of progression section). Unfortunately, the mention of cultural aspects remains tokenistic in nature and the focus remains, once again, squarely on linguistic goals, with guidelines not extending to the development of learners' intercultural understanding. Publication was followed by much controversy on the breadth, validity and robustness of the purported evidence base for the Reviews, and on the little affordance given to existing scholarly and practice-based evidence relating to the value and necessity of embedding intercultural goals in the language curriculum, especially when considering the specific challenges facing Languages in the English context: Indeed, on the OCRR, Woore et al. (2022) note that:

> students' motivation and their progress in other aspects of language learning should also be considered. It is no good students being able to apply the correct endings to a verb if this is accompanied by boredom or even hostility towards the target language and its culture - a problem we have encountered amongst Key Stage 3 students in the past. (p. 153)

With similar concerns raised by Blow and Myers (2022) about the revised GCSE Subject Content:

> turning language learning into learning a list of 1200 words makes it easier both to teach and learn, but that is surely a travesty of what realistic lan-

guage learning entails and what in language learning can be motivating to learners. It is our view that, far from increasing uptake of languages at GCSE, the revisions that make up the 2022 GCSE Subject Content may well demotivate learners and undermine continuation to further study. (p. 246)

The curriculum documents briefly explored above not only fail to address learner motivation, but risk heightening the problem—leaving a jarring gap where intercultural goals are concerned, and an apparent lack of intention to address this odd omission going forward (Coffey, 2022), instead providing a very unstable foundation on which teachers are supposed to build effective practice.

England therefore remains a 'notable exception' (Hennebry, 2014, p. 148) in addressing the broader goals of language education. A prescriptive curriculum, a narrow focus on linguistic goals and the failure to embed intercultural goals in language policy only serve to lead teachers to attend to the most pressing: preparing their pupils for academic success, rather than 'tak[ing] them on a journey of discovery into the target language and its culture, which they can approach with enjoyment, positivity and success' (Woore et al., 2022, p. 154).

4 Intercultural Teaching and Learning in the Secondary Classroom

Beliefs and Barriers

There is growing evidence that language teachers in England see intercultural learning as the prime objective of language learning (Koro, 2017) and as a strong contributor to fostering lasting engagement with, and motivation for language learning (Fielding, 2020).

However, it is also clear that curriculum and assessment frameworks have a strong influence on practice: to a large extent, teachers are expected to comply with, and enact policy in the classroom, and this can have an impact on their ability or willingness to engage in pedagogical innovation. This, together with a lack of theoretical framework to support the implementation of intercultural teaching (Byram & Wagner, 2018), has led to a marked dichotomy between teachers' beliefs and their practice in the classroom.

However, a recent survey (Koro, 2017) also noted that while teachers expressed strong views in favour of intercultural goals, cultural awareness ranked last in a list of desirable learners' skills to be developed and indicated that they prioritise those relating to the linguistic goals of language learning. Teachers were also quick to identify key barriers to implementing intercultural teaching:

- An unfavourable educational and policy landscape
- Inflexible curriculum and assessment frameworks
- A lack of available resources
- A lack of time to plan and keep up to date with the latest cultural 'trends'
- A lack of curriculum time for language lessons
- The influence of home context on learners' attitudes and intercultural opportunities
- English as a Lingua Franca and its impact on learners' motivation for language learning
- A perception that learners with lower linguistic attainment cannot access authentic/cultural content

Whether these barriers are real or perceived, many language teachers in England view intercultural teaching as a low priority and something that curriculum and assessment frameworks leave little flexibility for; reflecting the discourse seen in policy documents, intercultural teaching is therefore seen as an optional add-on (Hennebry, 2014), or fear of 'diluting linguistic objectives with socio-cultural ones' (Peiser & Jones, 2012, p. 183).

So How Do Secondary Language Learners Develop Their Intercultural Skills in England?

These barriers, combined with the complex contextual challenges discussed earlier, act as so many hurdles to intercultural learning, which remains a rarity in secondary classrooms (Peiser & Jones, 2012), and as a result, little research exists to explore the way it is enacted in this context (Porter et al., 2022). Where evidence exists, it shows that cultural elements, when included, are generally tokenistic, superficial and only introduced as a means to support linguistic learning (Scally et al., 2021), rather than with the goal to provide learners with opportunities to develop intercultural skills (Baker, 2015).

While there is research pointing to learners' interest for exploring other cultures (Koro, 2017, 2018), there is also evidence that learners are very aware that their opportunities for intercultural learning are fewer in the secondary school; furthermore, there is also evidence that sufficient cognitive challenge is rarely present in the secondary language classroom, with Wingate (2018) noting that there is a

> serious underestimation of pupils' cognitive and intellectual capability […] it is fair to speak of an MFL classroom culture of low expectations, lack of challenge and light entertainment. It is possible that this culture has gradually developed as a result of the negative perceptions of MFL in England and of dwindling student numbers and that it reflects teachers' desire to make language learning look easy and fun. (p. 452)

This paints a stark picture of intercultural language learning in England: One where context, policy and practice not only fail to reflect the beliefs of language teachers, the cognitive skills and interests of learners, and their need to develop intercultural competencies, but they also fail, in doing so, to address the very root of the motivation problem marring language study in England, by repeatedly missing out on the role that intercultural teaching could play. This has led many to argue for a complete reconceptualisation of language teaching, one that fosters intercultural goals (Byram & Wagner, 2018) in order to provide learners with a different and worthwhile rationale for and experience of language learning (Grüber & Hopwood, 2022).

5   The Need to Reconceptualise Curriculum, Policy and Practice Around Intercultural Goals: Can CLIL Offer a Suitable Solution in the English Context?

Reconceptualising the Goals of Language Teaching and Learning

Woore et al. (2020) argue that teachers' beliefs on the importance of intercultural learning should be reflected in the language curriculum in England, to ensure its effective and meaningful implementation. Blow and Myers (2022) also argue that, in order to avoid further demotivating England's language learners, there should be a requirement for linguistic content to be contextualised through 'cultural themes' and that this, in turn, would also provide the necessary 'imperative for teachers' to integrate intercultural pedagogy in the classroom (p. 244)—a move which Peiser and Jones (2012) see as necessary to ensure the 'rhetoric of curriculum policy […] become[s] a reality in the MFL classroom' (p. 185). While linguistic goals are important, policy should reflect the wealth of evidence on the potential benefits of intercultural language teaching (Woore et al., 2022) in order to reconceptualise the language learning endeavour as a more holistic and enriching one, through approaches which foster innovation, cognitive challenge and cultural exploration (Porter et al., 2022).

CLIL: An Innovative Approach in the English Context, and a Solution?

One such approach, Content and Language Integrated Learning (CLIL) could offer a possible way forward and contribute to greater learner motivation, if adapted to the unique context in England (Dobson, 2020).

CLIL can be defined as the use of the language of instruction to teach both content (often related to another area of the curriculum) and language. Like many integrated pedagogical models of language education, it is often viewed as an ideal way to develop learners' intercultural competence, because of its equal focus on language and culture, through the 4Cs model proposed by Coyle and her colleagues (Coyle et al., 2010): Content, Cognition, Communication and Culture.

There is growing evidence attesting to the benefits of a CLIL approach: an increase in learners' motivation for language learning (Dalton-Puffer, 2007), a greater degree of cognitive challenge (Hunt, 2011), a positive shift in learners' attitudes (Coyle et al., 2010), gains in cultural knowledge (Campos, 2009), the capacity to reflect on differing cultural perspectives (Koro, 2017) and opportunities to develop intercultural competence (Sudhoff, 2010). In light of these stated benefits, it can therefore be argued that the CLIL model, if fully realised, has much potential. However, despite some early interest and research in CLIL approaches in England, its uses remain experimental in nature and somewhat of an innovation (Bower, 2020; Dobson, 2020), notwithstanding the prevalence of the approach in international curricula, and despite evidence its implementation in England could contribute to addressing many of the challenges specific to the context (Dearing & King, 2007). The lack of mention of CLIL in more recent policy documents leaves teachers isolated and without the necessary guidance (Dobson, 2020) and local initiatives less likely to be sustainable in the longer term (Bower, 2020).

However, while CLIL has much potential, there are also a number of limitations worthy of note where current practice is concerned: It is often the preserve of learners who have already achieved higher linguistic proficiency—leaving out a vast majority of language learners, including those most needing motivation (Bruton, 2013); teachers often lack clarity on desired outcomes (Driscoll et al., 2013), and there is a disproportionate focus on teacher-talk and surface-learning exercises serving either the content or the language (Sobré, 2017) instead of the holistic needs of language learners; there is also disproportionate focus on receptive skills in many CLIL classrooms, with little opportunity for learners to use the language for meaningful purposes (Cenoz & Ruiz de Zarobe, 2015). In terms of intercultural goals, learners are seldom given opportunities to reflect on their own culture and to engage in the compare/contrast process, a key principle in intercultural teaching (Byram & Wagner, 2018), and the rationale for taking a CLIL approach tends to maintain a focus on the instrumental goals of language learning (Wilson, 2013).

Therefore, while culture is a central tenet of the CLIL framework, developing learners' intercultural skills is not (Porto, 2018). If we wish to still consider CLIL as a worthwhile innovation in the English context, we must therefore redefine its paradigm through intercultural principles.

6 Towards Intercultural CLIL Principles

In order to reconceptualise CLIL around intercultural goals, I propose the following renewed principles and argue that CLIL should stand for:

C – Content seen through the lens of culture

Meaningful intercultural content to foster engagement and memorable learning; providing higher value to the knowledge acquired contributes to higher levels of motivation in learners (Moya et al., 2016) and can give the intercultural CLIL classroom a transformative role.

L – Language to foster intercultural communication and collaboration

As language learning is a social process, the goal of language learning should be to enable (intercultural) interaction. Consequently, communication and collaboration should be central in the intercultural language classroom, as they can contribute to learners' intercultural and societal awareness through dialogue (Freire, 2004; Sorrells, 2013).

I – Intercultural experiences to foster affective engagement

Integrating culture in language education can foster learners' affective motivation (Doiz et al., 2014). An approach which promotes the importance of both language and culture through exploration and relatable experiences can provide an engaging way to contribute to learners' linguistic acquisition while supporting the development of their intercultural understanding (Koro, 2017, 2018).

L – Learning for meaningful, tangible outcomes

In order to have meaning and motivate, learning should have a purpose, and be relevant to learners. Effective approaches are therefore most likely to be project-based and require learners to work collaboratively and independently towards a shared goal; this can also enable them to experience more immediate success, rather than expecting sustained motivation on the premise of longer-term linguistic gains.

These reconceptualised, intercultural CLIL principles have the potential to provide a more holistic approach to language education, to offer learners meaningful, engaging and cognitively challenging content, and to motivate them intrinsically.

7   A Framework for Transformative Intercultural CLIL Pedagogy

Operating within a more holistic framework for language education can however seem quite a wide-reaching and daunting prospect for language teachers, which may explain why many tend to shy away from incorporating intercultural goals more readily in their everyday practice. Therefore, to support planning and implementation and to help teachers gauge learners' progress both in terms of linguistic knowledge and skills and in terms of intercultural attributes, a revised framework is proposed for intercultural CLIL pedagogy. This framework, inspired by Byram's intercultural competence model of *savoirs* (1997) and by the CLIL framework (Coyle et al., 2010), is summarised in Table 1.

To further elaborate, the framework can be summarised as follows:

- In the **introductory stage**, the aim is to set the scene for learners and generate interest and curiosity, through experiential activities and immersion in the language being taught. Activities focus on receptive language skills and promote affective motivation through the use of authentic, engaging and relatable content that is culturally relevant through a range of materials; these present learners with content that is cognitively accessible and familiar so as to raise confidence levels, which in turn promotes continued engagement and motivation despite the potential threat of increasingly challenging language and content as the sequence of lessons progresses. The content focuses on cultural, factual knowledge—facts, figures, images—as students have not yet developed the intercultural attitudinal attributes required to shift perspectives.

Table 1 Framework for transformative intercultural CLIL pedagogy

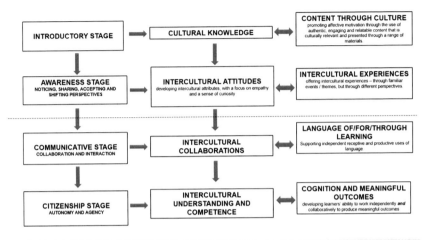

- In the **awareness stage**, the longest in the sequence, the aim is to build on learners' curiosity, through dialogic and collaborative activities. These will continue to focus on receptive skills, but guided language production can be built in; activities will help promote affective motivation through the use of a wider range of authentic materials presenting familiar events and themes, but through perspectives different to those of learners. Content is still cognitively accessible, but this may be achieved through careful scaffolding of tasks as the linguistic challenge is increased—offering additional opportunities to focus on building language learning skills. Despite the increasingly challenging language and content, there are opportunities for learners to verbalise emotions by switching between L1 and L2 where necessary, and to identify with similar perspectives to their own: this can in turn help learners start to develop key intercultural attitudinal attributes, with a focus on empathy, enabling them to gradually start shifting perspectives while maintaining affective motivation.
- In the **communicative stage**, the aim is to support more independent receptive and productive uses of language. Activities continue to promote affective motivation through the use of a wider and more complex range of authentic materials, presenting unfamiliar events and themes. Content is cognitively challenging, and with careful

mediation, learners can feel more confident applying their linguistic and intercultural skills in new contexts with increasing support from their peers—and decreasing support from the teacher. Despite the use of more complex language and content, learners can start to show sufficient adaptation to use the L2 for real purposes, and the sense of achievement this generates can further contribute to affective motivation. Empathy is consolidated as learners become able to shift more readily between perspectives.
- In the **citizenship stage**, the aim is to demonstrate intercultural understanding and competence through the realisation of meaningful outcomes. The focus is on productive skills and independent collaborations. Learners are given opportunities to synthetise their cultural and linguistic knowledge and skills and to apply their intercultural attitudinal attributes with the aim to share their learning with a specific audience—presenting unfamiliar content and differing perspectives in a familiar context. Content is for the most part determined by learners and can be produced through the L1, the L2 or a combination; along with the purposeful production of language, this can further contribute to their sense of achievement and to affective motivation. Learners' acceptance of the shifting between perspectives, necessary to the completion of the activities, can consolidate empathy and enable them to demonstrate a level of intercultural understanding and competence.

To illustrate this framework in practical terms, the following section provides a summary of the intervention study I carried out—and its key findings.

8   Through the Lens of Culture: Intercultural CLIL in Practice

Background and Rationale

Through my own experiences teaching languages in English secondary schools, it became clear that the goal of learning a language should be seen in broader terms and enable learners to develop intercultural as well as linguistic competence—yet the scope for achieving this through existing curriculum models was limited. As a practitioner, I was also aware that I had some agency in enacting the curriculum, and that, if I found the content and materials lacking, then it was in my power to explore ways to address this. When I delved a little more, I came across CLIL, but did not find much on the use of the approach in the context of secondary schools, and in particular, in the context of England—nor did much focus on intercultural goals. From my perspective, it seemed a missed opportunity to reserve such an innovative approach to those very pupils who needed motivation least: the youngest, or the most advanced learners. It also seemed obvious that exploring the value of using a CLIL approach with younger secondary learners at Key Stage 3 (ages 11–14) would be beneficial, due to their more developed linguistic and cognitive skills and being the age when they both tend to lose motivation for, and abandon language learning. Curious as to why an approach, prevalent internationally, was almost unheard of among colleagues, I conducted a practitioner study exploring its potential to develop learners' intercultural understanding, skills and attributes.

Participants

The aim was primarily to explore and improve my own practice, so one of the classes involved was my own. To broaden the scope of the study, I sought out language teachers interested in taking part through an online teaching forum. As a result, 94 secondary students and 19 teachers were selected for participation across four schools. To achieve broad comparability, and to facilitate the planned intervention approach, all participating groups were from state-maintained, mixed-sex schools in England with French the only language studied by participants. Finally, as the study sought to explore the value of a CLIL approach with younger, lower-attaining and unmotivated secondary students, only Year 8 classes (aged 12–13) fitting this profile were selected. Two of the classes participated in a first wave of intervention, with the remaining two classes doing this at a later stage.

Procedures

The study centred on a taught intervention exploring whether a series of lessons (Appendix 1) following an intercultural CLIL approach could contribute to the development of learners' intercultural understanding. Prior to the start of the study, language teachers involved were offered a choice of topics and cross-curricular links for the sequence to be taught, and they opted for the topic of 'French children in the second World War'. The theme, marrying History with French, offered scope to align with linguistic content prescribed in the respective schools' curriculum (the use of the perfect tense and narrating events in the past), as well as being the most likely to draw on the interests of students and on their prior historical knowledge (the period was also studied as part of the History curriculum). In planning the history content, subject specialist teachers were consulted to establish learners' existing historical knowledge, but the delivery of the sequence of lessons was conducted solely by the language teachers in the respective participating schools, due to practical constraints.

The taught intervention consisted of a series of 15 lessons with accompanying materials (Appendix 2). The sequence of lessons was delivered over a period of six to eight weeks, depending on the context of each participating school. To ensure participation and consistency of approach, I designed all lesson plans and materials for the sequence and shared these with participating teachers.

To gauge the impact—if any—of the intervention on learners' intercultural understanding, this was supplemented by teacher and student questionnaires, providing both qualitative and quantitative data. Teacher questionnaires were designed using emerging themes from a literature review exploring the place of intercultural understanding in language education. These aimed to explore teachers' beliefs, attitudes and perceptions, their current practice, including use of materials, and what barriers they perceived to intercultural teaching and learning. The study also used teacher interviews to explore these themes in more depth. Students' questionnaires were also designed to explore attitudes, perceptions and experiences of learning a language, and to establish their existing level of intercultural knowledge and understanding. Further to this, taught participants were asked to complete the same questionnaire again, with the addition of a quiz aiming to gauge any gains in cultural knowledge, providing quantitative data; other aspects such as lesson observations and students' work provided additional qualitative insights.

Design of the Intervention Lessons

The design of the sequence was guided by the principles of the reconceptualised intercultural CLIL paradigm, which, as I have explained earlier, consists of:

- **C** – Content seen through the lens of culture
- **L** – Language to foster intercultural communication and collaboration
- **I** – Intercultural experiences to foster affective engagement
- **L** – Learning for meaningful, tangible outcomes

The sequencing of the lessons followed the four stages of the intercultural CLIL framework detailed in Table 1, as follows:

- In the **introductory stage**, consisting of lessons 1 and 2, the scene was set for learners through a range of video clips on villages in France, to create a sense of discovery and immersion from the onset. This was followed by a focus on the village of Oradour-sur-Glane in the second half of the first lesson, during which—to generate interest and curiosity—students worked with their peers to comprehend a range of contradicting statements on the village; this was supported by the use of repetitive sentence structures, cognates and evocative pictures, and immersion in the target language.

In the second lesson, more contradicting statements were presented, followed by a collaborative task in which students were given 15 minutes in groups to deduct what had made the village so notable, and to articulate their hypothesis in French using a speaking frame. Once a group had correctly extrapolated that Oradour-sur-Glane had been one of the

French martyred villages during the Second World War, the class was set a further research task as homework, to find out more about the events and report back, this time in their L1 (English) in the next lesson.

- The **awareness stage** consisted of a further 4 lessons (lessons 3, 4, 5 and 6), conducted in the target language, with opportunities for learners to share thoughts and emotions in the L1. In order to further build on learners' curiosity through experiential immersion, each of these lessons welcomed them with sound or music (an air raid siren in lesson 3 for instance), followed by a range of presentation formats (slides, videos, animated clips, recordings, diary entries); in lesson 3, the focus was on the key events of the Second World War; this gave students a chance to share their existing knowledge on the topic, while still being presented with a different perspective, for instance with a focus on the Occupation period in France, which they were less familiar with. Students had to work in pairs to reconstruct a long text in the target language using the information presented, narrating the chronology of the war. In lessons 4, 5 and 6, students were then presented with the opportunity to build on their knowledge of Oradour-sur-Glane (familiar content) while relating it to new yet relatable content: the account of a boy who had survived the events in the village. To make his perspective accessible, real information was presented to students in diary format, again using repetitive sentence structures and cognates. Students worked on a range of individual, paired and group activities to further explore the events and understand the boy's account, which enabled them to start shifting perspectives and develop empathy gradually.
- In the **communicative** stage (lessons 6, 7 and 8), students had the opportunity to listen to voice recordings of other survivors of the event (created using text-to-speech software) and conducted a role-play in which they interviewed one of the survivors, using the facts gathered in the listening task and a speaking frame. They also explored the final pages of the boy's 'diary' independently, finding out what had happened to him at the end of the war. While the content was more challenging, their desire to discover the fate of a person they were now familiar with provided sufficient motivation, and the linguistic skills

they had developed the necessary confidence to decipher content successfully and with minimal teacher input. Empathy was consolidated through their discussions and ability to stand in the boy's shoes for the time of the lessons.
- In the **citizenship** stage (lessons 9 to 15), students were given the opportunity to recount the events in their own words and in their own language through the writing of an article for the school's newsletter (lesson 9), later presented to their peers (lesson 12). In order to further consolidate the development of empathy and intercultural understanding among learners, lesson 10 gave students opportunities to explore French songs and poems related to the Second World War, lesson 11 enabled them to discover other events having affected children in France during the Second World War, and lessons 13 to 15 provided insight into the period of the occupation through a structured film study using the French movie *la Rafle* (2010).

An insight into the lesson sequence and its key features can also be found in Appendices 1 and 2.

9 Findings

Affective Motivation for and Through the Exploration of Cultural Perspectives

There was evidence that the application of an intercultural CLIL framework led to the development of learners' affective motivation for and through the exploration of different cultural perspectives. The study found that learners valued intercultural opportunities, and that this, in turn, contributed to greater degrees of motivation, cultural knowledge and intercultural understanding. When surveyed, 56% stated they wanted to learn more about French-speaking countries and people, 70.6% said they liked learning about different people, and 82.6% enjoyed learning about different countries.

Following the sequence of CLIL lessons, students also indicated greater enjoyment of language learning through intercultural elements—moving from 4.3% to 26.1% post-intervention. This seemed to indicate that, while teachers often viewed linguistic competence as a pre-requisite to access intercultural content, the careful planning and design of interculturally rich materials can serve to develop learners' intrinsic motivation for the subject, if made accessible through the use of transparent language and engaging visuals.

A Better Understanding of the Broader Value of Language Learning

When students were asked to consider the broader value of language learning (Table 2), aspects related to instrumental motivation were given more prominence before the intervention (82.5% of first responses) while those relating to intercultural attitudes and attributes ranked much lower (17.5%). Following the intervention, these changed to 69.9% and 30.1%, respectively, indicating a shift from the instrumental towards the affective and intercultural.

The 'difference' factor often associated with the exploration of otherness seemed to be viewed more positively (from 13% to 17.4%), and

Table 2 Pre- and post-test students' first responses on the benefits of language learning (N = 60)

Benefits of language learning	Pre-test%	Post-test%
It can get you a better job later	43.2	23.1
It can help you get into university	14.3	24.5
You can use the language when you go on holidays	7.1	3.8
It gives you access to more jobs	17.9	18.5
INSTRUMENTAL ASPECTS – CUMULATIVE	**82.5**	**69.9**
It helps you meet people from different countries	3.6	14.8
It can help you understand and use your own language better	3.6	3.8
It can help you understand how people may do things differently	10.3	11.5
INTERCULTURAL ASPECTS – CUMULATIVE	**17.5**	**30.1**

even for those students who disliked learning a language, none stated this was because it was 'too different', perhaps also indicating a shift in attitudes (7.1% to none post-intervention). There was also evidence of an increase in learners' ability to engage with different perspectives and to demonstrate empathy following exposure to the intervention materials, both through their own language (English) and that of instruction (French), collaboratively and on their own.

The Role of Authentic, Culturally Relevant Materials

The survey presented some interesting findings on the impact of authentic, culturally relevant materials. While teachers noted the value of video clips for intercultural teaching (47.4%), movies, pictures, internet resources, songs and poems ranked much lower, with 10.5% each. However, it was clear from observing the pre- and post-intervention data that learners responded positively to the use of video clips (0 to 8.3%), movies (5.7 to 16.7%) and online materials (11.4 to 25%). This shift could be interpreted as a willingness to embrace more authentic, challenging and culturally rich materials, if given the opportunity. Also interesting was the evidence that, when presented with alternative materials, learners became significantly less interested in their usual textbooks (34.3 to 19.4%), worksheets (11.4 to 5.6%) and their teachers' own presentations (25.7 to 19.4%), indicating that they favoured culturally rich but linguistically challenging content over easier to access, linguistic-focused material.

Limitations

Of course, this study was small in scale and does not claim generalisability, and the scope of this chapter does not permit the presentation of all the findings; however, as an under-researched aspect, and to make the case for a more holistic and intercultural approach, I chose to present the learners' perspectives here. Furthermore, the study has the merit to present an insight into how teacher beliefs and practice can be reconciled.

While there are limits to the cultural skills and knowledge a teacher can impart in isolation, and many barriers to the implementation of intercultural learning, many of these barriers are not insurmountable, and the scope of intercultural practice should be motivation enough to overcome them.

Implications for Practice

There is a need for language educators to acknowledge the value of an intercultural approach to language education, and to shift to more holistic goals. While challenging, this shift is necessary as it can contribute to teachers' and learners' motivation, but also to the full realisation of the wider value of language learning in society.

Policy makers should provide teachers with the necessary guiding principles and frameworks to enact the curriculum in ways that consider the intrinsic role of intercultural understanding in the development of communicative competence. I would also argue that they should go further and consider the individual, affective dimension and dynamic processes involved in the development of intercultural understanding; only then will they be able to ensure learners have the opportunities and desire to truly engage with language learning and to develop intercultural skills.

The intercultural CLIL classroom can democratise access to innovative pedagogies in the English context and counterbalance the noted tendency to 'isolat[e] language in cognitive space' (Atkinson, 2010, p. 617) and to limit language education to narrow linguistic and instrumental goals.

The choice of materials in the intercultural classroom is also important to foster intercultural engagement and the development of the empathetic learner, and materials should be:

- authentic and varied in nature
- culturally relevant in content
- relatable to learners

- cognitively challenging
- accessible to all learners, regardless of their linguistic competence
- carefully scaffolded
- diverse in their representation of the 'polysemantic' nature of culture. (Byram & Wagner, 2018, p. 142)

10 Conclusion

Intercultural understanding can no longer merely be conceptualised as a positive by-product of language education but should be both its main tenet and objective. In order to engage and retain learners' affective motivation and their active engagement in language learning, and to fulfil the potential of language education to contribute to their holistic development, we need to move away from the instrumental towards the affective, from the utilitarian to the principled, from atomistic to more holistic approaches such as the intercultural CLIL one explored. This approach can combine the linguistic and the cultural, the pragmatic and the idealistic, the individual and the global to make for more rounded language learners.

Learning another language and exploring other cultures can be challenging processes, which both require careful planning from teachers; however, by putting the individual learner back at the heart of policy and practice, where it belongs, we could enable language education to fulfil its potential for learning that is meaningful and transformational, that can give language learners true motivation, and that will serve to support their journey to becoming interculturally competent in a globalised and changing world.

Appendix 1: Overview of Lesson Sequence

Lesson	Content and stage	Linguistic / Intercultural focus	Use of L1 / L2
Lessons 1 and 2	Contextualisation, students introduced to the village of Oradour-sur-Glane.	Collaborative investigative tasks completed independently in small groups.	Use of French as the main medium of instruction.
Lesson 3	Consolidation of knowledge on WW2, from a French perspective.	Receptive skills focus: use of video clips, extended reading task explored collaboratively as a whole class.	Use of French as the main medium of instruction.
Lessons 4 to 8	Exploration of the life of a child before, during and after the events of Oradour-sur-Glane.	Narration through diary entries, focus on empathy and linguistic aspects.	Use of French as the main medium of instruction.
Lesson 9	Student summary in the form of a newsletter article.	Productive task and focus on comprehension, analytical and synthesising skills.	Use of learners' L1.
Lesson 10	Refocus on broad historical content.	Engagement with lesser-used materials: songs and poems related to WW2, intercultural opportunities through authentic materials—reading and listening skills	Use of French as the main medium of instruction.
Lesson 11	Further study of historical period through intercultural lens.	Focus on receptive skills, reading and listening.	Use of French as the main medium of instruction.
Lesson 12	Students share their article through class presentation.	Presentation skills.	Use of learners' L1.
Lessons 13 to 15	Film study.	Focus on empathy and comprehension/listening skills.	Use of French as the main medium of instruction.

Appendix 2: Exemplar Materials from Lesson Sequence

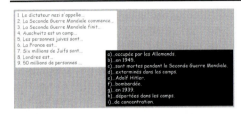

Le mystère d'Oradour-sur-Glane

Oradour est un ancien village qui date de la période romaine.
Oradour n'est pas un vieux village: il a été construit en 1947.
Oradour est un village, pas une ville célèbre comme Paris.
Oradour n'est pas un village anonyme: une rue à Paris porte son nom.

Le mystère d'Oradour-sur-Glane

est-ce que...		pendant
je peux...	aller	avant
tu peux...	visiter	après
il y a...	faire	depuis
c'est...	voir	génial
parce que...	jouer	amusant
à cause de...	se promener	terrible
grâce à...	acheter	affreux
quelque chose que	manger	intéressant
quelqu'un qui		joli

Presenting content through the lens of the target culture
Learners were introduced to the events leading to the second world war, using the target language, and presenting a different perspective to that they would have been familiar with.

Offering challenging content, manageable through the use of cognates
Here, learners were presented with a range of statements following the same sentence structure (repetition) and the use of cognates to support their understanding of more complex language (use of context).

Providing language needed by the students to carry out the planned activities
This is an example of a speaking frame learners were provided with to complete one of the collaborative tasks.

(continued)

(continued)

j'ai joué	I have played
Ils ont cassé	They have broken
ma sœur a aidé	My sister has helped
j'ai écouté	I have listened
Les alliés ont débarqué	The Allies have landed
Nous avons mangé	We have eaten
maman a caché	Mum has hidden
j'ai visité	I have visited
Nous avons rencontré	We have met
Paul a demandé	Paul has asked
vous avez parlé	Have you spoken
Ils ont massacré	They have massacred
Les allemands ont débarqué	The Germans have arrived
Ils ont emmené	They have taken away
J'ai attendu	I have waited

Using highly recyclable language, applied in the topic's context
Grammatical concepts were introduced as part of the content study, with learners developing their linguistic understanding through exposure and application.

Le film
Titre:
Date de sortie:
Genre:
Le film raconte l'histoire de _____.
Ça se passe à Paris, le _____ 1942.
C'est pendant l'occupation _____ de la France.
Le personnage principal s'appelle _____.

Promoting affective motivation through the use of authentic, engaging and relatable content from a wide range of sources and types of materials
Throughout the sequence, learners studied a range of songs, poems and a film (in French language, with English subtitles) on themes relating to the second world war, exploring a wide range of topics, for instance the Resistance movement, the occupation of France and the events of the roundup and deportation of Jewish people in Paris on July 16–17, 1942.

(continued)

(continued)

Offering intercultural experiences through familiar themes, but unfamiliar perspectives
Here learners were given an opportunity to explore a known theme, that of the second world war, but through an unfamiliar perspective in more depth, by focusing on the events in Oradour-sur-Glane.

Developing intercultural attributes, with a focus on empathy and a sense of curiosity
Here, learners were introduced to the events through the eyes (and the personal diary) of a child survivor from the massacre in Oradour-sur-Glane.

Supporting learners in *producing* cognitively challenging language
This was another example of a speaking frame used for a paired activity where learners had to take on the role of one of the survivors sharing their experience with a reporter.

(continued)

(continued)

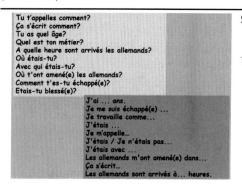

Tu t'appelles comment? Ça s'écrit comment? Tu as quel âge? Quel est ton métier? A quelle heure sont arrivés les allemands? Où étais-tu? Avec qui étais-tu? Où t'ont amené(e) les allemands? Comment t'es-tu échappé(e)? Etais-tu blessé(e)? J'ai ... ans. Je me suis échappé(e) ... Je travaille comme... J'étais ... Je m'appelle... J'étais / Je n'étais pas... J'étais avec ... Les allemands m'ont amené(e) dans... Ça s'écrit... Les allemands sont arrivés à... heures.	Supporting learners in *accessing* cognitively challenging language *This was a challenging listening task, involving authentic testimonials from survivors—the task was carefully scaffolded so that learners were successful in applying their listening skills.*
Oradour-sur-Glane You are going to prepare an article for the next school newsletter. In this article, you will explain what you have been learning so far in French lessons about World War 2 and the village of Oradour-sur-Glane, and what happened there. You will work in pairs. The best 3 entries will win a prize and will feature on the school's website. The winning entry will feature in the next Headteacher's newsletter.	Developing learners' ability to work collaboratively and independently to produce meaningful outcomes *Students had to produce their own account to share what they had learnt and were expected to supplement their work with their own research and illustrations.*

Illustrations adapted from Koro (2018)

References

All-Party Parliamentary Group on Modern Languages (APPGML). (2019). *A national recovery programme for languages,* March 4. https://nationalrecovery-languages.weebly.com/downloads.html

Atkinson, D. (2010). Extended, embodied cognition and second language acquisition. *Applied Linguistics, 31*(5), 599–622. https://doi.org/10.1093/applin/amq009

Baker, W. (2015). Research into practice: Cultural and intercultural awareness. *Language Teaching, 48*(1), 130–141. https://doi.org/10.1017/S0261444814000287

Bauckham, I. (2016). Modern foreign languages pedagogy review. Teaching Skills Council. https://ncelp.org/wpcontent/uploads/2020/02/MFL_Pedagogy_Review_Report_TSC_PUBLISHED_VERSION_Nov_2016_1_.pdf

Blow, D., & Myers, H. (2022). Comparative analysis of the 2022 DfE GCSE Subject Content for French, German and Spanish and its implications for schools. *Language Learning Journal, 50*(2), 238–248. https://doi.org/10.1080/09571736.2022.2045678

Bosch, R. (Director). (2010). *La Rafle* [Film]. Gaumont.

Bower, K. (2020). School leaders' perspectives on content and language integrated learning in England. *Language, Culture, and Curriculum, 33*(4), 351–367. https://doi.org/10.1080/07908318.2019.1667367

Bowler, M. (2020). *A languages crisis?* HEPI Report 123. Higher Education Policy Institute. https://www.hepi.ac.uk/2020/01/09/a-languages-crisis/

Broady, E. (2020). Language learning in the UK - taking stock. *Language Learning Journal, 48*(5), 501–507. https://doi.org/10.1080/09571736.2020.1812812

Bruton, A. (2013). CLIL: Some of the reasons why… and why not. *System, 41*(3), 587–597. https://doi.org/10.1016/j.system.2013.07.001

Byram, M. (1997). *Teaching and assessing intercultural communicative competence*. Multilingual Matters.

Byram, M., & Wagner, M. (2018). Making a difference: Language teaching for intercultural and international dialogue. *Foreign Language Annals, 51*, 140–151. https://doi.org/10.1111/flan.12319

Campos, A. T. S. (2009). Strategies to raise cultural awareness and create multicultural materials and activities in the language classroom. *Revista de Lenguas Modernas, 11*, 383–390.

Cardim-Dias, J., & Zodgekar, Y. (2022, August 31). Language learning in England: Why curriculum reform will not reverse the decline or narrow the gaps. [Blog post]. Retrieved August 24, 2023, from https://epi.org.uk/publications-and-research/15043/

Cenoz, J., & Ruiz de Zarobe, Y. (2015). Learning through a second or additional language: Content-based instruction and CLIL in the twenty-first century. *Language, Culture and Curriculum, 28*(1), 1–7. https://doi.org/10.1080/07908318.2014.1000921

Coffey, S. (2018). Choosing to study modern foreign languages: Discourses of value as forms of cultural capital. *Applied Linguistics, 39*(4), 462–480. https://doi.org/10.1093/applin/amw019

Coffey, S. (2022). 'Ambition for all'? Competing visions of 'ambition' and recognising language learning and teaching as a geo-historically situated social practice. *The Language Learning Journal, 50*(2), 142–145. https://doi.org/10.1080/09571736.2022.2045682

Coonan, M. C. (2007). Insider views of the CLIL class through teacher self-observation-introspection. *International Journal of Bilingual Education and Bilingualism, 10*(5), 625–646. https://doi.org/10.2167/beb463.0

Coyle, D., Hood, P., & Marsh, D. (2010). *Content and language integrated learning*. Cambridge University Press.

Dalton-Puffer, C. (2007). *Discourse in content and language integrated learning (CLIL) classrooms* (Vol. 20). John Benjamins Publishing.

Dearing, R., & King, L. (2007). *The languages review*. Department of Education and Skills.

Department for Education (DfE). (2013). *Languages programmes of study: Key stage 3. National curriculum in England*. DfE. https://www.gov.uk/government/uploads/system/uploads/attachment_data/file/239083/SECONDARY_national_curriculum_-_Languages.pdf

Department for Education (DfE). (2023). *French, German and Spanish GCSE Subject Content*, February. https://assets.publishing.service.gov.uk/government/uploads/system/uploads/attachment_data/file/1141722/French__German_and_Spanish_GCSE_subject_content.pdf

Dobson, A. (2018). Towards 'MFL for all' in England: A historical perspective. *The Language Learning Journal, 46*(1), 71–85. https://doi.org/10.1080/09571736.2017.1382058

Dobson, A. (2020). Context is everything: Reflections on CLIL in the UK. *Language Learning Journal, 48*(5), 508–518. https://doi.org/10.1080/09571736.2020.1804104

Doiz, A., Lasagabaster, D., & Sierra, J. M. (2014). CLIL and motivation: The effect of Individual and contextual variables. *Language Learning Journal, 42*, 209–224. https://doi.org/10.1080/09571736.2014.889508

Driscoll, P., Earl, J., & Cable, C. (2013). The role and nature of the cultural dimension in primary modern languages. *Language, Culture and Curriculum, 26*(2), 146–160. https://doi.org/10.1080/07908318.2013.799675

Eurostat. (2022). *Foreign language learning statistics*. Retrieved August 10, 2023, from https://ec.europa.eu/eurostat/statistics-explained/index.php?title=Foreign_language_learning_statistics

Fielding, R. (2020). Language teaching in monolingual policy settings: Teacher views of successful language learning and effective language programmes. *Language learning journal, 48*(5), 1–16. https://doi.org/10.1080/09571736.2020.1802771

Freire, P. (2004). *Pedagogy of the oppressed* (30th anniversary ed.). Continuum.

Graham, S., Courtney, L., Tonkyn, A., & Marinis, T. (2016). Motivational trajectories for early language learning across the primary-secondary school transition. *British Educational Research Journal, 42*(4), 682–702. https://doi.org/10.1002/berj.3230

Grüber, A., & Hopwood, O. (2022). Foreign language education policies at secondary school level in England and Germany: An international comparison. *Language Learning Journal, 50*(2), 249–261. https://doi.org/10.1080/09571736.2022.2044372

Hagger-Vaughan, L. (2020). Is the English Baccalaureate (EBacc) helping participation in language learning in secondary schools in England? *The Language Learning Journal, 48*(5), 519–533. https://doi.org/10.1080/09571736.2020.1752292

Hennebry, M. (2014). Cultural awareness: Should it be taught? Can it be taught? In P. Driscoll, E. Macaro, & A. Swarbrick (Eds.), *Debates in modern languages education* (pp. 135–149). Routledge.

Huber, J., & Reynolds, C. (2014). *Developing intercultural competence through education*. Council of Europe Pestalozzi Series, No. 3. Council of Europe Publishing. https://rm.coe.int/developing-intercultural-enfr/16808ce258

Hunt, M. (2011). Learners' perceptions of their experiences of learning subject content through a foreign language. *Educational Review, 63*(3), 365–378. https://doi.org/10.1080/00131911.2011.571765

Kim, D. (2020). Learning language, learning culture: Teaching language to the whole student. *ECNU Review of Education (Online), 3*(3), 519–541. https://doi.org/10.1177/2096531120936693

Koro, R. (2017). *To what extent is a CLIL approach useful in teaching intercultural understanding in MFL?* Doctoral dissertation, University of Reading.

Koro, R. (2018). Developing learners' intercultural understanding through a CLIL approach. *e-TEALS, 9*(s1), 77–107. https://doi.org/10.2478/eteals-2018-0014

Lanvers, U. (2020). Changing language mindsets about modern languages: A school intervention. *Language Learning Journal, 48*(5), 571–597. https://doi.org/10.1080/09571736.2020.1802771

Lanvers, U., Doughty, H., & Thompson, A. S. (2018). Brexit as linguistic symptom of britain retreating into its shell? Brexit-induced politicization of language learning. *The Modern Language Journal, 102*(4), 775–796. https://doi.org/10.1111/modl.12515

Lasagabaster, D. (2017). Language learning motivation and language attitudes in multilingual Spain from an international perspective. *The Modern Language Journal, 101*(3), 583–596. https://doi.org/10.1111/modl.12414

Long, R., & Danechi, S. (2022). House of commons library briefing paper: Number 07388, 7 September 2022: *Language teaching in schools (England)*. Retrieved August 13, 2023, from https://researchbriefings.files.parliament.uk/documents/CBP-7388/CBP-7388.pdf

Lupton, R., & Thomson, S. (2015). *The Coalition's record on schools: Policy, spending and outcomes 2010–2015*. SPCC WP13. Social Policy in a Cold Climate. https://sticerd.lse.ac.uk/dps/case/spcc/WP13.pdf

Markey, K., O'Brien, B., Kouta, C., Okantey, C., & O'Donnell, C. (2021). Embracing classroom cultural diversity: Innovations for nurturing inclusive intercultural learning and culturally responsive teaching. *Teaching and Learning in Nursing, 16*(3), 258–262. https://doi.org/10.1016/j.teln.2021.01.008

Moya, M. E. G., Ortiz, L. M., & Díaz, A. M. N. (2016). Evidence of intercultural communication competence in tenth grader's narrative texts. *Gist Education and Learning Research Journal, 13*(July–December), 111–130. https://doi.org/10.26817/16925777.315

Nechifor, A., & Borca, A. (2020). Contextualising culture in teaching a foreign language: The cultural element among cultural awareness, cultural competency and cultural literacy. *Philologica Jassyensia, 16*(2), 287–304.

Office for Standards in Education (Ofsted). (2021). *Research review series: Languages*, June 7. https://www.gov.uk/government/publications/curriculum-research-review-series-languages/curriculum-research-review-series-languages

Parrish, A. (2020). Curriculum change in modern foreign languages education in England: Barriers and possibilities. *Language Learning Journal, 48*(5), 534–554. https://doi.org/10.1080/09571736.2018.1557733

Parrish, A., & Lanvers, U. (2019). Student motivation, school policy choices and modern language study in England. *The Language Learning Journal, 47*(3), 281–298. https://doi.org/10.1080/09571736.2018.1508305

Peiser, G., & Jones, M. (2012). Rhetoric or reality: Intercultural understanding in the English Key Stage 3 Modern Foreign Languages curriculum. *Curriculum Journal, 23*(2), 173–187. https://doi.org/10.1080/09585176.2012.678499

Peiser, G., & Jones, M. (2013). The significance of intercultural understanding in the English modern foreign languages curriculum: A pupil perspective. *Language Learning Journal, 41*(3), 340–356. https://doi.org/10.1080/09571736.2013.836350

Porter, A., Graham, S., Myles, F., & Holmes, B. (2022). Creativity, challenge and culture in the languages classroom: A response to the Ofsted Curriculum Research Review. *Language Learning Journal, 50*(2), 208–217. https://doi.org/10.1080/09571736.2022.2046358

Porto, M. (2018). Intercultural citizenship in foreign language education: An opportunity to broaden CLIL's theoretical outlook and pedagogy. *International Journal of Bilingual Education and Bilingualism, 247*, 927–947. https://doi.org/10.1080/13670050.2018.1526886

Saniei, A. (2012). *Developing cultural awareness in language instructional materials*. Unpublished paper presented at the International Conference of Language, Medias and Culture.

Scally, J., Parrish, A., & Montgomery, A. (2021). Intercultural competence and languages: Inextricably linked or linked inexplicably? *Compare, 52*(3), 492–510. https://doi.org/10.1080/03057925.2020.1851000

Sobré, M. S. (2017). Developing the critical intercultural class space: Theoretical implications and pragmatic applications of critical intercultural communication pedagogy. *Intercultural Education, 28*(1), 39–59. https://doi.org/10.1080/14675986.2017.1288984

Sorrells, K. (2013). *Intercultural communication: Globalization and social justice.*.

Sudhoff, J. (2010). CLIL and intercultural communicative competence: Foundations and approaches towards a fusion. *International CLIL Research Journal, 1*(3), 30–37.

Wilson, R. (2013). Another language is another soul. *Language and Intercultural Communication, 13*(3), 298–309. https://doi.org/10.1080/14708477.2013.804534

Wingate, U. (2018). Lots of games and little challenge – A snapshot of modern foreign language teaching in English secondary schools. *Language Learning Journal, 46*(4), 442–455. https://doi.org/10.1080/09571736.2016.1161061

Wingate, U., & Andon, N. (2018). The need for new directions in modern foreign language teaching at English secondary schools. In S. Coffey & U. Wingate (Eds.), *New directions for research in foreign language education* (pp. 132–150). Routledge. https://doi.org/10.4324/9781315561561-9

Woore, R., Graham, S., Kohl, K., Courtney, L., & Savory, C. (2020). *Consolidating the evidence base for MFL curriculum, pedagogy and assessment reform at GCSE: An investigation of teachers' views*. Retrieved August 22, 2023, from https://ora.ox.ac.uk/objects/uuid:1f797d25-98b4-4b89-863a-779b2348ae20

Woore, R., Molway, L., & Macaro, E. (2022). Keeping sight of the big picture: A critical response to Ofsted's 2021 Curriculum Research Review for languages. *The Language Learning Journal, 50*(2), 146–155. https://doi.org/10.1080/09571736.2022.2045677

Part III

Northern Ireland

The Evaluation of the Young Persons' Stepping-Stone Programme: A Pilot ESOL 16+ Course for Newcomers in Northern Ireland

Declan Flanagan, Susan Logue, and Christina Sevdali

1   Introduction

In 2022, the United Kingdom (UK) received 5152 applications for asylum from unaccompanied asylum-seeking minors (UASMs)—many coming from Sudan, Iran, Eritrea, Afghanistan, Vietnam, Iraq, Albania, Ethiopia, and Syria. The majority are aged between 14 and 17, fleeing danger and war, and are victims of trafficking, exploitation, and

---

D. Flanagan (✉)
Health and Social Care (HSC) Trust, Belfast, Northern Ireland

S. Logue
School of Nursing and Paramedic Science, University of Ulster, Coleraine, Northern Ireland

C. Sevdali
School of Communication and Media, University of Ulster, Coleraine, Northern Ireland

© The Author(s), under exclusive license to Springer Nature Switzerland AG 2024
S. W. Chong, H. Reinders (eds.), *Innovation in Language Learning and Teaching*, New Language Learning and Teaching Environments,
https://doi.org/10.1007/978-3-031-66241-6_5

abandonment (Refugee Council, 2023). The Health and Social Care Board (HSCB, 2020) in Northern Ireland (NI) highlights a recent rise in (UASM) children, trebling from 20 in 2020/2021 to almost 60 in 2022, raising concerns about the capacity to provide immediate care placements and educational provision.

The Department of Education (DE) uses the term 'newcomer' to refer to children who lack satisfactory language skills, cannot access school curricula, and do not have a language in common with their teachers (Kernaghan, 2015). The Education Authority (EA) is responsible *only* for school placement, language support, and translation services for newcomer children at primary and post-primary levels. For UASM children aged 16+, the Health and Social Care Trust and other statutory authorities are accountable for allocating appropriate education and training opportunities (EA, 2022; HSCB, 2019).

Newcomers (16+ UASM) face challenges in accessing formal education due to their age, lack of formal education, English language proficiency, and literacy issues. The response from government-funded provisions has been inadequate, leading to a lack of sustained and bespoke options that provide clear educational pathways into vocational, further, and higher education. To address this, the Rowntree Foundation provided funding for a pilot 16+ English to Speakers of Other Language (ESOL) programme (Young Persons' Stepping-Stone Programme) within community education settings in Belfast between September 2021/June 2022. ESOL is defined as the teaching of English to learners within community education settings whose first language is not English and who are living in an English-speaking country. The programme's impact was measured by participants' English language ability and socio-emotional well-being skills, using statistical analysis of language and well-being assessment scores at the beginning and end of the programme.

2   ESOL Provision in Northern Ireland

Crangle (2023) argues that the low immigrant numbers before the Good Friday Agreement (GFA), pre-1998, led to a fabricated assumption that immigration was a non-issue, excluding migrant communities from public policy and education. This lack of visibility has been reflected in NI's universities, which have been reluctant to respond to changes in their local populations through their research functions. Belluigi and Moynihan (2023) argue that the lack of engagement in academic knowledge production has perpetuated the historical under-documenting of ethnic minorities and migrants' histories, leading to assumptions, stereotyping, and homogenisation, putting the burden of knowledge-making on non-academic individuals, communities, and volunteer groups. An example of this is reflected in the NI-ESOL provision, which is provided through formal (six regional further education (FE) colleges) and informal learning environments (community/voluntary/church groups) (Flanagan & O'Boyle, 2021).

A lack of minority visibility is reflected in the current provision, which has been reactive, ad hoc, and underfunded for decades, with significant issues persisting. These include funding mechanisms, favouring FE colleges over community/voluntary settings, protracted waiting lists and human capital principles underpinning 'product model' curricula. The latter reinforces essentialist pedagogy rather than a holistic 'whole learner', asset-based approach to language education and multilingual learners (Flanagan & O'Boyle, 2021). Moreover, newcomer children often face challenges during resettlement, including developmental delays, fear, and anxiety and are more likely to have experienced war, persecution, and additional adversities during post-migration (Hadfield et al., 2017). Trauma, including post-traumatic stress disorder, discrimination, and culture shock, is a common challenge that can persist long after resettlement (Kernaghan, 2015; Murphy & Vieten, 2017). Recent research has found a correlation between the well-being of immigrants and refugees and their proficiency in the second language and educational outcomes. Those with greater well-being, measured by higher self-control and interpersonal skills, have greater proficiency in the second language and are more successful in academic achievement (Kernaghan, 2015; Murphy & Vieten, 2017; Devlin, 2022).

The DfE (2024) has drafted an NI-ESOL policy to address refugee and newcomer issues and aims to provide high-quality, flexible, and accessible provisions for educational pathways. Recommendations include increased cross-departmental cooperation, offering accredited ESOL courses in post-primary schools, and investigating integrating ESOL into vocational training courses. Recommendations also include reviewing the needs of S/UASC and care leavers, completing initial assessments promptly for learners aged 16–18, and identifying opportunities to widen ESOL for young learners within voluntary/community settings. The policy also aims to ensure seamless, bespoke pathways for learners, considering the impact of interrupted education profiles. However, until such policies are enacted, these newcomers remain in an educational limbo, and it is left to alternative provisions which provide non-accredited language support within church, community, and voluntary settings (Soye, 2023).

3 Overview of the Stepping-Stone Project

The ESOL Young Persons' Stepping-Stone Project was a 24-week initiative aimed at developing English language ability and social skills for immigrant, refugee, and unaccompanied minors in NI. The project aimed to address language barriers and socio-emotional well-being issues faced by these individuals. The 24-week programme, which lasted from September 2021 to April 2022, focuses on facilitating English acquisition, personal development, guidance on educational and employment opportunities, and fostering a sense of belonging. The project was a unique collaboration between community education, charitable (well-being charity) and the university sectors (one NI University), allowing for the sharing of expertise and evidence-informed practice. The programme was provided to 12 young refugees and asylum seekers aged 16–19 from Syria, Iran, Iraq, Afghanistan, and Somalia who were unable to access the curriculum due to language proficiency issues or lack of secondary school/FE places. The current study set out to provide a structured education programme to facilitate English language learning, increasing confidence and integration into NI society. In addition, it conducted tailored and innovative language assessments and interventions to identify and target specific areas of language need and accelerate English language development. Moreover, the programme delivered personal development and well-being sessions to improve confidence and education/employability progression opportunities and create a sense of belonging. Finally, in doing so, the programme aimed to offer a holistic and positive education experience to equip participants with improved language skills and confidence (Fig. 1).

4 Methodology

The project began on 13 September 2021 with tutor training and preparation sessions, followed by classes at the end of September. Initial assessments identified areas of need for personal development and language skills. Personal development and linguistic sessions focused on these skills, with informal evaluations ongoing throughout the programme. Regular communication between tutors and project workers allowed for

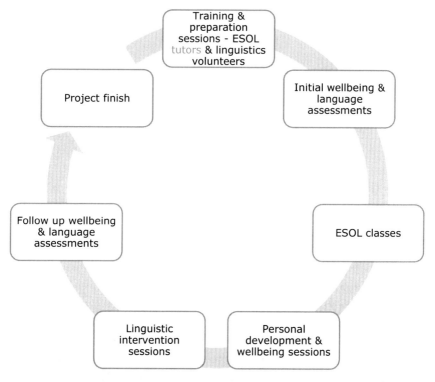

Fig. 1 The Project phases of the Young Persons' Stepping-Stone Project

adjustments as needed and follow-up assessments were conducted in February and March 2022 to measure progress with the project ending in April 2022.

Activities and Procedures

ESOL Provision

ESOL provision included adapting the 16+ routes to learning resources (Ma & Richardson, 2019) and involved 12 hours of classes per week, 4 hours per day, over 24 weeks. The curriculum was based on a Content and Learning Integration Learning (CLIL) approach, ranging from A1 beginner to B1 lower-intermediate (CEFR). The course focused on four skills: reading, writing, listening, and speaking, with subskills such as spelling, vocabulary, grammar, punctuation, and pronunciation. The course was designed to mirror a key stage 3, Year 8 (1st year secondary school curriculum). The topics were learner-focused and age-appropriate, with the vocabulary covered complementing each topic area. The Full-Service Community Network provided specialist training and support to tutors, focusing on scaffolding and differentiation activities. This allowed tutors to adopt a more holistic and student-centred teaching approach. Tutor support also included teaching phonology to young people, including sounds, word and sentence stress, intonation, and connected speech features (Fig. 2).

Well-being and Social Skills Sessions

The well-being and social skills sessions were delivered by a youth reach charity offering weekly, lasting 4 hours, on Wednesdays from 10 am to 2 pm. These sessions focused on building confidence, self-esteem, healthy relationships, community integration, and setting goals for the future. They included outdoor activities, digital storytelling sessions, and occupational therapy sessions. The learners also had access to a city-centre-based recreation space with games, seating areas, and kitchen facilities.

WHAT WE DO

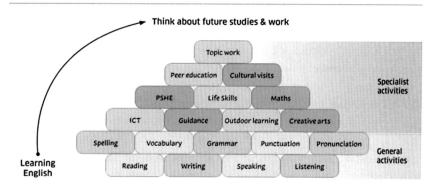

Fig. 2 16+ESOL routes to learning resources: Glasgow Clyde College (Ma & Richardson, 2019)

The programme included assessments to understand participants' wellbeing, such as the Outcome Stars Assessment and the Strength and Difficulties Questionnaire impact. The sessions were designed to complement topics covered in classes and promote group integration.

Linguistics Sessions

The linguistics sessions involved assessing the young people's language skills to identify specific language needs and providing extra language support through intervention activities to target these areas and complement the grammar covered in the ESOL classes. Language assessment involved three different areas, including informal observation of language use and understanding during linguistics sessions. Secondly, a formal assessment of language use with a focus on the grammatical features of English and, finally, consideration of the participants' home language was needed to identify where difficulties are likely to manifest due to crosslinguistic influence from the young person's first language.

Language intervention sessions were conducted in small group settings with native English facilitators (undergraduate linguistics students) to provide opportunities for the young people to hear, use, and get feedback on their English language skills to enhance language learning further.

Language intervention targeted areas of language need as identified through the language assessment. Intervention activities included lexical tasks such as matching pictorial representations of items with spoken or written forms to target vocabulary development and phoneme awareness activities to practise articulating phonological features of words and sentence forms in English. In addition, digital colouring and whiteboard actions were used to target the interpretation and production of morphological features (auxiliary and copular structures, inflectional morphology, subject-verb agreement) and word order in English. Finally, paper-based activities and board games focused on expressive accuracy and fluency of grammatical forms (complementing grammar covered in ESOL classes).

The project's impact was measured by the participants' development in English language ability and socio-emotional well-being skills. This impact was demonstrated by statistically analysing the language and well-being assessment scores at the beginning and end of the project. If the language assessment and well-being scores showed a positive effect (i.e., improvement) between earlier and later evaluation phases, this would provide evidence that the programme positively impacted the participants' language skills and well-being. In addition, the project measured whether a relationship was evident between the participants' English language ability and their well-being skills. This allowed those involved to evaluate whether well-being positively impacted language skills, as observed in previous studies on refugees' language development. This would provide further motivation for the delivery of a course, such as the present project, which incorporates the development of well-being alongside language skills. The impact was also evidenced via feedback from participants in the project, including the young people, the ESOL tutors, and the linguistics students. The following sections document how language skills and well-being were measured.

Measuring Language Development

The participants' English language skills were measured at the beginning and end of the project. This was done by completing a narrative storytelling assessment (Multilingual Assessment Instrument for Narratives; MAIN, Gagarina et al., 2012). This was administered by undergraduate linguistics student volunteers under the direction of linguistics researchers. In the task, the young people were asked to retell a story in English based on pictures representing different story events and characters. The language sample produced by participants was recorded and subsequently transcribed. A narrative storytelling task is a widely used instrument in language acquisition research (e.g., Gutiérrez-Clellen, 2002; Paradis et al., 2017). According to Schneider et al. (2006), using narrative tasks involves a type of expression more frequently found in natural everyday life, requiring participants to use word combinations and sentences instead of target language use in isolation (e.g., specific words or sentences). This, therefore, can allow more unrestricted, natural language to be produced and measured (Rocca, 2007).

In the current study, language samples from the MAIN task were used to evaluate language ability by measuring the Mean Length of Utterance (MLU). MLU is one of the most commonly used measures for evaluating language ability and a robust measure of language development (e.g., Bigelow, 2012; Eisenberg et al., 2001; Potratz et al., 2022). Measuring MLU involves calculating the number of morphemes per sentence used. This includes free morphemes such as nouns (e.g., 'cat', 'ball') and plural (-s on nouns, e.g., 'flower*s*') or inflected verbal forms (e.g., third person singular -s: 'The boy look*s* at the cat' or past tense -ed: 'The cat climb*ed* the tree'), etc. All morphemes are totalled and divided by the number of utterances produced (e.g., 70 morphemes produced over seven utterances = MLU of 10). The MLU score indicates language complexity and, thus, proficiency; therefore, a higher MLU score indicates greater language proficiency. The MLU of each participant was measured via the narrative task at the beginning and end of the project, and these were compared to observe their progress in English language proficiency.

Language development was also evaluated by analysing speech samples before and after intervention for using particular grammatical forms. This included use of the following grammatical forms: tense marking (e.g., past tense—'The cat climb the tree'/'The cat climb*ed* the tree'); subject-verb agreement (e.g., 'He have the ball now'/'He **has** the ball now'); article use (e.g., 'Cat sees a butterfly'/'**The** cat sees a butterfly');

and auxiliary and copula use (e.g., 'The cat angry'/'The cat *is* angry'). These language features were chosen as they represent key grammatical forms in English.

Measuring Well-being

Well-being was measured using two assessments: The *Outcomes Star* Assessment (Burns & MacKeith, 2013) and the *Strength and Difficulties Questionnaire* (Goodman, 1997). The Outcomes Star Assessment is utilised widely within the well-being sector (MacKeith, 2014). Few studies have measured its reliability or validity thus far; however, of those that have, it has been found to have good inter-rater reliability (MacKeith, 2014). The Outcomes Star Assessment covers six key areas: making a difference, hopes and dreams, well-being, education and work, communicating, and choice and behaviour. A 5-point rating scale for each area measures an individual's journey/stages. The five stages were categorised as *not interested, considering having a go, working on it, enjoying,* and *achieving*.

The Outcomes Star Assessment was administered by the participants' key worker in collaboration with the young person and with the help of interpreters where appropriate. The Strengths and Difficulties Questionnaire (SDQ) is one of the most widely used screening instruments for identifying psychosocial problems and strengths and their severity for an individual (e.g., Dickey & Blumberg, 2001; Rønning et al., 2004; Stone et al., 2015). It has been found to be a reliable and valid instrument as it has high internal consistency and high correlation with other instruments measuring the same psychosocial factors (Björnsdotter et al., 2013). This questionnaire comprises questions that can be used as an index of well-being in children, adolescents and young adults, assessing their problems and prosocial behaviours. The questionnaire produces five subscales: *hyperactivity, conduct, emotional problems, peer relationship problems,* and *prosocial behaviour*. The Strength and Difficulties Questionnaire was completed by the key worker in collaboration with the ESOL tutors. Scores for language proficiency were also analysed alongside well-being scores to measure any interactions between the two factors. This was done by investigating the correlations between the factors to determine the relationship each factor had with the other. Several learners were applying for refugee status and, this involved numerous appointments with the Home Office and non-government organisations (NGO), which did affect their attendance and fluctuation in participation when measuring their language development and wellbeing at the beginning and end of the programme.

5   Results

Language

As previously mentioned, language ability was measured via Mean Length of Utterance (MLU) using a narrative story retelling task (MAIN), which allowed us to evaluate the young people's English language proficiency through the use of complex language features in terms of grammatical features of English. A higher MLU indicates higher language proficiency. Twelve participants who started the project produced a language sample at the beginning of the study, and seven completed the second language sample. Only the seven participants who produced both language samples were included in the analysis. Results revealed that all seven participants showed higher MLUs between the two language samples, indicating that language proficiency had improved for all participants. In several cases, this score of language proficiency doubled, thus demonstrating that language ability improved considerably between the beginning and end of the project. This is shown in Fig. 3, where the blue column shows participants' language proficiency scores for the first assessment. In contrast, the orange column shows participants' language proficiency scores for the second assessment.

To determine a statistically significant mean difference in the MLU of participants between the beginning (Language Assessment 1) and the end (Language Assessment 2) of the project, a paired sample t-test was run on the sample of seven participants using the statistical package R (R Core Team, 2017). At the end of the language project, the results showed that the mean MLU score was higher (mean score = 13.02) compared to the beginning of the language project (mean score = 7.10), with a statistically

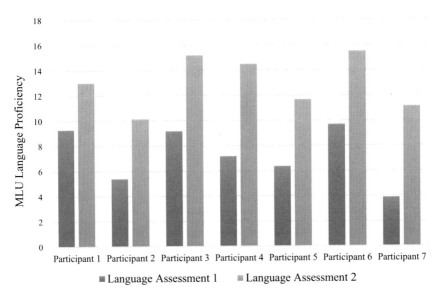

Fig. 3 Chart showing language complexity scores for Language Assessment 1 and Language Assessment 2

significant difference of −5.92 (95% CI, −7.21 to −4.62) in MLU, $t = -11.17$, $p<.001$. This is shown in Fig. 4, where the mean MLU score for the second language assessment (Language Assessment 2) is considerably higher than the mean MLU score for the first language assessment (Language Assessment 1).

Language ability was also measured in terms of using particular language features. Language samples from the recorded language assessments were analysed using target grammatical forms. The following table shows examples of these grammatical forms (tense, subject-verb agreement, articles, auxiliaries and copula) used in language assessments 1 and 2 (referring to pre- and post-intervention, respectively). In the language sample from Language Assessment 1, the young people frequently made errors of omission when attempting to use the target grammatical language features. In contrast, the language sample from Language Assessment 2 showed that the young people were starting to use these language features with increased accuracy, thus showing a clear improvement in grammatical proficiency (Table 1).

The Evaluation of the Young Persons' Stepping-Stone... 113

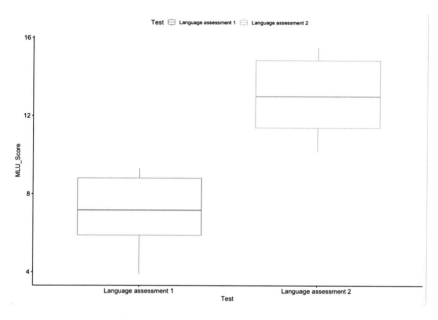

Fig. 4 Boxplot showing language proficiency scores (MLU Score) for Language Assessment 1 and Language Assessment 2

Table 1 Examples of expressive grammatical forms from Language Assessment 1 (pre-intervention) and Language Assessment 2 (post-intervention)

Types of grammatical forms	Language Assessment 1 (Pre-intervention)	Language Assessment 2 (Post-intervention)
Tense	'She's go to take'	'He ate the sausage'
		'He was surprised'
Subject-verb agreement	'He take the ball from the sea'	'And the dog takes the sausage'
Articles	'And cat is eating'	'The boy looked at his dog'
Auxiliary and copular forms	'The cat angry'	'He is so happy'
	'The boy coming'	'I don't know why he is sad'
		'She is going inside'
		'And the boy is so sad because the balloon is on top of the tree'

Well-being

As mentioned, well-being was measured through two assessments: the Outcomes Star Assessment and the Strength and Difficulties Questionnaire. Eight young people completed the first assessment, and eleven completed the follow-up assessment. Regarding the Outcomes Star Assessment, most young people reported that their primary focus in education and work was improving their English language skills. This was linked to their hopes and dreams, with many reporting that improvements in English would enable them to achieve their educational aspirations. This included medicine, architecture, dentistry, and art and design courses. In terms of well-being, many reported that they speak with friends, do sports activities, or exercise when they feel low. The young people and their key workers devised plans to help guide them in terms of their personal development and education. This involved making contacts with local associations, sports clubs and education centres. The follow-up assessment revealed that most young people reported doing well and feeling happy regarding their well-being and social skills. Two young people had difficulties settling into their home life, impacting their well-being. All of the young people reported that they were keen to continue learning English and were very happy with the improvements in their English skills.

Eight of the young people (Participants 1, 2, 3,4, 5, 6, 7, and 9) completed the first and second Outcomes Star assessments. Considering the overall well-being scores from the Outcomes Star Assessment (covering all six key areas), results showed that while two young people demonstrated slightly lower scores between the initial and follow-up assessments, the majority of young people showed an increase in overall well-being. This is shown below, where the blue column indicates the results of the first well-being assessment, and the orange column indicates the results of the second well-being assessment (Fig. 5).

As with the statistical analysis for language ability, a paired sample t-test was run using the statistical package R (R Core Team, 2017) to determine any significant mean difference in the overall well-being of the sample between the beginning (Well-being score 1) and the end

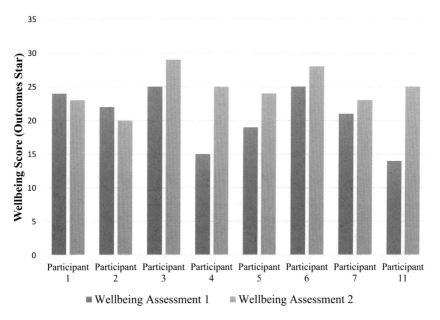

Fig. 5 Chart showing well-being scores from the Outcomes Star Assessment at the beginning and end of the project

(Well-being score 2) of the project. The results showed that the mean Outcomes Star well-being score was higher at the end of the project (mean score = 24.63) compared to the beginning of the project (mean score = 20.63), with a statistically significant difference of −4.0 (95% CI, −7.89 to −0.10) in well-being $t = -2.43$, $p = .05$. This is shown in Fig. 6 where the mean Outcomes Star well-being score for the second well-being assessment (Well-being Assessment 2) is higher than the mean Outcomes Star well-being score for first well-being assessment (Well-being Assessment 1).

Strength and Difficulties Questionnaire

The Strength and Difficulties Questionnaire measured several areas related to well-being. This included prosocial skills, emotional problems, conduct problems, hyperactivity, and peer problems. Each of these areas

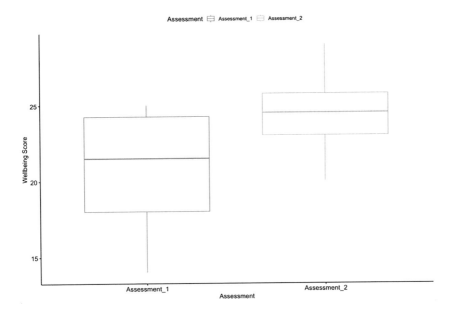

Fig. 6 Boxplot showing the mean Outcomes Star well-being scores at the beginning (Assessment 1) and end of the project (Assessment 2)

was evaluated at the programme's beginning and end. Two of the well-being scores were selected for further statistical analysis: *prosocial behaviour* and *emotional problems*. These well-being factors were selected for two reasons: (1) they represented two key fine-grained areas of well-being, and (2) the variation in scores for these measures allowed the impact of these factors to be more readily identified.

Prosocial behaviour occurs when people act to benefit others rather than themselves, which can include cooperation with others or caregiving behaviours. Eleven participants completed the prosocial behaviour assessment at the project's beginning and end. The scores for prosocial behaviour revealed that nearly half of the young people showed an improvement during the programme. In contrast, the same number of participants showed decreased prosocial behaviour. The blue column indicates the results of the first assessment, and the orange column indicates the results of the second assessment (Fig. 7).

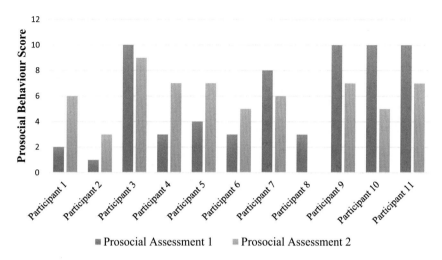

Fig. 7 Chart showing the scores for prosocial behaviour at assessments 1 and 2

A paired sample t-test was run on the sample of 11 participants to determine a statistically significant mean difference in the prosocial behaviour scores of participants between the beginning and the end of the project. The results showed that the mean prosocial behaviour score was not higher at the end of the project (mean score = 5.64) compared to the beginning of the project (mean score = 5.82), with a non-significant difference of −0.18 (95% CI, −2.00 to 2.37) in prosocial behaviour, $t = .19$, $p = .86$. This is shown in Fig. 8 where the mean prosocial behaviour score for the second assessment (Prosocal Assessment 2) is similar to the mean prosocial behaviour score for first assessment (Prosocal Assessment 1). The results for prosocial behaviour will be considered further in the discussion section.

The evaluation of *emotional problems* revealed that five young people demonstrated a reduction in emotional problems between the first and second evaluations. Three of the young people showed an increase in emotional issues, while three of the young people had no difference in their scores. As before, this is shown below, where the blue column indicates the results of the first assessment, and the orange column suggests the results of the second assessment (Fig. 9).

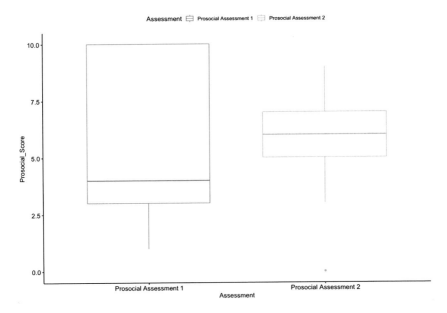

Fig. 8 Boxplot showing the mean prosocial behaviour scores at the beginning (Prosocial Assessment 1) and end of the project (Prosocial Assessment 2)

A paired sample t-test was run on the sample of 11 participants to determine any statistically significant mean difference in the emotional problem scores of participants between the beginning and the end of the project. The results showed that the mean scores for emotional problems were lower at the end of the language project (mean score = 2.64) than at the beginning (mean score = 3.45). However, this difference of -0.81 was non-significant (95% CI, -0.93 to 2.56), $t = 1.04$, $p = .32$. This is shown in Fig. 10, where the mean emotional problems score for the second assessment (Assessment 2) is similar to the mean emotional problems score for first assessment (Assessment 1). The results for emotional problems will be considered further in the discussion section.

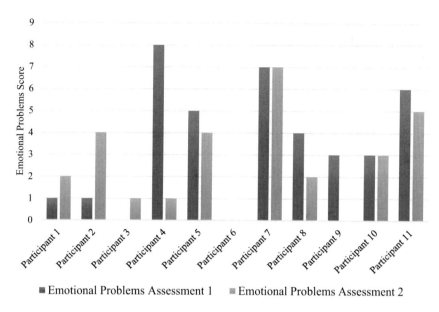

Fig. 9 Chart showing the scores for emotional problems at assessments 1 and 2

Language and Well-being

The analysis of results included a comparison between well-being and language scores to determine whether there were relationships between these factors, as shown in recent research (e.g., Han, 2010; McNally et al., 2019; Soto-Corominas et al., 2020; Zins et al., 2004). The final language assessment scores (MLU from the second language assessment) were compared with two final well-being scores for *prosocial behaviour* and *emotional problems*. As mentioned previously, these factors were selected as they represent key fine-grained measures of well-being, and the variation in scores would allow the impact of factors to be more readily identified. A comparison between the scores for prosocial behaviour and language ability showed that as the young people's prosocial behaviour increased, so did their language ability (see Fig. 11). This suggests an association between these factors whereby higher well-being, as measured via prosocial behaviour, is associated with greater language proficiency. This can be seen in Fig. 11, which reveals a steep gradient in the slope of

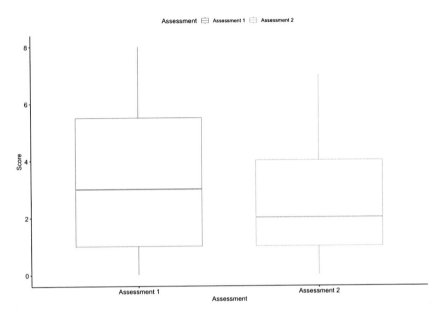

Fig. 10 Boxplot showing the mean emotional problems scores at the beginning (Assessment 1) and end of the project (Assessment 2)

effect, demonstrating that language proficiency scores increased with greater prosocial behaviour. Linear regression analyses were conducted using R to determine whether there was a statistically significant association between language ability and prosocial behaviour of the sample of participants (R Core Team, 2017). Results revealed a significant association between language proficiency and prosocial behaviour (p = .041) (Table 2). This positive association between factors is reflected by the upward slope of the effect in Fig. 11.

A comparison of language skills and emotional problems revealed that higher scores for emotional problems were associated with decreased scores on the language assessment. This is shown by the gradient in the slope of effect, revealing that young people with more significant emotional problems had lower language proficiency scores, and the young people with less emotional problems had higher language proficiency (Fig. 12). Therefore, as scores for emotional problems reduced, language ability increased. As before, a linear regression analysis was conducted

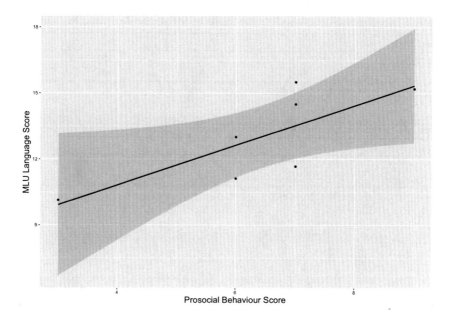

Fig. 11 Chart showing the interaction between prosocial behaviour and language proficiency

using R to determine whether the association between language ability and emotional problems was statistically significant (R Core Team, 2017). Results revealed that the association between language proficiency and emotional problems approached significance ($p = .064$) (Table 3). The downward slope of effect in Fig. 12 reflects this result and demonstrates that as emotional problems decreased, language ability increased.

6 Discussion

This study investigated the impact of the Young Persons' Stepping-Stone programme on the participants' language ability and well-being. Language ability in the study was determined by measuring MLU via the MAIN narrative story task. A paired sample t-test was run to determine significant differences between the language proficiency (MLU scores) of the sample between the beginning and end of the project.

Table 2 Impact of prosocial well-being from the fitted model on accuracy of MLU

Variables	B	Z	P
Intercept	7.216	2.195	.022*
Prosocial	.903	.330	.041*

p<.1, *p<.05, **p<.01, ***p<.001

Table 3 Impact of emotional problems from fitted model on accuracy of MLU

Variables	β	Z	P
Intercept	15.093	1.066	3.16e–05***
Prosocial	-.632	.2676	.064*

p<.1, *p<.05, **p<.01, ***p<.001

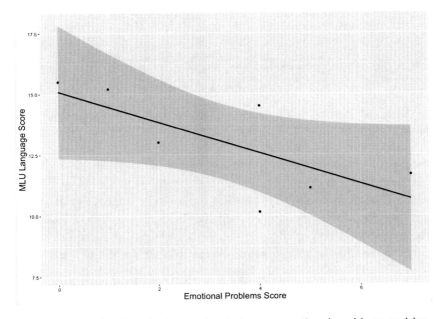

Fig. 12 Chart showing the interaction between emotional problems and language proficiency

Results of the study revealed that participant MLU scores significantly increased between the beginning and end of the programme ($p<.001$). This suggests that the programme had a significant positive effect on the young people's language ability. This result is reflected in the analysis of grammatical forms (tense, subject-verb agreement, articles, auxiliaries and copula) from the recordings of narrative speech used in the language assessments. In the language sample from Assessment 1, the young people frequently omitted these language features, while there was increased use and accuracy of these forms in Language Assessment 2.

While these results for language ability are encouraging, it should be noted that participant numbers in the language proficiency analysis were small (seven participants produced a language sample at the beginning and the end of the project). Future research, including a larger number of participants, would increase the generalisability of findings. In addition, other factors outside of the programme could have impacted the participants' language ability. This may include interaction in English with others outside the project and participation in social activities, which may have increased their exposure to and use of English. To take this into account, future studies could include a measure of other potential extraneous factors that may impact language ability. Additionally, only expressive language was measured in the language proficiency measure used in the study. While the narrative task used in the study is widely employed in research and aims to capture natural, everyday language, it cannot account for other aspects of language, such as linguistic comprehension or the use of specific forms of language. For a more holistic view of participants' English language proficiency, future research could include various tasks to provide further insights into language proficiency across domains.

Well-being was measured using two assessments: The Outcomes Star Assessment (Burns & MacKeith, 2013) and the Strength and Difficulties Questionnaire (Goodman, 1997). The Outcomes Star Assessment gave an overall measure of well-being by evaluating the following areas: making a difference, hopes and dreams, well-being, education and work, communicating, and choice and behaviour. This was administered at the beginning and end of the project, and a paired sample t-test was run to determine any significant difference between the assessments. Results revealed that overall well-being significantly increased for the young people who participated in the project ($p = .05$). As with the results for language ability, this outcome is very promising. However, similar to the language ability analysis, participant numbers were quite low (eight participants), and other factors outside of the programme could have impacted the participants' well-being (e.g., interaction with friends or participation in social activities). Future research, including more participants, would increase the generalisability of findings while measuring other factors that could take into account conditions outside of the programme that impact well-being.

While overall well-being measured via the Outcomes Star Assessment showed a significant improvement between the beginning and end of the programme, results for the fine-grained measures of well-being (prosocial behaviour and emotional problems) indicated a more complex picture. Findings for these measures were mixed across individuals. In some cases, the young people showed improvement, while specific aspects of well-being were somewhat reduced for others. However, refugee, immigrant, and unaccompanied minors will undoubtedly have ongoing issues that may be exacerbated by adapting to life in a new country and culture after a brief period. Due to this, young people may encounter a huge upheaval in their everyday life while coming to terms with the trauma and displacement they have experienced before arrival in NI. Therefore, some issues can be expected to be ongoing, and it may take some individuals longer to improve particular social skills. Additionally, from speaking with the participants during sessions, it was noted that a small number of young people were adjusting to changes in their home lives, which may have impacted scores on these measures of well-being. Future longitudinal research would provide a further understanding of the long-term effects related to fine-grained measures of well-being.

A comparison between well-being and language scores was also completed to determine relationships between these factors, as shown in previous research (e.g., Han, 2010; McNally et al., 2019; Soto-Corominas et al., 2020; Zins et al., 2004). To measure this, the final language assessment scores were compared with the two final fine-grained well-being scores (prosocial behaviour and emotional problems). When scores in prosocial behaviour were analysed alongside language scores, they revealed a significant interaction (p = .041), demonstrating a relationship between these factors. The results for emotional problems and language ability revealed that the association between these factors approached significance (p = .064). These results indicate that as well-being increased (either through increased prosocial skills or decreased emotional problems), so did language proficiency, suggesting that well-being positively impacts language proficiency for this population. This result reflects other research studies which have found that those with greater well-being (in these cases, higher self-control and interpersonal skills and lower incidences of problem behaviours) have greater second language proficiency (e.g., Han, 2010; McNally et al., 2019; Soto-Corominas et al., 2020; Zins et al., 2004).

More broadly, global displacements and the arrival of asylum seekers and refugees are placing significant pressure on public services, particularly education in the 'global North'. In addition, government departments (DE/DfE) can no longer view and implement temporary, piecemeal, reactionary ESOL provisions. While welcome, any forthcoming NI-ESOL policy must be scrutinised, incorporating practitioners' and learners' voices and recommendations to ensure a more transformative, holistic approach, especially for 16+ newcomers. The Stepping-Stone Programme emphasises the importance of English language acquisition and social and well-being skills for immigrant, refugee, and unaccompanied minors' participation in society. Without such programmes, educational opportunities can be limited, and a young person's sense of belonging can be impacted. The results of this project revealed that language ability and overall well-being increased for all the young people who participated, and it could be deemed a tentative success with the need for sustained annual funding to make further changes, amendments, and additions to improve this programme. The lack of guarantee of further funding leaves these bespoke ESOL programmes uncertain, emphasising the need for more ring-fenced funding for community and voluntary sectors.

Acknowledgements The content of this chapter is derived from an article that is to appear in Flanagan, D. Logue, S and Sevdali, C. (2024). The evaluation of the Young Persons' Stepping-Stone Programme: a pilot ESOL 16+ course for newcomers in Northern Ireland. *Language and Education Journal* (Forthcoming). This chapter's originality, and thus its difference from the article, is its entire focus on the evaluation of the programme. It primarily focuses on methodology and analysis—measuring the project's impact on the participants' development in English language ability and socio-emotional well-being skills. The chapter displays in detail how this is achieved by statistically analysing the language and well-being assessment scores at the beginning and end of the project—the first study to do so in Northern Ireland. The findings section of this chapter is identical to that in the article.

References

Belluigi, D. Z., & Moynihan, Y. (2023). *Academic research responsiveness to 'ethnic minorities' and 'migrants' in Northern Ireland. Study report.* QUB Belfast.

Bigelow, K. M. (2012). *Reliability of the mean length of utterance measure in samples of children's language.* Theses and Dissertations. 3274, Brigham Young University, Utah, USA.

Björnsdotter, A., Enebrink, P., & Ghaderi, A. (2013). Psychometric properties of online administered parental Strengths and Difficulties Questionnaire (SDQ), and normative data based on combined online and paper-and-pencil administration. *Child and Adolescent Psychiatry and Mental Health, 7*(1), 40.

Burns, S., & MacKeith, J. (2013). *Family star organisation guide* (2nd ed.). Triangle Consulting Social Enterprise.

Crangle, J. (2023). *Migrants, Immigration and Diversity in Twentieth-Century Northern Ireland British, Irish or 'Other'?* (Palgrave Studies in Migration History). Palgrave Macmillan.

Devlin, N. (2022). *Newcomer pupils in Northern Ireland briefing paper.* Research and Information Service, Northern Ireland Assembly.

Dickey, W. C., & Blumberg, S. J. (2001). Revisiting the factor structure of the Strengths and Difficulties Questionnaire: United States. *Journal of the American Academy of Child & Adolescent Psychiatry, 43*(9), 1159–1167.

Education Authority. (2022, 1 March). http://aims.niassembly.gov.uk/questions/printquestionsummary.aspx?docid=365822

Eisenberg, S. L., Fersko, T., & Lundgren, C. (2001). The use of MLU for identifying language impairment in preschool children: A review. *American Journal of Speech-Language Pathology, 10*, 323–342.

English for Speakers of Other Languages (ESOL) Policy for Northern Ireland. (2024). Forthcoming, Department of the Economy (DfE) Northern Ireland.

Flanagan, D., & O'Boyle, A. (2021). Evaluation of a bespoke work-related English language course for newcomers in Northern Ireland. *Professional and Academic English, 28*(2), 71.

Gagarina, N., Klop, D., Kunnari, S., Tantele, K., Välimaa, T., Balčiūnienė, I., Bohnacker, U., & Walters, J. (2012). MAIN, 'Multilingual Assessment Instrument for Narratives'. *ZAS Papers in Linguistics, 56*.

Goodman, R. (1997). 'The Strengths and Difficulties Questionnaire', A research note. *Journal of Child Psychology and Psychiatry, 38*, 581–586.

Gutiérrez-Clellen, V. (2002). Narratives in two languages: Assessing performance of bilingual children. *Linguistics and Education, 13*, 175–197.

Hadfield, K., Ostrowski, A., & Ungar, M. (2017). What can we expect of the mental health and well-being of Syrian refugee children and adolescents in Canada? *Canadian Psychology/Psychologie Canadienne, 58*, 194–201.

Han, W.-J. (2010). Bilingualism and socio-emotional well-being. *Children and Youth Services Review, 32*, 720–731.

Health and Social Care Board (HSCB). 2019. *Delegated statutory functions composite report*: 1 April 2018–31 March 2019. http://www.hscboard.hscni.net/download/PUBLICMEETINGS/HSC%20BOARD/board_meetings_2019/september_2019/Item-08-02-DSF-Overview-Report-March2019.pdf

Health and Social Care Board (HSCB). (2020). *Delegated statutory functions composite report*: 1 April 2019–31 March 2020. http://www.hscboard.hscni.net/download/PUBLIC-MEETINGS/HSC%20BOARD/board_meetings_2020/ITEM-9-02-DSFOverview-Report-March-2020.pdf

Kernaghan, D. (2015). *Feels Like Home: Exploring the experiences of newcomer pupils in primary schools in Northern Ireland*. Barnardo's Northern Ireland.

Ma, L., & Richardson, M. (2019). *ESOL 16+ routes to learning*. Scottish Refugee Council. www.scottishrefugeecouncil.org.uk

MacKeith, J. (2014). Assessing the reliability of the Outcomes Star in research and practice. *Housing, Care and Support, 17*(4), 188–197.

McNally, S., Darmody, M., & Quigley, J. (2019). The socio-emotional development of language-minority children entering primary school in Ireland. *Irish Educational Studies, 38*, 519–534.

Murphy, F., & Vieten. U. M. (2017). *Asylum seekers and refugees' experiences of life in Northern Ireland*. Report of the first study on the situation of asylum seekers and refugees in NI – 2016.

Paradis, J., Rusk, B., Duncan, T. S., & Govindarajan, K. (2017). Children's second language acquisition of English complex syntax: The role of age, input, and cognitive factors. *Annual Review of Applied Linguistics, 37*, 148–167.

Potratz, J. R., Gildersleeve-Neumann, C., & Redford, M. A. (2022). Measurement properties of mean length of utterance in school-age children. *Language, Speech, and Hearing Services in Schools, 53*(4), 1088–1100.

R Core Team. (2017). *R: A language and environment for statistical computing*. R Foundation for Statistical Computing.

Refugee Council. (2023, 25 September). Facts about separated children. https://www.refugeecouncil.org.uk/information/refugee-asylum-facts/separated-children-facts/

Rocca, S. (2007). *Child second language acquisition: A bi-directional study of English and Italian tense-aspect morphology*. John Benjamins Publishing Company.

Rønning, J. A., Handegaard, B. H., & Sourander, A. (2004). The Strengths and Difficulties Self Report Questionnaire as a screening instrument in Norwegian community samples. *European Child & Adolescent Psychiatry, 13*, 73–82.

Schneider, P., Hayward, D., & Vis Dube, R. (2006). Storytelling from pictures using the Edmonton Narrative Norms Instrument. *Journal of Speech-Language Pathology and Audiology, 30*(4), 224–238.

Soto-Corominas, A., Paradis, J., Al Janaideh, R., Vitoroulis, I., Chen, X., Georgiades, K., Jenkins, J., & Gottardo, A. (2020). Socioemotional well-being influences bilingual and biliteracy development: Evidence from Syrian refugee children. In *Proceedings of the 44th annual Boston University Conference on Language Development*. Cascadilla Press.

Soye, E. (2023). *'Embracing the Stranger': Challenges and opportunities for NI Churches*. Embrace. https://www.embraceni.org/wp-content/uploads/2023/03/Embracing-the-Stranger-Report-2023.pdf

Stone, L. L., Janssens, J. M. A. M., & Vermulst, A. A. (2015). The Strengths and Difficulties Questionnaire: Psychometric properties of the parent and teacher version in children aged 4–7. *BMC Psychology, 3*, 4. https://www.unicef.org/reports/state-of-worlds-children

Zins, J. E., Weissberg, R. P., Wang, M. C., & Walberg, H. J. (Eds.). (2004). *Building school success through social and emotional learning. What does the research say?* Teachers College Press.

Content and Language Integrated Learning: A Comparative Study in Northern Ireland

Sarah O'Neill

1   The Area of Innovation: CLIL in UK Schools

Content and Language Integrated Learning (CLIL) is an educational approach with a dual focus on the teaching and learning of *both* content *and* language (Coyle et al., 2010), in which an 'additional' language, "is used as a tool in the learning of a non-language subject" and where "both language and the subject have a joint curricular role" (Marsh, 2002, p. 58).

Sarah O'Neill is a PhD Research Student at the School of Arts, English and Languages, Queen's University Belfast. Her research is funded by the Department for the Economy (NI) in conjunction with the Arts and Humanities Research Council Priority Area Leadership Fellowship (Modern Languages) held by Professor Janice Carruthers. Award number: AH/P014313/1. The author is grateful to the DfE and AHRC for their support.

S. O'Neill (✉)
Queen's University Belfast, Belfast, UK
e-mail: sarah.oneill@qub.ac.uk

© The Author(s), under exclusive license to Springer Nature Switzerland AG 2024
S. W. Chong, H. Reinders (eds.), *Innovation in Language Learning and Teaching*, New Language Learning and Teaching Environments,
https://doi.org/10.1007/978-3-031-66241-6_6

CLIL research in UK schools has predominantly focussed on the teaching and learning of modern foreign languages (MFL) (Bower, 2013, 2019, 2021; Coyle, 2011, 2013; Dobson, 2005), with few studies considering CLIL provision through English as an additional language (EAL) (Coyle et al., 2021; Rutgers et al., 2020) or indigenous, community or heritage languages (Mac Gearailt et al., 2021). CLIL programmes are offered "in only a small minority of schools" in England (Bower, 2019, p. 45) and in an "experimental and limited manner" in Scotland (San Isidro, 2021, p. 5). In England, the redirecting of policy support and funding for language initiatives (Dobson, 2020) and a shortage of teaching professionals with language skills (UK Government, 2021) entail that "conditions for developing CLIL are limited" (Coyle et al., 2021, p. 4).

There is no known CLIL provision in schools in Northern Ireland, despite repeated calls for a pilot scheme (Gillespie et al., 2012; Jones, 2020), as is currently the case in the Republic of Ireland (DES, 2019). Language learning in Northern Ireland is compulsory for pupils aged 11–14 only, and typically timetabled as a separate subject area for 1–3 hours per week (Collen, 2023). To the author's knowledge, the present study is the first to compare CLIL and 'typical' approaches to language teaching in the context of Northern Ireland.

Due to its cross-curricular nature, CLIL eschews a siloed positioning of languages as a separate subject on the curriculum; instead, conceptualising language as a communicative tool to be used for learning and learned while using (Coyle et al., 2010; Coyle, 2011). The Northern Ireland curriculum describes the cross-curricular skill of 'communication' as "central to the whole curriculum" (CCEA, 2019, p. 25), thus offering a potentially favourable environment for CLIL.

2 The Context for Innovation

For the pupils and teachers involved in this intervention study, this was their first experience of CLIL. In each of three participating post-primary schools in Northern Ireland, an intervention class engaged with a CLIL ecotourism module taught through French by the language teacher (Mehisto & O'Neill, 2023); whilst a comparator class taught by the same teacher continued to learn French using the school's regular scheme of work.

French is the most commonly taught language (other than English) in Northern Ireland, with nine out of ten post-primary schools offering fully timetabled classes (Tinsley, 2019, pp. 19, 26). The intervention ran from January to June 2020, and involved pupils aged 13–14 in Year 10, which is the final year of Key Stage 3 (KS3) and of compulsory language learning in Northern Ireland. The intervention therefore coincided with pupil decisions as to whether to continue studying French at Key Stage 4 (KS4).

The post-primary school system in Northern Ireland has retained academic selection, with pupils attending either selective 'grammar' or non-selective 'secondary' schools (Henderson & Carruthers, 2022). The system is further divided on the basis of religion, with some 93% of all pupils attending a school considered to be predominantly Roman Catholic or predominantly Protestant (Hughes & Loader, 2022). A relatively small integrated sector, accounting for 7% of pupil enrolments (DENI, 2022) seeks to purposively balance pupil intake on the basis of religion.

An invitation to participate in the study was extended to the Heads of Language Departments of all schools on the NICILT[1] mailing list. Of those responding, three schools were purposively selected to achieve a balance in terms of pupil gender, religious ethos and academic selection. Pseudonyms have been assigned to all participating schools, teachers and pupils.

'Ferngrove Integrated' is an urban, co-educational (mixed gender), non-selective school in the integrated sector. It is located in one of the most socio-economically deprived areas in Northern Ireland (NISRA, 2017) and has a higher-than-average intake of pupils with Free School Meal Entitlement (FSME) at 56%, compared with the national average of 37% for non-grammar post-primary schools (DENI, 2021).

'Cavalier College' is a co-educational urban grammar school with a predominantly Protestant ethos and pupil population. Pupil intake is based on an academic selection process. Pupils in this school are from a

---
[1] Northern Ireland Centre for Information on Language Teaching and Research.

higher-than-average socio-economic background (6.9% FSME compared with a national average of 13.7% for grammar schools, DENI, 2021). In this study, the socio-economic background of pupils was perceived to be linked to subject relevance.

'Sanctus High' is a rural, non-selective school with a Roman Catholic ethos. Pupils in this school reported a stronger positive disposition towards languages than the other schools in the study and were more likely to indicate that they would take French at GCSE. This school withdrew early from the intervention, for reasons which will be discussed below.

3   The Impetus for Innovation

> *What attracted me was I frankly would do anything to try and keep an interest in languages [...] really anything, I am willing to try anything that will improve, or at least inject, a slightly different energy into the whole thing.*
> **Pre-Intervention: Teacher at Sanctus High**

These are the words of one participating teacher when asked what had attracted her to the CLIL intervention. All three teachers sought to improve pupil motivation in Year 10 (final year of KS3) and to increase the uptake of languages at GCSE. The impetus for change, or in the words of the teacher at Cavalier College, the desire for "a new way of thinking, a new way of doing things", was described in terms of pupil disillusionment with languages, the 'struggle' to encourage continuation at GCSE and A Level, and a sense that the current curriculum at KS3 is not, or no longer, fit for purpose:

> *The likes of the material that we are covering at KS3 now, is, it's stale for us. We don't believe in it. We see that it's just box-ticking exercises to get to, to get to a certain stage [...] And I think, for us to be able to look at something like these [CLIL materials], it would make us fresher.*
> **Pre-Intervention: Teacher at Sanctus High**

The decline in the uptake of language qualifications is a matter of UK-wide concern (British Academy, 2019) and has been described in policymaking, research and media discourse as a "languages crisis"

(Lanvers & Coleman, 2013). Research charting the proportion of the pupil population taking a language at GCSE and A Level in England and Northern Ireland evinces an overall decline since 2005 (Henderson & Carruthers, 2022), which was the first GCSE examination cohort to 'opt in' to studying a language at KS4, following the removal of languages from the statutory curriculum for 14–16-year-olds.

The proportion of the pupil cohort taking a GCSE in French, in particular, has fallen more steeply than other languages, deteriorating from 45.5% (2005) to 21.6% (2018) in Northern Ireland (Henderson & Carruthers, 2022). Results from the pre-test questionnaire in the present CLIL study show that the proportion of participating pupils intending to take GCSE French in the integrated and grammar schools was smaller still, at 14% and 17% respectively. By contrast, 34% of Sanctus High pupils expressed an intention to study GCSE French. These pupils were also more highly motivated than those in other schools, but withdrew from the study for reasons discussed below.

In addition to a decline in uptake, pupil disaffection with language learning in lower secondary has been well documented across the UK for over two decades, particularly in England (for a review of UK research on pupil motivation, see Lanvers, 2017). Research has found that pupil perceptions of the difficulty and personal relevance of languages are predictive factors of uptake at GCSE and that intervention programmes can encourage higher uptake (Taylor & Marsden, 2014). There is also evidence to suggest that "teaching-related issues" and "systemic teaching difficulties" are contributing factors to pupil disaffection (Lanvers, 2017, pp. 521, 524). The teachers participating in this CLIL intervention study were hopeful that changes to their teaching practice could have a positive impact on pupil motivation and uptake at GCSE.

4   Comparing CLIL and 'Typical' Language Lessons

Participating schools were provided with teaching and learning materials for the delivery of approximately 24 half-hour CLIL lessons on the topic of ecotourism. The CLIL materials comprised a Google Site (https://sites.

google.com/view/ecotourisme/accueil), in addition to a scheme of work and pupil booklet, excerpts of which are available online: http://bit.ly/soneillCLIL.

The topic of ecotourism was drawn from 'Learning for Life and Work' (LLW), one of the nine 'areas of learning' on the Northern Ireland curriculum at KS3 (CCEA, 2019). The Northern Ireland curriculum conceptualises LLW as both a statutory subject in its own right and as an overarching purpose to be realised through all areas of the curriculum (CCEA, 2020), making it particularly suited for integration with language learning.

All three schools took a topic-based approach to typical lesson content. Whilst 'ecotourism' did not feature on the schools' regular schemes of work, they did cover the topics of 'travel' and 'transport'. These provide a useful point of comparison between CLIL and typical lessons. The description below is based on commonalities identified across all three schools through teacher interview, pupil focus groups and an analysis of the teaching and learning materials typically used by these teachers.

Teachers typically employed a PPP (presentation-practice-production) paradigm (Anderson, 2016), whereby vocabulary items and grammar points were presented explicitly using PowerPoint; practised, often ludically, using a variety of interactive games, picture-matching, gap-fills, anagrams and low stakes quizzes; followed by a productive phase in which learners applied their learning to single sentence translations or single paragraph responses to stimulus questions, scaffolded by pre-taught key phrases and model answers. Spoken French was modelled on these written activities, with pupils typically memorising their written answer and reciting it in response to a stimulus question.

Lesson objectives were language-oriented and lesson content typically consisted of word lists, predominantly nouns, which were tested on a weekly basis. For example, pupils were explicitly taught a list of countries and modes of transport so that they could 'talk about where you go on holiday' and 'how you travel'. Grammar teaching focused on the accurate use of grammar in isolation, for example choosing the correct preposition in a gap-fill exercise (e.g. 'I go *to* France/Canada'—je vais *en* France *but* je vais *au* Canada; 'I go *by* car/foot'—je vais *en* voiture *but* je vais *à* pied), with greater emphasis placed on verbs and tenses in the grammar school.

By contrast, the teaching of vocabulary and grammar in CLIL lessons was embedded in authentic texts and audio-visual materials. The teachers appreciated the use of real-world resources with an applied purpose, which they felt added greater context to learning and could stimulate pupil interest. Learners were explicitly taught reading strategies to enable them to recognise vocabulary in context and to deduce meaning using decoding strategies, which included paratextual features, cognates and near-cognates, and skimming and scanning techniques. They applied these strategies to the authentic materials, decoding vocabulary in context and learning how to parse texts into chunks of language that could be reused and recombined in productive tasks.

CLIL lesson objectives focussed on developing subject knowledge and conceptual understanding, as well as cultural and language-oriented goals. Discovery tasks introduced pupils to key vocabulary, which included the three categories of the CLIL Language Triptych (Coyle et al., 2010, p. 36): language of learning (key words for recognition/mastery), language for learning (phrases for self-expression and the negotiation of meaning) and language through learning (language emerging through use).

For example, the unit on sustainable transport focussed on the key words 'ecological' and 'polluting' and familiarised learners with the verbs of instruction and opinion phrases necessary for the various tasks ('rank', 'classify', 'I think that', 'In my opinion'); the teacher's scheme of work also left space to record any new language emerging through classroom interactions. Grammar points were drawn from context and selected for communicative intent, e.g. the formation of the comparative for the purposes of comparing the environmental impact of different modes of transport.

Each unit contained scaffolded rich tasks culminating in a project that applied the principles of collaborative learning, critical questioning and enquiry-based learning (Ball et al., 2015; Coyle et al., 2010; Mehisto & Ting, 2017; Mehisto & O'Neill, 2023). For example, pupils completed the sustainable transport unit by working collaboratively to research, design and present an Interrail journey across Europe.

5 What Worked Well and What Did Not

Teachers were interviewed before and after the intervention, and pupils completed a pre-/post-test questionnaire. Five or six pupils from each CLIL class also participated in post-intervention focus groups. The data were analysed to explore any relationship between pupil motivation, GCSE choices and the type of pedagogic approach (CLIL/non-CLIL), and to investigate what worked well, what did not, and what policy implications could be drawn from the intervention.

Due to the withdrawal of Sanctus High and difficulties matching pre- and post-test questionnaire responses for one class, 55 learners out of a total sample of 138 returned a matched pre- and post-intervention questionnaire (Table 1). The sample size of the non-CLIL group is very low, increasing the probability of Type II error.

Although the impetus for innovation was a desire to boost pupil motivation and increase uptake at GCSE, no significant association was found between the type of approach (CLIL/non-CLIL) and pupils' overall enjoyment of French lessons or their intention to take French at GCSE. However, Wilcoxon Signed Rank tests (Wilcoxon, 1945) identified significant changes in pupils' intrinsic motivation; the level of cognitive challenge, and pupil progress in language learning, as discussed below.

Intrinisic Motivation

Although no significant change could be observed in CLIL and non-CLIL pupil's overall enjoyment of French, a significant deterioration in intrinsic motivation was identified among the CLIL pupils who had enjoyed French prior to the intervention ($T = 20$, $p = 0.012$, $r = 0.36$); 50% of these pupils returned a lower score on the intrinsic motivation scale following the intervention. These were the pupils who had responded that, overall, they had enjoyed their typical French lessons. It is likely that the typical approach was working for these pupils and the introduction of CLIL may have upset this status quo.

Table 1 Counts and frequencies of pupils completing a matched pre-/post-questionnaire by school type, gender, FSME and type of approach

Matched pre/post-questionnaire	School type		Gender			FSME		Type of approach	
	Grammar	Non-grammar	Female	Male	Non-binary	Yes	No	CLIL	Non-CLIL
Count	26	29	20	32	3	18	37	43	12
Frequency	47%	53%	36%	58%	6%	33%	67%	78%	22%

The teacher in Sanctus High withdrew from the intervention following two introductory CLIL lessons, having surmised that it 'just wasn't working' for her learners; 100% of pupils at Sanctus High had responded that they 'enjoyed French overall' in the pre-test, and these pupils returned significantly more positive responses than those in other schools (Fig. 1). One-third of these pupils attributed their enjoyment of French to their teacher, a Head of Department with 23 years' experience. It would appear that her typical approach was highly motivating for learners, and that the intervention had a disruptive effect.

It must be noted that no negative effect was found for the CLIL group overall: 44% of all CLIL pupils reported no change; indeed, the intrinsic motivation of one-third of those who had not enjoyed their typical lessons improved. These findings suggest that experimental intervention may work best for those learners who are disaffected with the status quo, whilst those who enjoy the typical approach may experience a deterioration in motivation. Teachers may wish to consider which learners stand to benefit, and which perhaps have the least to lose, when piloting a new approach.

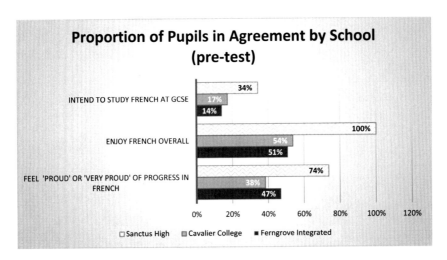

Fig. 1 Proportion of pupils in agreement by school (pre-test)

Level of Cognitive Challenge

The level of cognitive challenge in CLIL lessons was a concern for teachers in both non-selective schools, and the difficulty level of CLIL was a factor in the withdrawal of Sanctus High from the intervention. However, the case of Ferngrove Integrated demonstrates how careful scaffolding and the explicit teaching of learning strategies can support learners in engaging with higher levels of challenge.

Prior to the intervention, only three pupils (8%) at Ferngrove Integrated and none of the pupils at Sanctus High felt that their French lessons were too difficult. The level of challenge in typical French lessons appears to have purposively been kept low in these schools due to teacher beliefs around pupils' tolerance threshold.

> *They're put off by something that's too difficult, they just won't engage.*
> **Pre-Intervention: Teacher at Ferngrove Integrated**

> *That's something that I find difficult when dealing with them, they're not great with challenge.*
> **Pre-Intervention: Teacher at Sanctus High**

Sanctus High withdrew from the intervention after only a few lessons; the teacher cited the level of cognitive challenge as a factor in her decision to withdraw: "The level of your work, if you like, was just too high." At Ferngrove Integrated, the Wilcoxon Signed Rank test identified a significant and moderate increase in subject difficulty for the CLIL group ($T = 19$, $p = 0.017$, $r = 0.41$). This effect was not observed in the grammar school, where 35% of pupils had felt their typical lessons were too difficult, and which typically covered a higher volume of material, placing more emphasis on grammar teaching than the non-selective schools.

Teachers at the non-selective schools perceived the quantity and length of target-language texts used in CLIL as challenging for their pupils. The teacher at Sanctus High cited the amount of reading as influential in her decision to withdraw from the project, whilst the Ferngrove Integrated teacher also expressed concern at pupil reactions to sentence-level and text-level work:

For some of them, they were just intimidated by the complete, sheer amount of French that they were seeing in front of them.
Post-Intervention: Teacher at Ferngrove Integrated

In both non-selective schools, teachers perceived pupil literacy levels in English (L1) as a barrier to their use of reading strategies in French (L2). The Ferngrove Integrated teacher observed that pupils lacked the metalanguage to describe parts of speech "What's a verb? What's an adjective?"; whilst the teacher at Sanctus High reported that pupils could not decode cognate infinitives such as 'observer' and 'respecter' and struggled, more generally, with grammatical concepts:

Those youngsters could not understand the infinitive, the whole… they just aren't getting it. My youngsters don't get verbs. They do not understand verbs. They don't understand tenses. My children do not understand that there's a correlation between 'I go' and 'I went'.
Post-Intervention: Teacher at Sanctus High

This teacher felt that the amount of reading was unsuitable for her 'practically minded' learners and was leaving many of them behind. The use of authentic texts; the level of cognitive challenge, and the difficulties that her learners experienced in decoding cognates and near-cognates, posed what she considered to be insurmountable challenges in her particular context.

Prior to the intervention, the teacher in Ferngrove Integrated had raised similar concerns around the level of challenge that CLIL materials would pose:

The top set in our school might be the bottom set or, you know, kind of lower ability in a different school. So […] I'm just concerned, you know, not overwhelming them, […] and making sure that they feel that they're having success with the materials.
Pre-Intervention: Teacher at Ferngrove Integrated

To mitigate these concerns, this teacher supplemented the CLIL resources with visual scaffolding, using PowerPoint slides to display key information, model tasks and exemplify responses; she also introduced low-stakes quizzes to gamify vocabulary practice. Her activities exemplify the "careful scaffolding" and supportive role that Graham suggests teachers should adopt in order to support learners in building self-efficacy by using personal agency to master challenging tasks (Graham, 2022, citing Bandura, 1994, p. 6).

Following the intervention, this teacher felt the explicit teaching of reading and writing strategies had been one of the most successful aspects of the CLIL intervention and was something she would adopt in her future teaching.

> *I liked the sentence builder aspect. I liked the reading strategies and being able to put the reading strategies into use, [...] that's something that I would use, that I would make sure pupils are aware of and would use as, like, a technique going forward, and I think that it would be useful at GCSE as well.*
> **Post-Intervention: Teacher at Ferngrove Integrated**

The level of challenge in typical language lessons at the non-selective schools appears to have been kept purposively low. Although CLIL raised the level of challenge significantly in Ferngrove Integrated, this increase was observed in relation to the proportion of pupils agreeing that French was 'their most difficult subject'; which rose from 12% in the pre-test to 35% in the post-test. The proportion of pupils who found French lessons 'too difficult' remained stable. This would suggest that whilst difficulty *relative to other subjects* increased significantly for the CLIL class; this did not surpass pupils' tolerance threshold. It seems that pupils were able to tolerate a higher level of challenge than had been offered in their typical French lessons.

Low challenge environments in the language classroom have been described as, "a serious underestimation of pupils' cognitive and intellectual capability" (Wingate, 2016, p. 452) and social cognitive theory suggests that a lack of challenging tasks and personal agency may, in fact, undermine the development of self-efficacy in language learners (Graham, 2022). Yet, through the CLIL intervention and appropriate scaffolding, as provided by the teacher in Ferngrove Integrated, these learners demonstrated that they could rise to meet a higher level of cognitive challenge in the language classroom.

Collaborative Project-Based Learning

Collaborative project-based learning was linked to significant gains made by the CLIL group in both spoken French and cross-curricular skills. Wilcoxon Signed Rank tests found that CLIL pupils reported significant improvements in their progress in speaking in French ($T = 318$, $p = 0.026$, $r = 0.24$) and cross-curricular skills ($T = 292.5$, $p = 0.010$, $r = 0.28$). The latter was framed as 'learning skills that you can use in other subjects, not just in French'. By contrast, non-CLIL pupils reported a significant deterioration on progress in both speaking in French ($T = 0$, $p = 0.020$, $r = 0.50$) and cross-curricular skills ($T = 0$, $p = 0.046$, $r = 0.45$).

Each unit of the CLIL module culminated in a collaborative project with learners working in groups to deliver an oral presentation in French. For example, pupils worked together to design and present an Interrail itinerary through Europe, developing their own visual and textual supports using PowerPoint slides and presenter's notes. For CLIL pupils in the participating schools, this was the first time they had experienced collaborative, project-based learning in the language classroom.

When asked to design their ideal course for French, pupils in the focus groups unanimously voted to include group work activities and interactive games. This was despite the fact that the focus group composition comprised pupils with strongly opposed views on learning French. CLIL pupils developed research and presentation skills during the project phases that could be applied across the curriculum; moreover, in their comments, they linked collaborative project-based learning to greater subject enjoyment.

> *It was more enjoyable, too [...] because we were doing more group work.*
> **Post-Intervention: Pupil at Ferngrove Integrated**

Their teachers also observed higher levels of enjoyment and engagement in the group work phases:

> *I would say that they definitely enjoyed it, more than they would have enjoyed following our normal course. I think there's no question about that. And I think*

> *the key to that was, number one, the amount of group activity that there was involved in it.*
>
> **Post-Intervention: Teacher at Cavalier College**

Collaborative, project-based learning represented a step-change in the development of spoken language skills. Grammar pupils described how, in typical French lessons, they would compose written answers to oral questions which they memorised and recited in one-to-one dialogue with their teacher. One pupil expressed frustration at not being able to generate spontaneous speech, and a desire to be "able to hold a conversation with a French person, without being, having revised it for the past week".

By contrast, CLIL emphasised peer-to-peer interactions in the target language. The triadic focus on language of, for and through learning fostered an expectation that pupils would be supported to generate their own language during the lesson to meet their communication needs. Rather than one-to-one question and answer assessment, pupils were assessed in groups during the presentation phases, enabling them to use cue cards and slides as visual scaffolding to support their spoken language and to rely on each other for prompts.

The introduction of collaborative project-based learning appears to be one of the successes of the intervention, especially in relation to pupil enjoyment and progress. Group and project work were not found to be a feature of typical French lessons. The grammar teacher attributed this to the quantity of material to be covered in preparation for the GCSE syllabus, which led to a "fear of surrendering time" to non-direct instruction:

> *If we didn't feel that the GCSE curriculum was so dense at it is, and therefore the pressure was on us to cover those topics at KS3 [...] And that shapes so much of our approach in the classroom and the pressure that we feel to not be able to do things like group work.*
>
> **Post-Intervention: Teacher at Cavalier College**

The teachers in this study reported a wash-back effect from the GCSE syllabus driven by the quantity of material to be covered and felt obliged to use direct instruction due to time pressures. Their concerns around the nature and content of the external exams are echoed by other teachers across Northern Ireland (Collen, 2023, p. 31). However, the statutory curriculum for modern languages at Key Stage 3 (Northern Ireland) details that "young people should have opportunities [...] to become effective and creative communicators", "research and manage information" and "work effectively with others" (CCEA, 2007). This intended KS3 curriculum does not appear to be fully realised in typical language lessons at these schools. It is perhaps timely for designers of curriculum and assessment to consider an alternative approach to the speaking examination at GCSE; assessment via group discussion and peer-to-peer role play, for example, could provide the impetus for more collaborative activity in the language classroom.

Topic Content

CLIL introduced new topic content to language lessons through integration with the subject Learning for Life and Work. The ecotourism module featured destinations in Northern Ireland local to participants, with the intention of increasing the topic relevance for learners. However, this inadvertently exposed a socio-economic divide between the life experiences and opportunities of pupils in the selective and non-selective schools.

In her post-intervention interview, the grammar teacher attributed pupil enjoyment of the CLIL module to two factors: group work and the topic content, which she felt was highly relevant to pupils. In the focus group, grammar pupils related numerous anecdotes connecting lesson content to their personal experiences.

> *The overtourism part [...] In wintertime, I was jumping in the pier, and it was just covered in people!*
> **Post-Intervention: Pupil at Cavalier College**

> *The gentrification-[...] of, like, the [PLACE NAME]. I felt that really resonated with me.*
> **Post-Intervention: Pupil at Cavalier College**

Although the tourist destinations used in the CLIL module were located within the same council area as Ferngrove Integrated, it became apparent during focus group discussions that some pupils had rarely left their urban housing estate and never visited attractions within ten miles of their homes. By contrast, all of the grammar pupils in the focus group had visited these sites, despite living over 60 miles away, and indeed, some had a second home in the area.

Ferngrove Integrated was located in an area ranked within the top ten most deprived areas of Northern Ireland for income deprivation (NISRA, 2017) with a higher-than-average FSME enrolment; whilst Cavalier College had lower-than-average FSME. Studies in Northern Ireland provide robust evidence linking school type and pupil FSME profile (Henderson, 2020) and demonstrating a relationship between school type/FSME profile and language learning (Henderson & Carruthers, 2022).

Despite geographical proximity to sites covered in the CLIL ecotourism module, the teacher at Ferngrove Integrated felt the topic lacked relevance for her pupils. She attributed this to pupils' socio-economic background and limited travel opportunities, linking these to a wider problem with the relevance of French and language learning in general.

> *It was out of their realm of interest and I already think that there's a bit of [...] an elitism with French, that they've never been to France, so it's kinda out of their – they're not interested in it, some of them have barely left, you know, their estate in [TOWN NAME], never mind going away to France, so trying to put them in a place to think about going Interrailing, it's just not, not, not in their interests really.*
> **Post-Intervention: Teacher at Ferngrove Integrated**

Research has demonstrated how signifiers of social class are (re)produced in discourse around the value of languages, pupils' social practices and their imagined futures (Coffey, 2018, drawing on Bourdieu, 1986, 1998). The description of ecotourism as 'out of their realm of interest', could be analysed in terms of the Bourdieusian framework of 'field' and 'habitus', the social positioning of these pupils, and how these influence their disposition towards the topic. In combining French with tourism, this teacher felt that the CLIL ecotourism module was doubly beyond the 'field' of her pupils' lived experience.

However, Coffey argues that "there is scope for individual agency to effect change [...] within the parameters of the imaginable" (Coffey, 2018, p. 473), and indeed, when asked about their imagined futures, pupils at Ferngrove Integrated acknowledged their limited travel opportunities, but most expressed a desire to travel in future. These pupils were keen to learn more about the world past and present, requesting topics such as Francophone Africa and the French Revolution. They did not want to merely memorise facts, but to engage critically with topics, posing questions, such as, "How much it [the French Revolution] impacted France and the way it is now?"

The discord between the circumstances and ambitions of pupils in Ferngrove Integrated indicates a desire for educational opportunities beyond those offered by their personal circumstances. However, their typical language lessons appear to be limited to content relevant to their immediate realm of experience. The languages programme of study for KS3 in England describes language learning as 'a liberation from insularity and provides an opening to other cultures' (DE, 2013, p. 1); whilst OFSTED claims it "helps to equip pupils with the knowledge and cultural capital they need to succeed in life" (OFSTED, 2021). Similarly, the modern languages curriculum at KS3 (Northern Ireland) "prepares pupils for moving comfortably between a range of cultural environments" (CCEA, 2007). Teachers and curriculum designers may wish to consider to what extent the topic content and the overarching purposes of their curricula align.

6 Lessons Learned

This intervention study introduced a CLIL approach to language learning in three schools in Northern Ireland, in order to compare CLIL to typical language lessons in each school. Results from pupil questionnaires, teacher interviews and pupil focus groups found significant differences between CLIL and non-CLIL groups in relation to the level of cognitive challenge and pupil progress in speaking and cross-curricular skills, and indicate that CLIL offers new, and potentially beneficial, opportunities to integrate collaborative project-based learning and rich topic content in the language classroom.

Teachers interested in introducing CLIL should be aware that the motivation of learners who enjoy typical language lessons may deteriorate in response to change. They may wish to consider piloting CLIL with a year group that has no prior experience of language learning, or with learners who are disaffected with typical lessons, and are advised to monitor the motivational trajectory of participants.

Explicit strategy instruction and collaborative project-based learning were identified as particularly successful elements of this CLIL intervention. Whilst these pedagogies are not unique to CLIL, they do form part of an "enriched pedagogy" toolkit associated with the CLIL approach (Ball et al., 2015; Coyle et al., 2010; Mehisto & Ting, 2017). CLIL offers a means of embedding such practices in classrooms where direct instruction, low cognitive challenge and limited topic content may otherwise dominate.

Teachers interested in experimenting with CLIL should anticipate an increase in the level of cognitive challenge, particularly if typical lessons represent a low challenge environment. This can place an additional workload on the teacher in the delivery and maintenance of a "high-challenge, high-support" environment (Gibbons, 2009) characterised by both a challenging curriculum and carefully planned scaffolding which meets learners' emerging needs. The findings of the present study suggest that, in return, teachers may observe significant gains in pupil progress.

This study also invites those who teach, build curriculum and design assessment to engage critically with the *how* and *what* of language learning. If the *why* of language learning is "a liberation from insularity and provides an opening to other cultures" (DE, 2013), as in England, or "to become effective and creative communicators" (CCEA, 2007), as in Northern Ireland, are these purposes best served by a diet of topics emphasising noun-intensive vocabulary work and grammar in isolation? Is an oral assessment culture of teacher-pupil dialogue effective in developing creative communication in the target language? The pedagogies introduced through this CLIL intervention offer alternative approaches that are potentially more effective in developing pupils' communicative and cross-curricular skills.

Finally, learners in this study expressed an interest in meaningfully integrating language learning with subject content beyond their immediate experiences and circumstances. Teachers may wish to consider affording their pupils greater autonomy in the selection of lesson content. The collaborative, project-based approach to learning introduced through this CLIL intervention offers teachers a means of co-creating stimulating curricula with pupils, integrating language learning with content that engages and interests learners.

References

Anderson, J. (2016). Why practice makes perfect sense: The past, present and potential future of the PPP paradigm in language teacher education. *English Language Teaching Education and Development, 19*, 14–22. http://wrap.warwick.ac.uk/169557/

Ball, P., Kelly, K., & Clegg, J. (2015). *Putting CLIL into practice: Oxford handbooks for language teachers*. Oxford University Press.

Bandura, A. (1994). Self-efficacy. In V. S. Ramachaudran (Ed.), *Encyclopedia of human behavior* (Vol. 4, pp. 71–81). Academic Press.

Bourdieu, P. (1986). *Distinction: A social critique of the judgement of taste*. Routledge.

Bourdieu, P. (1998). *Practical reason. On the theory of action*. Stanford University Press.

Bower, K. (2013). *To what extent does Content and Language Integrated Learning (CLIL) as a language-based project approach promote pupil motivation in the teaching of MFL in three secondary schools in England?* The University of Hull.

Bower, K. (2019). 'Speaking French alive': Learner perspectives on their motivation in Content and Language Integrated Learning in England. *Innovation in Language Learning and Teaching, 13*(1), 45–60. https://doi.org/10.1080/17501229.2017.1314483

Bower, K. (2021). Contact and Language Integrated Learning in England: Missed opportunities and ways forward. In *Language learning in Anglophone countries* (pp. 267–287). Springer International Publishing. https://doi.org/10.1007/978-3-030-56654-8_14

British Academy. (2019). Languages in the UK: A call for action (From the four UK-wide National Academies: The British Academy; with the Academy of

Medical Sciences; the Royal Academy of Engineering; and the Royal Society). https://www.thebritishacademy.ac.uk/sites/default/files/Languages-UK-2019-academies-statement.pdf

CCEA. (2007). *Statutory requirements for modern languages at Key Stage 3.* https://ccea.org.uk/key-stage-3/curriculum/modern-languages

CCEA. (2019). *Statutory curriculum at Key Stage 3.* https://ccea.org.uk/learning-resources/statutory-curriculum-key-stage-3

CCEA. (2020). *The big picture of the curriculum at Key Stage 3.* https://ccea.org.uk/learning-resources/big-picture-curriculum-key-stage-3

Coffey, S. (2018). Choosing to study modern foreign languages: Discourses of value as forms of cultural capital. *Applied Linguistics, 39*(4), 462–480. https://doi.org/10.1093/applin/amw019

Collen, I. (2023). *Language trends Northern Ireland 2023: Language teaching in primary and post-primary schools.* British Council. https://doi.org/10.57884/Z4WV-XA65

Coyle, D. (2011). *ITALIC research report investigating student gains: Content and Language Integrated Learning.* University of Aberdeen, Esmée Fairbairn Foundation.

Coyle, D. (2013). Listening to learners: An investigation into 'successful learning' across CLIL contexts. *International Journal of Bilingual Education and Bilingualism, 16*(3), 244–266. https://doi.org/10.1080/13670050.2013.777384

Coyle, D., Bower, K., Foley, Y., & Hancock, J. (2021). Teachers as designers of learning in diverse, bilingual classrooms in England: An ADiBE case study. *International Journal of Bilingual Education and Bilingualism.* https://doi.org/10.1080/13670050.2021.1989373

Coyle, D., Hood, P., & Marsh, D. (2010). *Content and Language Integrated Learning.* Cambridge University Press.

DE. (2013). *Languages programmes of study: Key Stage 3 national curriculum in England.* https://www.gov.uk/government/publications/national-curriculum-in-england-languages-progammes-of-study

DENI. (2021). *Education school meals census, 2020/21.* https://www.education-ni.gov.uk/sites/default/files/publications/education/School%20Meals%20Infographic%20202021.PDF

DENI. (2022). *School census key statistics 2021/22.* https://www.education-ni.gov.uk/sites/default/files/publications/education/School%20Census%20Key%20Statistics%20202122.pdf

DES. (2019). *Content and Language Integrated Learning (CLIL). Irish pilot project 2019/20*. https://assets.gov.ie/46716/3f0c358a6d7c4ca6a97ece81774 acfdd.pdf

Dobson, A. (2005). *Content and Language Integrated Project (CLIP), External evaluation report – A commentary on progress and issues*. CILT.

Dobson, A. (2020). Context is everything: Reflections on CLIL in the UK. *The Language Learning Journal, 48*(5), 508–518. https://doi.org/10.1080/09571736.2020.1804104

Gibbons, P. (2009). *English learners, academic literacy, and thinking: Learning in the challenge zone*. Heinemann Educational Books.

Gillespie, J. H., Johnston, D., & Ó Corráin, A. (2012). *Languages for the future: Northern Ireland languages strategy*. Department of Education NI. https://www.education-ni.gov.uk/publications/languages-future-northern-ireland-languages-strategy-final-report

Graham, S. (2022). Self-efficacy and language learning – What it is and what it isn't. *Language Learning Journal, 50*(2), 186–207. https://doi.org/10.1080/09571736.2022.2045679

Henderson, L. (2020). Children's education rights at the transition to secondary education: School choice in Northern Ireland. *British Educational Research Journal, 46*, 1131–1151. https://doi.org/10.1002/berj.3620

Henderson, L., & Carruthers, J. (2022). Socio-economic factors, school type and the uptake of languages: Northern Ireland in the wider UK context. *The Language Learning Journal, 50*(6), 712–731. https://doi.org/10.1080/09571736.2021.1888151

Hughes, J., & Loader, R. (2022). Is academic selection in Northern Ireland a barrier to social cohesion? *Research Papers in Education*. https://doi.org/10.1080/02671522.2022.2135016

Jones, S. (2020). Finding our true North: On languages, understanding and curriculum in Northern Ireland. *Curriculum Journal*. https://doi.org/10.1002/curj.93

Lanvers, U. (2017). Contradictory others and the habitus of languages: Surveying the L2 motivation landscape in the United Kingdom. *The Modern Language Journal, 101*(3), 517–532. https://doi.org/10.1111/modl.12410

Lanvers, U., & Coleman, J. A. (2013). The UK language learning crisis in the public media: A critical analysis. *The Language Learning Journal, 45*(1), 3–25. https://doi.org/10.1080/09571736.2013.830639

Mac Gearailt, B., Mac Ruairc, G., & Murray, C. (2021). Actualising content and language integrated learning (CLIL) in Irish-medium education; Why, how and why now? *Irish Educational Studies, 42*(1), 39–57. https://doi.org/1 0.1080/03323315.2021.1910971

Marsh, D. (2002). *Content and Language Integrated Learning: The European dimension – Actions, trends and foresight potential*. http://europa.eu.int/comm/education/languages/index.html

Mehisto, P., & O'Neill, S. (2023). Critical pedagogy: Fostering learner engagement, critical thinking and language learning. In N. Pachler & A. Redondo (Eds.), *Learning to teach foreign languages in the secondary school: A companion to school experience* (pp. 165–178). Routledge.

Mehisto, P., & Ting, T. Y. L. (2017). *CLIL essentials for secondary school teachers*. Cambridge University Press.

NISRA. (2017). *Northern Ireland multiple deprivation areas 2017*. https://www.ninis2.nisra.gov.uk/public/documents/DeprivationLGD.pdf

OFSTED. (2021). Research review series: Languages. https://www.gov.uk/government/publications/curriculum-research-review-series-languages/curriculum-research-review-series-languages

Rutgers, D., de Graaff, R., van Beuningen, C., & Fisher, L. (2020). The knowledge base of CLIL teaching in multilingual primary settings. *ELT Research Papers, 20*(2). https://www.teachingenglish.org.uk/sites/teacheng/files/L019_ELTRA_FINAL.pdf

San Isidro, X. (2021). CLIL as a pathway for cross-curricular and translingual classroom practices: A comparative quantitative study on Scottish and Spanish teachers' views. *Language Teaching Research*. https://doi.org/10.1177/13621688211032431

Taylor, F., & Marsden, E. J. (2014). Perceptions, attitudes, and choosing to study foreign languages in England: An experimental intervention. *Modern Language Journal, 98*, 902–920.

Tinsley, T. (2019). *Language trends Northern Ireland 2019: Findings from surveys of primary and post-primary schools*. British Council.

UK Government. (2021). Skilled worker visa: Shortage occupations for healthcare and education. https://www.gov.uk/government/publications/skilled-worker-visa-shortage-occupations-for-health-and-education/skilled-worker-visa-shortage-occupations-for-healthcare-and-education

Wilcoxon, F. (1945). Individual comparisons by ranking methods. *Biometrics Bulletin, 1*, 80–83. https://doi.org/10.2307/3001968

Wingate, U. (2016). Lots of games and little challenge – A snapshot of modern foreign language teaching in English secondary schools. *The Language Learning Journal, 46*(4), 442–455. https://doi.org/10.1080/09571736.2016.1161061

Part IV

Scotland

Developing a Rationale for Teaching Local Languages to Young Language Learners: A Case Study of Teaching and Learning Chinese Language and Culture in a Scottish Primary School

David Roxburgh

1 Introduction

This chapter is based on my recent research and scholarship in Scotland concerning language provision in its primary education sector (ages 5–12) and, in particular, ideas which continue to develop the concept and promotion of 'local languages'. This thinking has arisen from research from a number of interested colleagues (Pedley et al., 2024) and aims to explore innovations in ways of teaching the languages already in use in schools and their local communities as a means of further highlighting purpose and relevance, particularly with young learners. As will be discussed, this thinking aligns very well to aspects of current Scottish

---

D. Roxburgh (✉)
Strathclyde Institute of Education, University of Strathclyde, Glasgow, UK
e-mail: david.roxburgh@strath.ac.uk

© The Author(s), under exclusive license to Springer Nature Switzerland AG 2024
S. W. Chong, H. Reinders (eds.), *Innovation in Language Learning and Teaching*, New Language Learning and Teaching Environments,
https://doi.org/10.1007/978-3-031-66241-6_7

languages national policy (Scottish Government, 2012) which, in addition to second (L2) provision, seeks to develop opportunities for learners to engage in a third (L3), opening doors to languages that better reflect the growing language diversity seen throughout the country. However, though the policy offers scope to think differently, the majority of schools are still grappling with what L3 means in practice with many drawing upon mini versions of their existing L2 provision within traditional European languages. This is despite the strong potential to draw upon others that are under-represented or, indeed, absent from languages curricula, but seen and used in pupils' domestic, educational, and local environments. Though the rationale behind L3 provision is innovative, it requires further fleshing out and, therefore, this chapter argues that practices around notions of 'local languages' are a strong means of creatively supporting and exemplifying the space provided by L3 provision and fairly light touch policy in contrast to L2 offerings. As an illustration of this approach, there is a particular focus on one case study in the context of teaching Chinese language and culture (referred to from now on as CLC) in a Scottish primary school. The discussion of this study, the impetus for change that led to this way of thinking, what worked well, and lessons learned offers insights that are applicable to other languages. This chapter will be of interest to a variety of audiences including pre-service and in-service school practitioners, local, regional and national advisers, teacher educators, and those researching the field of language learning across the UK and beyond.

2 What Is Meant by Local Languages in Scotland?

At the outset of this chapter, there is a need to explain how I understand the concept of local languages as the recurring theme that provides the impetus for the thinking underpinning the various discussions of theory and practice.

In the wider literature base, for example, Bühmann and Trudell (2008), Mahboob and Lin (2018), Mehmedbegovic (2017), local languages generally refer to those spoken by the people in a particular region or locality;

usually not widely spoken outside of their immediate area or community and often not recognised as official languages of a country or region. They can include indigenous languages, dialects, or regional variations of widely spoken languages. In this sense, local languages are an important part of a community's cultural heritage and can play a crucial role in preserving its unique identity and traditions. In many cases, these languages are at risk of disappearing due to the dominance of more widely spoken languages or the impact of political and economic factors.

These points certainly have relevance in Scotland, given the historical dominance of English as its official language, but with similar recognition in 2005 being afforded to Gaelic, a language which, like English, has been associated with Scotland for around 1500 years. It is spoken by around 1.1% of the population as a whole (National Records of Scotland, 2015) with updated data due for release from the 2022 census in due course. The on-going, overall decline of Gaelic users, despite various initiatives and central funding, feeds into the larger debate on how languages, other than English, can be sustained and promoted. However, on potentially a more positive note, regular and changing patterns of migration means that the mix of languages in use is shifting and that language diversity in Scotland increases year on year. For example, the most recent Scottish school census (Scottish Government, 2023) lists over 164 languages spoken by Scottish pupils, ranging from Polish, the most widely used after English, with almost 18,000 pupils, to a range of languages grouped together in the category of 'other' given fewer than 300 speakers such as Basque, Kannada, and Wolof. In the school census, 10.8% of the school population reported to have a language other than English as their 'main home language'.

Therefore, at the simplest level, 'local languages' in Scotland encompass those spoken within close-knit communities, including languages with deep historical ties to Scotland like English, Scots, Gaelic, as well as languages introduced through migration such as Polish, Urdu, Chinese, Yoruba, Arabic, and Spanish, including their variants. These languages serve various purposes, from local business transactions to cultural activities. Visit Britain (2020) identifies Scotland's top international tourism markets as the USA, Germany, France, the Netherlands, and China, meaning the languages associated with these regions could also be considered local due to their prevalence among visitors. Given this definition, and the growing linguistic diversity in Scotland and greater connectedness globally than in the past, any language in the world is potentially a local language in Scotland. This speaks positively to the diversification of languages globally and the need to think differently of ways to celebrate and promote this in school systems.

3 The Scottish Curriculum Context: Giving Space to Think About Local Languages

Over the past two decades, Scotland has witnessed increased linguistic diversity, coinciding with the introduction of the 'Curriculum for Excellence' (CfE) and language teaching guidelines. The current policy, known as the '1+2 languages approach', (Scottish Government, 2012) ensures that all Scottish pupils learn one additional language (L2) from Primary 1 (age 5) to the end of Secondary 3 (age 15). At this point, they can choose to pursue language exams in the senior phase (ages 16–18). In the primary sector, the focus has predominantly been on traditional European languages like French, German, Spanish, and Italian, aligning with the 1+2 policy and ensuring a smooth transition into secondary school. The L2 curriculum is guided by formal 'experiences and outcomes' outlined in national education documents (Education Scotland, 2015). In line with practices in the UK, and other global education systems, these outcomes apply universally to all languages with some examples given below for illustration (Education Scotland, 2015, p. 4, 5, and 8 respectively):

- I can deliver a brief presentation on a familiar topic using familiar language and phrases (listening and talking, Second level: ages 9–12).
- I can work on my own or with others to demonstrate my understanding of words and phrases containing familiar language (reading, First level: ages 6–8).
- I use my knowledge about language and success criteria to help me, and I can check that I have written familiar words and phrases accurately (writing, Second level: ages 9–12).

In contrast to other parts of the UK, provision is made in Scottish schools for another additional language (L3) starting from no later than Primary 5 (age 9). The 1+2 policy highlights that there should be no hierarchy of language provision and that the L3 should allow a choice of language(s) that suits a school's needs. In contrast to the formalised statements of learning for L2, guidance for L3 provision (Education Scotland, 2019) is far less prescriptive with broader indications of content and outcomes including:

- The choice of any language is available to schools;
- Coverage is far less constrained by notions of specific continuity and progression;
- Different models of delivery are possible to suit local needs;
- Based ideally on the same L3 being taught across Primaries 5–7 though not exclusively so;
- Encouragement to use local resources e.g., local speakers of the language, working alongside primary teachers trained to some extent in language pedagogies;
- Greater emphasis on the 'cultural' base as a motivation for further language learning; and
- Strengthened arguments for the incorporation of language learning through interdisciplinary approaches that mirror existing core curricular practices in Scottish primary schools.

The L3 classroom in Scotland exposes students to a variety of languages reflecting diverse communities. Recent data (Glen & Hugh, 2021) show that 64% of primary schools offer some form of L3 experience. Popular languages include Spanish, French, German, Chinese, Gaelic (learners), Italian, and Urdu. Additionally, 'other' languages such as British Sign Language, Scots, Polish, Japanese, Arabic, Portuguese, Latin, Russian, Dutch, and Ukrainian (due to the recent refugee influx) are being taught. While L3 broadens language horizons, it raises concerns about effective learning, teacher proficiency, training, support, and cultural awareness (ADES, 2016; Valdera Gil & Crichton, 2018). This approach offers opportunities for reimagining language education, albeit with limited attention within Scottish research circles at present. As a result, this requires innovative language learning in Scottish classrooms, aligning with curriculum goals and fostering enthusiasm in primary schools, which can later be built upon as learners transition to the secondary education phase.

4 Arguing for Innovation Through the Teaching of 'Local Languages'

As explained previously, the focus of '1+2' implementation initially was on achieving the early start for L2 and ensuring continuity and progression across primary schooling and into the secondary phase. In this respect, L2 provision looks quite similar to primary language provision in many other contexts. However, the possibilities presented by L3 have revealed this to be a potentially innovative space where we can think differently. In looking at a theoretical model for this chapter and its L3 focus, I draw upon ecological theories of second language learning (SLA) in the first instance. Steffensen and Kramsch (2017, p. 1) recognise this range of theories as being a 'convenient metaphor to promote sociocultural or sociocognitive approaches to second language learning', identifying their broad aspects as covering:

- The emergent nature of language learning and use;
- The crucial role of affordances in the environment;
- The mediating function of language in the educational enterprise; and
- The historicity and subjectivity of the language learning experience, as well as its inherent conflictuality.

Such ecological models are not without their critics, and can often tend to be seen as 'catch-alls' upon which to hang many issues in the area of language acquisition. However, such models are being revisited in an attempt to give further discussion round the ways in which context plays a fundamental role in shaping language learning environments (Chong et al., 2023). One of the more recent representations of this includes the 'transdisciplinary framework' promoted by the Douglas Fir Group (2016) which is useful in linking to the particular nature of the L3 experiences outlined in this chapter from the stance of promoting 'local languages' by recognising that:

> *SLA must now be particularly responsive to the pressing needs of people who learn to live—and in fact do live—with more than one language at various points in their lives, with regard to their education, their multilingual and multiliterate development, social integration, and performance across diverse contexts.* (p. 20)

The Douglas Fir Group (DFG) framework, as shown in Fig. 1, highlights that local multilingualism is the preferred starting point for second language acquisition.

At the heart of this model is the individual engaging with others in multilingual contexts of action and interaction, making communication in more than one language meaningful, and ensuring one of the conditions that they see as critical to success in language learning—namely that learners have regular recurring contexts to use their new languages. The DFG framework is based largely on theories concerning adult language learners, but raises challenging questions about the implications for traditional languages provision in schools, where language learners, conventionally, had few opportunities to meet or enter into regular meaningful communication with those whose languages they were learning. In contrast, pedagogies based on 'local languages' constitute a good fit for this model as they afford a number of potential benefits. Firstly, they can promote inclusivity: all children can be involved in sharing the languages they already know and exploring together these and other languages in use in local communities. Secondly, this can generate transformational experiences for pupils, in terms of seeing themselves as bilinguals—perhaps already speaking two or more languages fluently—or as emergent bilinguals, becoming able to use more than one language in everyday life in family, classroom, or community. Thirdly, they can prompt the emergence of new pedagogies to achieve these goals, involving co-learning and co-teaching for all concerned: the pupils themselves, primary class teachers, parents, community members, and language specialists.

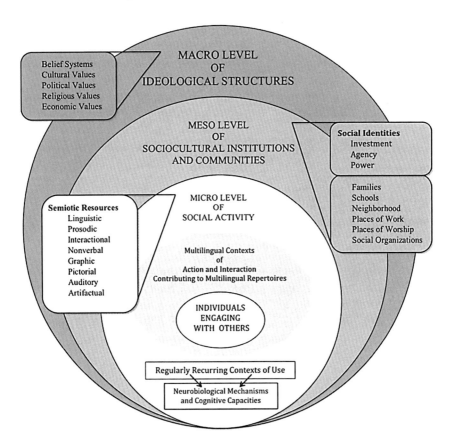

Fig. 1 Representation of the transdisciplinary framework (Douglas Fir Group, 2016, p. 25)

Another point for reflection comes from Phipps (2019) who challenges conventional notions of language learning when she raises key questions about, 'Who do we want to talk to?' and 'How will we learn?' These questions prompt a re-evaluation of language learning in Scotland and the UK, which has traditionally focused on languages like French, German, and Spanish. While teaching methods have evolved from grammar translation to communicative language teaching, they still rely on specialist teachers with a deep understanding of second language acquisition (SLA). The introduction of primary language education has disrupted this norm, as most primary teachers lack such specialisation. Despite these challenges, the teaching approaches have remained largely unchanged. Phipps advocates for rethinking not only which languages we learn and why, but also how we learn them, arguing against a technical approach and suggesting co-teaching and co-learning as more viable alternatives. Interestingly, some Scottish primary schools have already started implementing these approaches. The remainder of this chapter will explore these points further, using CLC as an example and drawing insights from a case study on innovative language teaching methods.

5   The Impetus for Change: Looking to Update the Teaching of CLC in Scottish Primary Schools

The case for change is drawn from two complementary bases. Firstly, wider reflection on other L3 language projects/ thinking with other colleagues that saw the group come together to identify, form and explore initial notions and understandings of 'local languages' and approaches (Anderson, in preparation; Pedley, 2021; Pedley et al., 2024). However, this chapter links to a larger investigation (Roxburgh, 2021) into the teaching of CLC in five Scottish primary schools, each adopting a variant of an L3 approach in their delivery to suit their local context, resource base, staff expertise and confidence. The original research adopted a mixed methods approach: a survey of 374 pupil perspectives through a wide-ranging baseline questionnaire and 14 focus group discussions, interviews with 18 class teachers from across Primaries 5–7, these being the expected stages for the implementation of L3 provision; 11 'Hanban'/ exchange teachers (visiting specialists in CLC from China working across Scotland and connected to a Confucius Institute) and 3 Professional Development Officers supporting schools with their delivery were also interviewed. Since the establishment of the first in 2012, there are now 43 'Confucius Classrooms' in Scottish schools in 21 out of 32 local authorities assisted by activities organised by the Confucius Institute for Scotland's Schools (CISS). According to the latest figures available, exposure to CLC has been estimated at over 409 schools and around 53,513 schoolchildren (Scottish Government, 2019) with the funding of both CISS and Confucius Classrooms given by the Scottish and Chinese Governments through an annual grant.

In four of the schools involved in my research (Roxburgh, 2021), Chinese was typically presented as the language of a faraway, exotic culture that pupils might one day experience themselves, essentially as tourists and I would like to briefly reflect on some of the underlying causes behind why children might feel this way about their learning. Though I draw upon only a very few examples, the quantitative and qualitative data sets were extensive and analysed by total, gender, stage, school and by length of pupils' study of CLC, as appropriate, with the complete data available online for those interested.

As shown in Fig. 2, the highest response was to agree. The overall view on the statement (SA/ A) was positive for a clear majority of pupils at 58.3%, however this still leaves a very sizeable minority of pupils either ambivalent or in disagreement at 41.7% (N/D/SD). Therefore, across the sample as a whole, there seemed to be a clear variation in pupils' understanding of why they were learning CLC. Whilst it would be legitimate for others to ask how children might respond to this question across the other subjects that make up the primary curriculum, it does seem pertinent for language learning and the hopes and expectations we might have for this going forward.

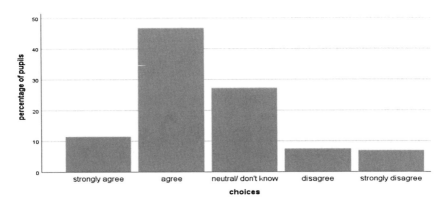

Fig. 2 I understand why I am learning CLC (by total, N = 374)

Developing a Rationale for Teaching Local Languages to Young...

Table 1 Categorisation of pupils' open-ended responses to reasons for learning CLC (by total, N = 374)

Initial categorisation	Responses = 403	%	Wider groupings
Communication when working or living in China	132	35.3%	Communicative goals
Communication when in China for travel purposes	44	11.8%	
Communication with users of Chinese living in/ visiting the UK	43	11.5%	
Communication when visiting other Chinese speaking countries	16	4.3%	
Enhanced cultural knowledge	5	1.3%	Cultural goals
Enjoyable/ interesting/ important to learn a language	10	2.7%	General interest
China is an economic power	7	1.9%	Awareness of China's global presence
Chinese is a major world language	19	5.1%	
Future personal benefits	19	5.1%	
No response	58	15.5%	Limited/ no importance
Do not know	25	6.7%	
Stated as not important	25	6.7%	

In Table 1, it is evident that the majority of pupil respondents viewed the communicative aspect of CLC as the primary motivation for its study. Only a minority (35.3%) considered its use in a work context in China, while few pupils saw its relevance within the UK, suggesting a disconnect in their perception of its applicability across different settings. Whilst a strong economic rationale can be associated as a motivation for learning Chinese, there seems to be less awareness of the country's growing influence in that respect within responses. Approximately 29% of pupils expressed uncertainty about the importance of CLC, including those who did not provide any response.

The third piece of data, represented in Fig. 3, considers children's future aspirations for their study of CLC. We would hope that, if

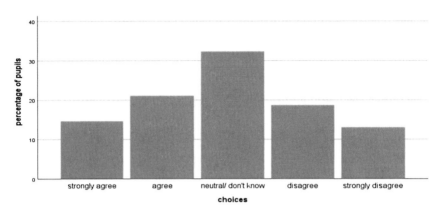

Fig. 3 I would like to continue learning CLC in secondary school (by total, N = 374)

experiences have been positive, there will be impetus for continuing study in secondary schools (all primary schools in the research did have provision for this transition to take place). The data broadly shows a split of three thirds for positive/ neutral and negative views on taking their learning forward. Given the time and resource applied to the promotion of CLC in Scottish schools by local authorities, the Scottish and Chinese Governments, there is again a need to interpret why these mixed views may have arisen.

When looking across all the data sets, important messages for the pedagogy used to promote CLC, and no doubt other L2 or L3 languages arise. In my study, there was an over predominance of what might be termed 'traditional' pedagogies where children received a series of lessons that were disjointed, focused on transmission of language and culture and often highly repetitive from one year to the next. Authors such as Kramsch (1998, 2009) might define these inputs as the promotion of large C culture where big, consistent messages are delivered about a country, its people and way of life, based round what she terms the 4 Fs: facts, folklore, festivals, and food. Though the visiting exchange teachers and Scottish teachers in the study felt these were starting points to try and hook or engage children into the learning of CLC (or other languages), the interviews picked up on a number of issues with this sort of approach e.g., notions of cultural stereotypes coming through very strongly in the

Developing a Rationale for Teaching Local Languages to Young…

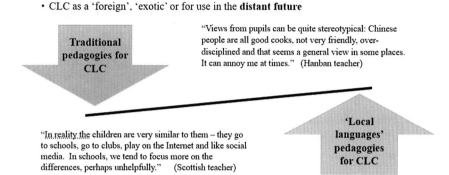

Fig. 4 Traditional vs. innovative pedagogies promoting CLC (Roxburgh, 2021)

views of China offered by children. If handled poorly, such approaches reinforce language and culture as foreign and exotic with purposes that seem quite remote to children's interests and the local diversity that they may see around them. Figure 4 tries to illustrate the tensions seen through the research and the need for a better balance in the pedagogies used in schools in my research.

Therefore, the promotion of 'local languages' constitutes opportunities for pupils to explore and share languages in use in their own classrooms, at school or in its community. Critical to success in transforming these into learning opportunities is the primary class teacher's work as a facilitator and consolidator, coupled with an understanding of how to link this learning to the broader primary curriculum.

6 Information About the Specific Case Study School

In contrast to the other schools in my study, the work of 'School 3' adopted a distinctive approach, focusing on local contexts where Chinese was in use. Interdisciplinary projects incorporated opportunities to meet and talk to Chinese speakers living in or visiting the area, with positive outcomes in terms of pupil motivation, developing competence in

Chinese through 'here-and-now' interaction, and changing pupils' and teachers' thinking about learning multilingually. All of these factors contributed to successful integration of 'local languages' into a planned programme of learning where children were given fairly extensive opportunities to use their language skills in the local area.

School 3, a Confucius Classroom, received extra funding and served as a model for nearby schools. Pupils in Primary 4–7 (ages 8–12) had weekly one-hour lessons from a teacher passionate about the subject, with additional input from a visiting exchange teacher linked to a university Confucius Institute. Located in Stirling, a hub for Scottish tourism and a university city, the school had a small, established Scottish Chinese community within its catchment area and familiarity with people of Chinese heritage was common among the children.

7   What Worked Well?

The CLC project, outlined below, highlights three key underpinnings that support the concept of 'local languages' as outlined in previous sections.

Looking at Purposeful Uses for Language Learning Within Local Contexts

Having established CLC in the school in 2015, staff leading its introduction had begun to think about ways for pupils to lead on the sharing of their learning with others, which initially started off with the scripting and recording of podcasts, under the guise of a 'Languages Café' to be promoted on the local authority's resource net and then on social media platforms. Pupils' efforts came to the attention of Professional Development Officers at 'Scotland's National Centre for Languages' (SCILT) who could see the potential for this to support on-going initiatives to promote business links with organisations interested in language learning through its 'Business Language Champions' programme. The aim here was to bring together local groups in innovative partnerships that fostered young people's development in communication, employability skills, and global mindsets.

This gave rise to a project between School 3 and Historic Environment Scotland (HES), the lead public body established to protect and promote the country's historic environment and facilitated by its Education Officer who collaborated alongside school staff and pupils throughout. The premise behind the project was to link to Stirling Castle, one of Scotland's most popular tourist attractions with domestic and international visitors, including an increasing number from China. The project was framed round the experience of HES colleagues who saw that communication in English was acting as a barrier for certain visitor groups. This gave rise to the idea of linking the CLC curriculum of School 3 to a familiar, local resource that the pupils would have visited and be aware of, but opening pupils' eyes to this landmark in new ways. This would highlight the value of language skills in the workplace to these young language learners, especially within the tourist sector which was very important for both the Stirling local and wider Scottish economy. When linking back to the Douglas Fir Group model (2016), such an approach can be seen to put these young learners at the heart of the language experience in terms of drawing upon contexts that are multilingual, emphasise the recurring use of languages, and which draw upon their localness in recurrent ways that allow pupils to see languages as being very much used in the 'here and now' rather than seeming of delayed use until their adult future.

Meaningful Interdisciplinary Learning: Making Connections with Languages Across the Curriculum

In the Scottish curriculum, interdisciplinary learning (IDL) promotes the integration of knowledge and skills from various subjects through project-based learning. However, as Arnold et al. (2018) have noted, languages are frequently left out of IDL initiatives. Therefore, incorporating 'local languages' into such thinking can enhance students' language skills and expand the application of these across the curriculum in innovative ways.

The teachers, Professional Development Officers, and staff from HES saw this project as a means of making language learning engaging and purposeful with pupils initially gaining an understanding of the work of Stirling Castle tour guides and becoming familiar with its history, layout, and key features thus supporting pupils' Social Studies experiences. The initial aim was to assist existing guides by teaching them a range of basic greetings that they could use with Chinese visitors. However, the cross-curricular benefits were quickly seized upon as a means of developing languages through wider literacy, Expressive Arts and technology skills that saw pupils work in groups collaboratively to produce simple Chinese versions of a castle map; an interactive quiz; signage and information leaflets. The project work culminated in pupils getting involved in designing, scripting, and helping produce short videos in Chinese that played out some historical scenarios, tying to the long history of the castle with HES providing costumes to heighten the drama and excitement of being involved in this work. This links well to the notions of the 'semiotic resource base' promoted in the DFG model (2016) in terms of the various forms of communication, symbolic and representational media types that the children were exposed to and drew upon throughout the project. Linking to the 'social identities' base of the DFG framework, working with the HES organisation meant that children were engaging with people employed in the castle in their different roles e.g., guides, gift shop workers etc. thus gaining a sense of the wider world of work and the potential application of languages to these jobs. These curriculum experiences made children value their community even more and highlighted that CLC went beyond just notions of potentially travelling to China, thus also meaningfully addressing the questions raised earlier by Phipps (2019) of who do we want to talk to and why?

Linking Native Speakers' Expertise to the Pedagogical Base of Primary Teachers with Limited Ability in CLC

Whilst the Scottish L3 model offers opportunities to expand the range of languages that pupils are exposed to, it also raises challenges about how the language base of these experiences is to be managed, given that primary school teachers' abilities to deliver these minority languages will often be limited or, indeed, non-existent. This is where the notion of drawing upon other resources available comes into play, again as highlighted by the DFG framework (2016) in its reference to 'social communities'.

School 3 had some teachers with varying degrees of basic Chinese competence that would have assisted pupils' early introduction to the language. However, it was through the connection to the visiting exchange teacher resource, available through CISS, that a useful model of co-teaching was possible. My initial research (Roxburgh, 2021) spent quite some time looking at the role of such teachers in schools, given that these groups have been in operation across the UK for more than a decade. In my review of literature, a number of tensions and issues were identified beyond notions such as cultural difference and acclimatisation to also include consideration of teacher identity, classroom roles, and professional development. In contrast to existing literature reviewed (Roxburgh, 2021), my research took this further to consider the roles in the teaching of CLC from two perspectives: the visiting teachers from China and the Scottish teachers hosting these groups in their classrooms and schools.

For the most part, the majority of schools involved in my study placed the success of CLC practices squarely, and unfairly, on the shoulders of these visiting teachers, allowing them to deliver a series of one-off inputs that Scottish teachers were then unable to follow up or develop on their own. In this way, most Scottish teachers could be described as interested/ disinterested passive observers of the CLC work being carried out with their pupils. My interviews with the visiting teachers from China echoed themes from my initial literature review where they felt isolated in the schools in which they worked; lacked knowledge of the Scottish curriculum and suitable pedagogies and, therefore, felt unconfident to move away from the sort of transmission models of content that they had experienced themselves in China and which then presented issues in delivery, meaning, and purpose. Though the exchange teachers I interviewed came with high hopes of professional development, a number were disappointed by what CLC was achieving and recognised the imbalance that existed in the roles of both sets of teachers involved. From the views of the Scottish teachers interviewed, the lack of their own language ability and/ or perceptions of the difficulty of learning Chinese meant there was a real sense of nervousness in taking CLC forward on their own. When combining the views of both teacher groups, this created a position where the delivery often stalled and/ or became very repetitive.

School 3, however, was a good example of where both sets of teachers were able to come together to build upon each other's strengths, i.e., the native language ability and cultural awareness of the visiting Chinese groups and the expertise of Scottish teachers, to create contexts that promoted IDL that emphasised CLC in the here and now as a 'local language'. Rather than seeing the language element as a simplified version of L2 practices, lessons were delivered that covered some of the basic elements but also taught very specific language for use in IDL projects, such as that of Stirling Castle, which did not conform to specific schemes of study. Critics of this approach may argue that it flies in the face of progression and continuity, but what it did achieve was to give pupils experience of learning vocabulary, phrases and extended sentences in a context that was very meaningful to them, that they then repeated and developed through use in practice and taught to other users new to the language e.g., staff at the Castle, Chinese visitors etc. This approach was acting as a motivator and also allowed pupils to gain from the discussion of the language with the visiting teachers, thus seeing how language develops for a specific purpose. Notions of L3 continuity, in this respect, would be better seen as the positive impacts that would likely create momentum and enthusiasm for those wishing to continue CLC into secondary school and beyond.

Engagement with IDL pedagogies was positive for both teacher groups. Scottish teachers found it valuable as a familiar and effective approach, expanding projects beyond CLC. This extended into other subjects, reinforcing broader curricular objectives. Additionally, they saw themselves as learners alongside their pupils, which encouraged participation for everyone. Visiting Chinese teachers experienced professional growth and fulfilment, moving beyond the delivery of standard L2 topics that seemed to form so much of routine delivery in other schools in my research. They observed IDL in action, gaining insight into core teaching approaches in Scottish primaries and used their language expertise adaptively, emphasising purpose and relevance, thus addressing challenges in the delivery outlined earlier in the chapter.

This model of co-construction of the learning, involving pupils, their Scottish teachers, visiting groups from China and HES staff at Stirling Castle, again sits well within the DFR framework (2016) and conveys a very powerful message about the value of 'local languages' and the sort of innovation that this allows in the Scottish curriculum. Though this particular project was quite involved it could easily have been smaller in scale, applied to other languages and topics going on in the local community, but also drawing upon other native speakers in place of the professional groups mentioned here to instead include family members, business groups, students etc. as alternative models of native speakers, but still under the direction of Scottish school staff.

8   Applying Lessons Learned from 'Local Languages' in Other Educational Contexts

Experimental initiatives, such as this, raise challenging questions for those working in schools and Higher Education about the purposes of language learning, particularly in the primary sector; about 'effective' approaches and about how promising work can be sustained and developed well beyond the particular CLC context presented here. Regardless of language focus, this chapter has highlighted a number of points for all those involved in language education aimed at the needs of younger learners including:

- Pre-service and in-service education for teachers working in primary schools needs to embrace different ways of looking at language teaching that move on from standard notions of L2 provision;
- Drawing upon models of practice that are consistent with the expected features of primary pedagogy to give confidence to teachers who are not language subject specialists;
- Reflecting more on issues around purpose, motivation, and engagement of young learners so as to build up a positive base for transitioning to secondary contexts and beyond;

- Adopting a community-focused approach and valuing the 'local' nature of languages in ways that highlight the 'here and now' use of learning in contexts more familiar to pupils than simply touristic experiences which may or may not happen;
- Seeing the school community as a rich resource base for genuine collaboration between different people and organisations that highlights the use and purpose of language learning;
- Drawing upon a wider range of people from the community with native language competence that would create a sustainable pool of language and cultural expertise to draw upon where primary teachers' own bases may be limited;
- Making existing use of good quality interdisciplinary practices as a feature of primary pedagogy to avoid the traditional isolation of languages; and
- Sharing good practice resources and materials that evidence approaches to 'local languages' and its relevant pedagogies.

Though the design of the '1+2 policy' opens up space for different practices in the Scottish context and for L3 models in particular, this chapter has tried to exemplify shifts in thinking that will hopefully support discussion and reflection in other contexts around the principles of early language learning and the ways this can be improved.

References

Anderson, L. (in preparation). *Engaging bilingual parents in the teaching and learning of second additional languages: An ethnographic case study*. Doctoral thesis, University of Strathclyde.

Arnold, W., Bradshaw, C., & Gregson, K. (2018). Language learning through projects. In S. Garton & F. Copland (Eds.), *The Routledge handbook of teaching English to young learners* (pp. 288–302). Routledge. https://doi.org/10.4324/9781315623672

Association of Directors of Education – Scotland (ADES). (2016). *The 1 + 2 language learning policy: Progress review*. https://www.gov.scot/publications/1-2-language-policy-progress-review/

Bühmann, D., & Trudell, B. (2008). *Mother tongue matters: Local language as a key to effective learning*. UNESCO. https://unesdoc.unesco.org/ark:/48223/pf0000161121

Chong, S., Isaacs, T., & McKinley, J. (2023). Ecological systems theory and second language research. *Language Teaching, 56*(3), 333–348. https://doi.org/10.1017/S0261444822000283

Douglas Fir Group. (2016). A transdisciplinary framework for SLA in a multilingual world. *Modern Language Journal, 100*, 19–47. https://doi.org/10.1111/modl.12301

Education Scotland. (2015). *Curriculum for excellence: Modern languages experiences and outcomes*. https://education.gov.scot/Documents/modern-languages-eo.pdf

Education Scotland. (2019). *Language learning in Scotland: A 1+2 approach: Guidance on L3 within the 1+2 policy (updated May 2019)*. https://education.gov.scot/media/1cugpk4v/modlang12-l3-guidance-may19.pdf

Glen, L., & Hugh, S. (2021). *Education Scotland updates*. https://scilt.org.uk/Portals/24/Library/LANGS%20ex%20coala/2021_November/Keynote%204%20Nov.pdf

Kramsch, C. (1998). *Language and culture*. Oxford University Press.

Kramsch, C. (2009). Cultural perspectives on language learning and teaching. In K. Knapp & B. Seidlhofer (Eds.), *Handbook of foreign language communication and learning* (pp. 219–246). De Gruyter Mouton. https://doi.org/10.1515/9783110214246.2.219

Mahboob, A., & Lin, A. M. Y. (2018). Local languages as a resource in (language) education. In A. Selvi & N. Rudolph (Eds.), *Conceptual shifts and contextualized practices in education for glocal interaction. Intercultural communication and language education*. Springer. https://doi.org/10.1007/978-981-10-6421-0_10

Mehmedbegovic, D. (2017). Engaging with linguistic diversity in global cities: Arguing for "language hierarchy free" policy and practice in education. *Open Linguistics, 3*(1), 540–553. https://doi.org/10.1515/opli-2017-0027

National Records of Scotland. (2015). *Scotland's Census 2011: Gaelic report (part 1)*. Scottish Government. https://www.scotlandscensus.gov.uk/media/cqoji4qx/report_part_1.pdf

Pedley, M. (2021). Mother Tongue Other Tongue poetry competition: Insights for language education. *Scottish Languages Review, 36*, 9–20. https://scilt.org.uk/Portals/24/Library/slr/issues/36/36-02%20Pedley.pdf

Pedley, M., Roxburgh, D., Anderson, L., & McPake, J. (2024). The transformative power of local language encounters: Implications for teacher education. In C. Leslie & S. Mourão (Eds.), *Researching educational practices, teacher education and professional development for early language learning: Examples from Europe*. Routledge. https://doi.org/10.4324/9781003289043

Phipps, A. (2019). *Decolonising multilingualism: Struggles to decreate*. Multilingual Matters. https://doi.org/10.21832/9781788924061

Roxburgh, D. (2021). *An analysis of the promotion of Chinese culture within an L3 language experience at the P5–7 stages in selected Scottish primary schools*. Doctoral thesis, University of Strathclyde. https://stax.strath.ac.uk/concern/theses/nz806004j

Scottish Government. (2012). *Language learning in Scotland: A 1+2 approach*. Scottish Government. https://www.gov.scot/publications/language-learning-scotland-12-approach/

Scottish Government. (2019). *Scottish Parliament written answer, John Swinney, 12 September 2019, S5W-24838*. https://www.parliament.scot/chamber-and-committees/questions-and-answers/question?ref=S5W-24838

Scottish Government. (2023). *Pupil Census 2022 supplementary statistics*. Scottish Government. https://www.gov.scot/publications/pupil-census-supplementary-statistics/

Steffensen, S. V., & Kramsch, C. (2017). The ecology of second language acquisition and socialization. In P. A. Duff & S. May (Eds.), *Language socialization* (3rd ed., pp. 17–32). Springer. Encyclopedia of Language and Education. https://doi.org/10.1007/978-3-319-02255-0_2

Valdera Gil, F., & Crichton, H. (2018). Mother tongue plus two languages: Are Scottish primary teachers confident to deliver? *The Language Learning Journal*. https://doi.org/10.1080/09571736.2018.1448430

Visit Britain. (2020). Number of overseas trips to Scotland in 2019, by country of origin (in 1,000s) [Graph]. *Statista*, 14 September. Retrieved May 8, 2023, from https://www-statista-com.proxy.lib.strath.ac.uk/statistics/427315/number-of-overseas-trips-to-scotland-by-country-of-origin/

Student Perceptions of the Effectiveness of Technology Enhanced Learning in Blended Learning Contexts During the COVID-19 Pandemic

Fiona Nimmo

1 Introduction

At varying points throughout the COVID-19 pandemic, the global higher education (HE) sector reacted swiftly to ensure the provision of effective, high-quality, teaching and learning environments to help enhance and transform education pedagogy, whilst dealing with the challenges associated with the pandemic. In the months of March to June 2020, during the first UK lockdown, the number of UK citizens working remotely rose from 5% to 50%, in an attempt to help curb the spread of the virus and in keeping with UK Government guidelines (Royal Society for Public Health, 2021). This meant that many UK HE institutions had to make the radical shift from on campus to online delivery, all within unprecedented time scales, and not without challenges, as noted in the

---

F. Nimmo (✉)
University of Strathclyde, Glasgow, UK
e-mail: fiona.nimmo@strath.ac.uk

following statement from the Quality Assurance Agency for Higher Education:

> Pre-COVID-19, technology-enhanced learning in the UK had tended not to be driven from the top as a central part of a university's strategic agenda. There might be disciplines or schools where innovation flourished but whole-institution approaches to delivery excellence were rare, with a few very notable exceptions. Universities vary widely in their levels of digital maturity and there is a substantial knowledge and experience gap, both within and across institutions. (2020)

For many years, Learning Management Systems (LMS) such as Moodle and Blackboard have been utilised by the HE sector to help manage course content, assessment, and communication (Pinho et al., 2018). Given that LMS are primarily concerned with course management processes rather than real-time synchronous learning, my University, the University of Strathclyde (UoS), along with many other HE institutions, had to find alternative approaches to course delivery when lockdown restrictions were imposed. For my department, English Language Teaching (ELT), this included utilising Zoom for synchronous online activity, and more ubiquitous use of the Microsoft 365 Suite; a desktop and cloud-based application which is accessed via the worldwide web (Microsoft, 2022).

Additional forms of TEL that were adopted and popularised during the pandemic included classroom response systems (CRS) such as Clicker, Kahoot!, Socrative, Mentimeter, Lino, and Padlet, all of which can be accessed through QR and web randomised joining codes (Joshi et al., 2021; Nieto-Escamez & Roldán-Tapia, 2021; Pichardo et al., 2021; Saikat et al., 2021). There is also Google Workspace; a free suite of tools designed to provide flexible and collaborative communication (Google, 2022). Applications include Meet, Hangout, Chat, Slides, and Jamboard (an interactive whiteboard). These forms of TEL, which are by no means new in concept, have been shown to improve skills and knowledge (Muñoz et al., 2017), enhance learning and engagement (Eden, 2016), and encourage positive behaviour and motivation (Acmar & Bhagat, 2021; Wollmann et al., 2016).

It is not only TEL, however, that the HE sector had to become very quickly accustomed to during the pandemic, but also the mode of delivery. As Bozkurt et al. (2020) point out, the emergency response to the pandemic needed to be adapted to ensure that no learner was disadvantaged or left behind, and the learning design and delivery modified to help deepen learning through collaborative, interactive, and social activity. One way to achieve this was for institutions to adopt the blended learning model; a practical method combining synchronous and asynchronous activity. In this mode, students complete independent preparatory tasks prior to synchronous sessions. Potential benefits of blended learning include fostering critical thinking (Aristika & Juandi, 2021; Bernstein & Issac, 2018) and stimulating active student engagement (Bond et al., 2021; Heliporn et al., 2021; Nerantzi, 2020; Oraif & Elyas, 2021). Challenges include digital readiness and poor internet connectivity (Gupta & Gupta, 2020), limited peer and instructor interaction (Wang et al., 2021), and motivational issues (Aristika & Juandi, 2021; Sun & Chen, 2016).

2 Method

I focused on student perception to ascertain which TEL was perceived by students as most effective, as this could help with motivation and engagement. I began by drawing up a PICOSS table (Table 1) to help focus my ideas and develop my research design. I selected two main databases for the screening and selection process: SCOPUS and ERIC, as these databases were more applicable to the topic under investigation. To help me with the initial scoping exercise, I searched for key terms and synonyms related to research design, setting, outcome, and target population, all of which are key scoping processes outlined by Armstrong et al. (2011).

I began with SCOPUS (Table 2), Elsevier's abstract and citation database, as it is currently the largest database of peer-reviewed literature. My inclusion criteria centred around journal articles focusing on student perception of the various TEL utilised during the pandemic. I chose not to limit my search to the UK as HE institutions worldwide were experiencing similar issues. I excluded non-English medium journals in an attempt to avoid translation issues and misinterpretation (Neimann Rasmussen

Table 1 PICOSS table

Review title	Student perception of the effectiveness of technology enhanced learning in blended learning contexts during the COVID-19 pandemic—a scoping review
Research Qu	Which TEL was perceived by students as effective during the COVID-19 pandemic
Population	Higher education students and global HE settings
Intervention	Any potential transferable TEL
Comparator	The stated interventions compared with each other or no intervention
Outcomes	Any enhanced student experience and potential transferable TEL
Study design	Quantitative and qualitative with student perception as the primary focus
Setting	Higher education English institutions worldwide

Table 2 SCOPUS

No.	Concept strings	Journal articles returned
1	"technology enhanced learning" or *digital or *technology or "emerging technology" or "e-learning" or "learning through technology"	717,927
2	"blended learning" or "flipped learning" or the "flipped classroom"	1594
3	"student engagement" or "learning outcomes" or "student experience" or "engagement" or "student satisfaction"	1080
4	"higher education" or "university" or "UG" or "PG" or "graduates" or undergrad* or postgrad*	1073
5	"pandemic* or COVID* or Coronavirus*"	396

& Montgomery, 2018). I set the parameters from March 2020, at the start of the COVID-19 pandemic, to March 2022, at which time Scotland was still experiencing COVID restrictions and ELT staff were still working remotely with no immediate plans to return to on campus delivery. I also excluded schools, adult education, private language schools, and further education, as I wanted to keep my focus on HE, but did not exclude gender, age, or nationality within this setting. This returned 135 journal articles.

I followed a similar process with ERIC, using the Thesaurus feature to refine my criteria (Table 3). When search terms were unavailable, I ran a

Table 3 ERIC

No.	Concept strings	Journal articles returned
1	Set 1: "technology enhanced learning" or *digital or *technology or "emerging technology" or "e-learning" or "learning through technology"	71,475
	Set 2: *digital or *technology or "emerging technology" or "e-learning" or "learning through technology"	121,324
		Set 1 and 2 combined using 'or' = Set 3: 150,324
2	Set 4: "blended learning" or "flipped learning" or the "flipped classroom"	5746
		Set 3 and 4 combined using 'and' = Set 5: 3927
3	Set 6: "student engagement" or "learning outcomes" or "student experience" or "engagement" or "student satisfaction"	28,140
	Set 7: "student engagement" or "learning outcomes".	17,220
		Set 6 and 7 combined using 'or' = Set 8: 40,833
		Set 5 and 8 combined using 'and' = Set 9: 713
4	Set 10: "higher education" or "university" or "UG" or "PG" or "graduates" or undergrad* or postgrad*	104,995
5	Set 11: COVID* or Coronavirus* or pandemic*	4633
	Set 12: pandemic*	4228
		Set 11 and 12 combined with 'or' = Set 13: 5430
		Sets 9, 10, and 13 combined using 'and' = Set 14 generating 9 journal article returns. Once this was limited to peer-reviewed articles only, the final total was 7.

free text search for key terms and concepts, entering "exact" and *stem words, with 'or' between each term, for example,*digital or "emerging technology" or "e-learning", and screened abstracts in the drop-down menu. I combined concept strings with 'and', for example, Sets 1 and 2 (Table 3), repeating the process for key concepts and Set criteria. The final return was 7 (Table 3). I now had 142 journal articles, across two databases (Fig. 1).

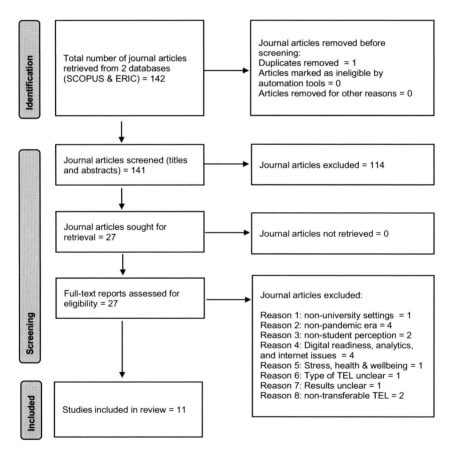

Fig. 1 Prisma Statement. (Adapted from Page M. J., McKenzie J. E., Bossuyt P.M., Boutron I., Hoffmann T. C., Mulrow C. D., et al. (2021). The PRISMA 2020 statement: an updated guideline for reporting systematic reviews. *British Medical Journal, 372*:71)

3 Data Extraction

There are, generally speaking, only two types of data in a systematic review: descriptive data (study characteristics) and analytical data (outcomes), and it is important to ensure that only data relevant to the research question is extracted (Boland et al., 2014). My next step, therefore, was to create a data extraction tool. I did this using Notion (Notion Labs Inc., 2021) to allow transfer of relevant data, adding the labels below.

1. Descriptive Data = Study Characteristics (participants, setting, data collection method).
2. Analytical Data = RQ: Which TEL was perceived by students as effective in blended learning contexts during the COVID-19 pandemic, including any negative feedback.

4 Screening and Selection

I systematically screened titles and abstracts, eliminating any papers that did not fall within my inclusion criteria, and, with just one duplication, the final SCOPUS total was 24 and ERIC 3. I now had 27 journal articles. I annotated and highlighted relevant sections of the papers to assist in the data extraction process, using a colour-coded key: yellow for the research design, pink for effective TEL, and green for perceived TEL weaknesses. For the final stage, I referred to my PICOSS screening and selection tool using Notion (Notion Labs Inc., 2021) as this included my inclusion and exclusion rationale. I also designed a Notion qualitative assessment tool, adding this to my Notion records, using a High, Medium, Low rating. This helped me to identify whether the topic, methodology, and data collection method were appropriate, relevant, and transferable. As can be seen in Fig. 1, the Prisma statement (Page et al., 2021), the final number of journal articles for inclusion in my study, was 11.

5 Results

Descriptive Data

As can be seen in Table 4, the articles selected for inclusion in my study were conducted across 12 nations. These were Oman (Ahshan, 2021), Spain and Peru (Feijóo et al., 2021; Latorre-Cosculluela et al., 2021), Turkey (Giray, 2021), Hong Kong (Kohnke & Moorhouse, 2021), The Philippines (Lapitan et al., 2021), Ukraine (Lytvyn et al., 2021), Poland (Ożadowicz, 2020), Thailand (Wichanpricha, 2021), Sri Lanka (Yatigammana & Wijayarathna, 2021), Turkey, India, and Costa Rica (Benito et al., 2021).

A range of qualitative and quantitative data was used across the 11 studies (Table 4). Seven of them employed questionnaires; Ahshan (2021) with 153 undergraduate (UG) Engineering students, Giray (2021) with 290 UG Engineering students, Lapitan et al. (2021) with 168 UG Engineering students, Latorre-Cosculluela et al. (2021) with 376 UG students cross-discipline, Ożadowicz (2020) with 90 UG students across various Environmental and Engineering faculties, Wichanpricha (2021) with 254 UG students on an academic English language course, and Yatigammana and Wijayarathna (2021) with 903 UG Commerce & Management Studies & Computing Technology students. One study conducted opinion polls with 3681 students across a number of institutions and disciplines, although the level of students is unknown (Lytvyn et al., 2021), and one study conducted interviews with 9 postgraduate (PG) English Language Centre students (Kohnke & Moorhouse, 2021). Two of the studies employed a mixed methods approach (Benito et al., 2021; Feijóo et al., 2021). This involved questionnaires and focus groups with 2367 UG and PG students across the disciplines (Benito et al., 2021), and questionnaires and interviews with 30+ UG students from The Faculty of Engineering in Spain and Peru (Feijóo et al., 2021).

Table 4 Descriptive data

Author(s)	Country where studies were conducted	No. of participants	UG/PG	Faculty	Q	I	F	OP
Ahshan (2021)	Oman	153	UG	Engineering	✓			
Benito et al. (2021)	Turkey, India, & Costa Rica	2637	UG & PG	Across the disciplines (number unknown)	✓		✓	
Giray (2021)	Turkey	290	UG	Engineering	✓			
Kohnke and Moorhouse (2021)	Hong Kong	9	PG	English Language Centre		✓		
Lapitan et al. (2021)	The Philippines	168	UG	Engineering	✓			
Latorre-Cosculluela et al. (2021)	Spain	376	UG	Across the disciplines (number unknown)	✓			
Lytvyn et al. (2021)	Ukraine	3681	unknown	Across a number of academic institutions (number & disciplines unknown)				✓
Feijóo et al. (2021)	Spain & Peru	30+ (precise number unknown)	UG	Engineering	✓	✓		

(continued)

Table 4 (continued)

Author(s)	Country where studies were conducted	No. of participants	UG/PG	Faculty	Q	I	F	OP
Ożadowicz (2020)	Poland	90	UG	The Faculty of Energy and Fuels, The Faculty of Geology, Geophysics & Environmental Protection, The Faculty of Electrical Engineering, Automatics, Informatics & Biomedical Engineering	✓			
Wichanpricha (2021)	Thailand	254	UG	Online Academic English Course (cross-discipline)	✓			
Yatigammana and Wijayarathna (2021)	Sri Lanka	903	UG	Commerce & Management Studies & Computing and Technology	✓			

UG undergraduate, *PG* postgraduate, *Q* questionnaire, *I* interview, *F* focus group, *OP* opinion poll

Analytical Data: Student Perception of TEL During the COVID-19 Pandemic

The findings are outlined and discussed in turn, below, under the two main themes arising from the data: 'Tools to enhance the learning process' and 'Preferred learning modality'.

Tools to Enhance the Learning Process

More than 90% of students in the Feijóo et al. study responded positively to computer response systems (CRS) such as Mentimeter, Kahoot, and Socrative as teaching and learning tools conducive to student engagement and motivation, with 35% noting the use of CRS helps them overcome shyness and improves their "achievements and transferable skills" (2021, p. 13). Students in the Kohnke & Moorehouse study similarly noted CRS as effective in encouraging student engagement, with one student commenting that "polls and word cloud(s) encourage everyone to contribute" (2021, p. 239). Ninety-nine percent of respondents in the Ahshan study expressed a preference for Jamboard whilst 94% noted a preference for Mentimeter (2021, p. 18). Fifty-five percent of all respondents in the Ahshan study perceived CRS tools as "compelling" in blended learning contexts (2021, p. 19).

Participants in the Wichanpricha study noted a preference for learning Academic English through MS Teams as opposed to a traditional classroom setting (mean = 3.51), as they felt it was more interesting (mean = 3.71) (2021, p. 131). They further noted that MS Teams helped improve their English language skills (mean = 3.87), speaking confidence (mean = 3.82), and critical thinking ability (mean = 3.56) and enabled them to have a better understanding of academic content (mean = 3.72) (Wichanpricha, 2021, p. 131). Respondents in the Ahshan study noted that student engagement was achieved through Google Meet (93%) and Google Chat (59%) but found a combination of TEL (43%) to be most effective (Google Chat, Breakout room, Jamboard, Mentimeter) (2021, pp. 18–19). Students in the Kohnke & Moorehouse study similarly found a combination of tools to be most effective (Zoom, Padlet, Lino,

Mentimeter, GoSoapBox, Kahoot, Breakout rooms, and Google Docs) (2021, pp. 235–239).

Participants in the Ożadowicz (2020) study ranked Webinars as most effective for student engagement (77%), closely followed by video demonstrations (52%), and quizzes and tests through Quizizz and the LMS (51%) (2020, p. 15). Least favoured TEL included mind maps using Padlet and Prezi (35%), teleconference meetings (21%), and course resources (18%) (Ożadowicz, 2020, pp. 15–16). This appears at odds with the Giray study where the most positively perceived aspect of blended learning was ease of access to on-demand course materials (33%) (2021, p. 6662). Participants in the Yatigammana & Wijayarathna study also rated on-demand materials as useful (48%) (2021, p. 68). Similarly, students in the Latorre-Cosculluela study rated accessibility of learning materials (mean = 8.24) as the most positive aspect of flipped learning (2021, p. 195).

In addition to revisiting video recordings, 51% of respondents in the Giray study accessed online resources such as Udemy and YouTube to enhance learning performance (2021, pp. 6664–6665). The majority of students in the Lapitan et al. study were in agreement that videos helped achieve learning outcomes (CHE211 84.7%, CHE216 97.4%) as they were engaging (CHE211 62.7%, CHE216 79.3%) and afforded opportunities to work autonomously (CHE 211 66%, CHE 216 87.1%) (2021, p. 122). Respondents in the Yatigammana & Wijayarathna study were also in agreement that videos were key to active engagement (78.8%), with 66% welcoming the 8–15-minute video (2021, pp. 67–68). Further comments are highlighted below:

> (Student 1) *I can able to ask live questions from lecturers during the lecture time and able to watch recorded lectures when I absent to participate.*
> (Student 2) *Ability to listen to a lecture more than once, Ability to ask questions in real time lecture, Easy to self-learning.* (Yatigammana & Wijayarathna, 2021, p. 66)

Student 2 above emphasises the benefit of learner autonomy in the asynchronous mode (Yatigammana & Wijayarathna, 2021). Students in the Latorre-Cosculluela et al. study similarly noted learner autonomy as a key benefit, rating it second highest in regard to skills for the twenty-first century (mean = 8.11) (2021, p. 195). Learner autonomy also ranked highly in the Wichanpricha study (mean = 3.98) (2021, p. 132) and in the Giray study (mean = 3.89) (2021, p. 6664).

Preferred Learning Modality

The majority of students in the Benito et al. study enjoyed the blended learning experience (61%) attributing this to the LMS (Moodle), as this was compatible with their mobile devices (2021, p. 60). Participants in the Lapitan et al. study also enjoyed the blended learning experience with 92.3% of respondents stating that the online plenary sessions were " engaging" (2021, p. 122). The most preferred mode of learning in the Yatigammana & Wijayarathna study was Zoom using pre-recorded video lectures (58.8%) (2021, p. 64).

In regard to assessment, Feijóo et al. found that 20.7% of students highly agreed and 51.7% agreed that the use of CRS was effective in assessing learning in the flipped learning model, with 24.1% returning a neutral response and only 16.7% disagreeing with this statement (2021, p. 12). Benito et al.'s study also discussed assessment in a flipped learning context, with 52% of the respondents agreeing that online assessments were as rigorous and fair as on campus (2021, p. 60). This is at odds with the Feijóo et al. study where 63.4% of respondents indicated a preference for on campus assessment (2021, p. 12). Participants in the Giray study perceived assessment as a negative aspect of flipped learning, with one student commenting that online exams are not "fair" or "reliable" (2021, pp. 6663–6664). Latorre-Cosculluela et al. similarly found that a substantially high index of agreement was not obtained in regard to perceived improved grades (mean = 7.40) (2021, pp. 195).

Sixty-two percent of respondents in the Ahshan study (2021, p. 20) and 61% of respondents in the Benito et al. study rated synchronous online sessions as effective, with 7.3% of the latter noting the most enjoyable aspect was the opportunity to interact digitally with faculty staff and students (Benito et al., 2021, p. 60). In the Lytvyn et al. study, participants were asked to select from three categories their opinion of synchronous learning: 'real time', returning 74% of responses; 'easy interaction' returning 16%; and 'asking questions, instant answers, motivation, and help', returning 10% (2021, p. 620). From among the three proposed drawbacks, respondents rated 'physical compliance with the schedule' at 44%, and both 'poor implementation of individualisation' and 'appropriate training' at 28% (Lytvyn et al., 2021, p. 621).

From among the proposed benefits of asynchronous learning, students ranked the benefits in order of importance, 'flexibility' (29%), 'time mobility' (28%), 'cost-effectiveness' (27%), and 'anti-localization' (16%) (Lytvyn et al., 2021, p. 622). Drawbacks were also rated in order of importance, with 'limitation of contact' rating highest at 83%, 'isolation' at 10%, and 'the need for self-discipline' at 7% (Lytvyn et al., 2021, p. 623). Regarding barriers to synchronous learning, in qualitative results, students in the Wichanpricha study felt that online learning through the medium of MS teams was demotivating (11.02%), ineffective (16.54%), and less understandable (16.4%), citing lack of concentration (8.66%), drowsiness (1.97%), and apathy (1.57%) as their rationale (2021, p. 134). Findings in the qualitative study highlighted a preference for on campus learning (51.8%) (Wichanpricha, 2021, p. 134). These findings differ significantly to the quantitative data which clearly demonstrated a preference for blended learning using MS Teams (Wichanpricha, 2021). In the Kohnke & Moorehouse study, which focused on the Hyflex model, students highlighted challenges in communication, paralinguistic cues, and uncertainties around turn-taking, with one student noting that this hindered their ability to collaborate, monitor progress, and receive and act upon feedback (2021, pp. 236–237).

Respondents in the Yatigammana & Wijayarathna study were very satisfied (78.7%) or somewhat satisfied (14.9%) with the new blended learning model with the remaining students returning a neutral response (2021, p. 67). The majority of students in the Feijóo et al. (2021) study were also satisfied with the blended learning model. This is at odds with participants in the Ahshan study who felt that asynchronous learning was insufficient for active student engagement (38%), although 99% were in favour of this modality when it involved open discussion and instructor contribution (2021, pp. 21–22). According to Lapitan et al. the blended learning model helps establish active learning habits, as noted by one of the participants in this study:

> The best thing about the online learning strategy is the balance between synchronous meetings and asynchronous videos. Since the pre-recorded videos are sharp and concise, they can be repeated multiple times before the synchronous meeting can start. This way, I can better understand the lesson and prepare for the meeting, but still anticipate for the synchronous session in order to gather more detailed information about the topics. (2021, p. 126)

Fifty-seven percent of respondents in the Benito et al. study expressed a preference for hybrid learning compared to 12% fully online and 31% face-to-face (2021, p. 61). This was similarly echoed in the focus group where 79% of students expressed an overall positive response toward hybrid learning, and only 4% recommending fully online (Benito et al., 2021, p. 64). Students acknowledged, however, that the course had not been designed for online course delivery and "appreciated their instructors' efforts to offer them the best experience possible under the emergency conditions" (Benito et al., 2021, p. 64). Advantages of online learning were not having to travel to study (34%), flexibility (27%), and autonomy (18%) (2021, p. 60). Aspects of face-to-face tuition that students missed included, "dressing up for school", "physical interaction", and "student-to-student dialogue" (Benito et al., 2021, p. 64).

The majority of students in the Wichanpricha study also noted flexibility as a key aspect of online learning, noting that MS Teams was more convenient than on campus tuition (mean = 4.08) (2021, p. 131). Participants in the Giray study similarly noted flexibility, for example, less travel (23%) and location convenience (12%) (2021, p. 6663), as did participants in the Kohnke and Moorhouse (2021) study but noted their preference was for in-person learning. Their rationale was the need to communicate more often with classmates in mixed mode instruction but acknowledged that mixed mode learning helped develop alternative learning strategies (Kohnke & Moorhouse, 2021). Some students felt mixed mode was an added burden but also found it beneficial, as highlighted in the comment below:

Actually, things take longer, as some [fellow students] are attending online and [others], like me, in class. So now I message my classmates, and we talk about what we should be doing [to help] each other to complete assignments. I feel like we were closer. (Kohnke & Moorhouse, 2021, p. 239)

A key finding in the Ahshan study was that blended learning provided opportunities for peer and instructor interaction, with 99% of respondents noting that answering questions and participating in group discussion helped them actively engage (2021, p. 21). Students in the Giray study perceived a higher level of instructor support on campus (mean = 3.70) compared to online (mean = 3.15) and a higher level of peer interaction on campus (mean = 3.82) (2021, p. 6659). This appears at odds with the participants in the Wichanpricha study who perceived online learning to encourage more peer and instructor interaction (mean = 3.86) and more teamwork (mean = 3.70) (2021, p. 132). They also moderately concurred that learning online through MS Teams was as productive as learning in a traditional classroom setting (mean = 3.41) (Wichanpricha, 2021, p. 131). Students in the Giray study noted, however, that they experienced challenges with motivation (15%), learning performance (14%), self-discipline (9%), team assignments (4%), and e-exams (15%) (2021, pp. 6662–6669).

Respondents in the Latorre-Cosculluela et al. (2021) study perceived flipped learning as helpful in the development of competencies for the twenty-first century. Competencies included character building, collaboration, communication, citizenship, critical thinking, and creativity (Latorre-Cosculluela et al., 2021, pp. 195–196). Participants in the Latorre-Cosculluela et al. study similarly returned a high rating for academic improvement in blended learning contexts; motivation (mean = 7.94), critical thinking (mean = 8.04), self-evaluation (mean = 7.71), communication (mean = 7.65), collaboration (mean = 7.92), and peer learning (mean = 7.96) (2021, pp. 194–196). More than 40% of students in the Benito et al. study expressed a desire to retain elements of blended learning post-pandemic:

(a) online access to recorded classes (73.0%); (b) all learning materials in digital form (73.5%); (c) flexibility in attendance to lectures (63.8%); (d) discussion boards (45.4%); (e) digital interaction with other students (44.7%); (f) online access to professors from other campuses/universities (40.6%); and (g) online access to industry experts (42.2%). (2021, p. 60)

Participants in the Yatigammana & Wijayarathna study were also in support of continued blended learning in the post-COVID-19 era (52%), with 32% undecided and only 16% rejecting this learning modality (2021, p. 69).

6 Discussion and Implications for the Future of HE Pedagogy

This review has considered student perceived effectiveness of technology enhanced learning in blended learning contexts during the COVID-19 pandemic. Eleven case studies, across 12 nations, were analysed, all of which used quantitative or qualitative data collection methods.

The findings demonstrate an overall positive agreement among students on the benefits of TEL in regard to graduate attributes and active student engagement (Ahshan, 2021; Feijóo et al., 2021; Kohnke & Moorhouse, 2021; Lapitan et al., 2021; Latorre-Cosculluela et al., 2021; Ożadowicz, 2020; Wichanpricha, 2021; Yatigammana & Wijayarathna, 2021), collaboration and communication (Ahshan, 2021; Benito et al., 2021; Kohnke & Moorhouse, 2021; Lapitan et al., 2021; Latorre-Cosculluela et al., 2021; Lytvyn et al., 2021; Wichanpricha, 2021; Yatigammana & Wijayarathna, 2021), critical thinking (Latorre-Cosculluela et al., 2021; Wichanpricha, 2021), learning performance and outcomes (Benito et al., 2021; Feijóo et al., 2021; Giray, 2021; Lapitan et al., 2021; Latorre-Cosculluela et al., 2021), and autonomy and motivation (Benito et al., 2021; Feijóo et al., 2021; Giray, 2021; Lapitan et al., 2021; Latorre-Cosculluela et al., 2021; Lytvyn et al., 2021; Wichanpricha, 2021; Yatigammana & Wijayarathna, 2021). Similar findings have been reported in literature, for example, enhanced student experience (Eden, 2016), improved performance and outcomes (Muñoz et al., 2017), active student engagement (Bond et al., 2021; Heliporn et al., 2021; Nerantzi, 2020; Oraif & Elyas, 2021), motivation (Acmar &

Bhagat, 2021; Wollmann et al., 2016), and deep learning (Aristika & Juandi, 2021; Bernstein & Issac, 2018).

In regard to learning modality, the preference was for synchronous or hybrid learning (Ahshan, 2021; Benito et al., 2021; Lapitan et al., 2021; Lytvyn et al., 2021; Yatigammana & Wijayarathna, 2021) using video conferencing software such as Zoom (Yatigammana & Wijayarathna, 2021), MS Teams (Wichanpricha, 2021), and Google (Ahshan, 2021). A combination of tools, including CRS tools such as Clicker, Jamboard, Mentimeter, Padlet, Quizzlet, Kahoot, and Lino, were deemed most effective (Ahshan, 2021; Kohnke & Moorhouse, 2021), with a combination of tools being reported as "engaging" (Lapitan et al., 2021, p. 123) and "compelling" (Ahshan, 2021, p. 19). Students in the Feijóo et al. (2021) study acknowledged the benefit of CRS in assessing learning in flipped learning contexts. Assessment in this learning modality was divided, however, with students in one study perceiving assessment in blended learning contexts to be as rigorous and fair as on campus (Benito et al., 2021), whilst two others advocated on campus only (Feijóo et al., 2021; Giray, 2021).

An overwhelming majority of students were satisfied with the blended or hybrid learning model during the pandemic (Ahshan, 2021; Benito et al., 2021; Feijóo et al., 2021; Lapitan et al., 2021; Latorre-Cosculluela et al., 2021; Wichanpricha, 2021; Yatigammana & Wijayarathna, 2021), with students in the Latorre-Cosculluela et al. (2021) study noting flipped learning helped foster graduate attributes and transferable skills. Whilst the majority of students across the studies were in favour of the blended learning modality, others noted a preference for on campus (Giray, 2021; Kohnke & Moorhouse, 2021). Challenges associated with blended learning included peer and instructor interaction (Kohnke & Moorhouse, 2021), motivation, learning performance, self-discipline, and collaboration (Giray, 2021). This is in keeping with previous studies where similar aspects were reported: motivation (Aristika & Juandi, 2021; Sun & Chen, 2016), learning performance and self-discipline (Aristika & Juandi, 2021), and student and instructor interaction (Wang et al., 2021).

Students in the Lapitan et al. (2021) and Kohnke and Moorhouse (2021) studies were invited to suggest improvements to the blended learning model with a view to enhancing the student experience for future cohorts. Suggestions included, "tasks being completed in advance of face-to-face sessions", synchronous activity limited to "no more than one hour" (Kohnke & Moorhouse, 2021, p. 240), and "more quizzes", "guided problems… and other forms of assessments (to) be included to compensate for low scores in exams" (Lapitan et al., 2021, p. 128). Participants in the Benito et al. (2021) study expressed a desire for elements of their blended learning experience to be retained post-pandemic, as did participants in the Yatigammana and Wijayarathna (2021) study. Participants in the Giray (2021) study noted that digital interaction environments and access to online resources were useful in both online and on campus education.

Overall, student perception across all 11 studies on the effectiveness of TEL in blended learning contexts during the COVID-19 pandemic was extremely positive. Given the overall positive findings, 5 of the 11 institutions indicated that they planned to retain the blended learning model (Kohnke & Moorhouse, 2021; Feijóo et al., 2021; Giray, 2021; Lapitan et al., 2021; Latorre-Cosculluela et al., 2021) as "some of the strategies and practices implemented during the lockdown period have entailed such a positive impact on the teaching practice that they have arrived to stay for the future" (Feijóo et al., 2021, p. 15). Reflecting on insights emerging from the data, Lapitan et al. observed that the blended learning model could be adapted and applied to "future events such as disruption of classes due to inclement weather conditions… and emergency situations" (2021, p. 130). Similarly, Latorre-Cosculluela et al. point out that on campus learning could be replaced with "online classes (and)… students continue to perceive certain benefits for the development of their skills for the 21st century" (2021, p. 200).

7   Conclusion

Whilst the COVID-19 pandemic unquestionably brought about transformational change in the way we work with our students, it is still too early to predict how substantial and long-lasting this will prove to be. It is reasonable to assume, however, that the post-pandemic face of the global HE sector is likely to be more digitally orientated, given the substantial investment already made in the development and utilisation of CRS, LMS, and software applications. This is reflected in the findings of the studies where 5 of the 11 institutions indicated that they planned to retain the blended learning model for the foreseeable future (Kohnke & Moorhouse, 2021; Giray, 2021; Lapitan et al., 2021; Latorre-Cosculluela et al., 2021; Feijóo et al., 2021). Similarly, students in both the Benito et al. (2021) and the Yatigammana and Wijayarathna (2021) studies expressed a desire for elements of the blended learning model to be retained post-pandemic. The future of TEL, therefore, in its various forms and modalities, looks set to remain a firmly embedded feature of HE pedagogy and practice for the foreseeable future, and I am personally looking forward to testing out the perceived effective TEL discussed in this chapter within my own UK HE context.

Reflections and Recommendations

I have learned a great deal from conducting this study, not least the value of a scoping review as a tool to inform innovative processes. I focused on student perception given that the students had been thrust into a massive online learning experiment of unprecedented scale and scope during the pandemic, and their comments and insights would help ensure a more focused and positive learning experience. I chose case studies from across the globe as HE institutions worldwide were experiencing similar issues to the UK, and transferable TEL more likely to emerge from widening the pool.

There are, however, some recommendations and points to note for those wishing to conduct a similar review. These relate mainly to the exploratory nature and the statistical robustness of the findings. For example, this was the first time I had conducted a scoping review and as such the Boolean operators selected may have limited the range and extent of the database returns. If I were to conduct further research, perhaps focusing on instructor perception of the effectiveness of TEL in blended learning contexts, terminology such as 'Gamification', 'HyFlex', and 'Hybrid' would be included in the search criteria as these terms were unknown to me at the outset of the process. Finding a key journal related to the topic under investigation and using the keywords contained within the paper as Boolean operators can help with the selection and screening process, and mining text with, for example, JSTOR's Text Analyser can also help locate key topics and terminology.

Interestingly, there were no UK journal articles returned during this scoping review. This may be attributed, however, to my initial limited knowledge regarding the specifics of TEL modes and practices. As previously discussed, my rationale for focusing on English-medium journal articles was to avoid translation issues and misinterpretation, but I acknowledge that in doing so I may have excluded key data. It is also worth noting that scoping reviews are generally conducted by a team of domain experts with specialist knowledge of methodological practices (Lasserson et al., 2022), and if there is only one reviewer, it could risk errors, introduce bias, and impact on the rigour of the findings (Neimann Rasmussen & Montgomery, 2018). It was not possible to work as a team in the present study as it was undertaken as part of a larger Doctoral research project. Employing a well-designed statistical tool, however, such as the PICOSS screening and selection tool, should help mitigate any weakness in the research design.

As a final note, I hope the very positive findings from this study will help inform not only my own UK HE pedagogical practice across ELT departmental and cross-Faculty offerings but also that of the wider global HE sector. Moving forward, I will continue to review and develop TEL within the ELT blended learning model to ensure continued quality enhancement, an overall positive student experience, and to equip learners with the twenty-first-century capabilities necessary to become work-ready graduates and employees.

Conflict of interest: There was no conflict of interest.

Data availability statement: All data relating to this study is available from the corresponding author upon reasonable request.

References

Acmar, D. E., & Bhagat, R. (2021). Opportunities and challenges to educators when transitioning to a TEL environment – Case of Kuwait. *International Journal of Multidisciplinary Studies an Innovative Technologies, 5*(1), 50–88.

Advance Higher Education. (2022). https://www.advance-he.ac.uk/guidance/teaching-and-learning/technology-enhanced-learning

Ahshan, R. (2021). A framework of implementing strategies for active student engagement in remote/online teaching and learning during the COVID-19 pandemic. *Education Sciences, 11*(9), 483. https://DOI.org/10.3390/educsci11090483

Aristika, A., & Juandi, D. (2021). The effectiveness of hybrid learning in improving of teacher-student relationship in terms of learning motivation. *Emerging Science Journal, 5*(4), 443–456. https://doi.org/10.28991/esj-2021-01288

Armstrong R., Hall, B. J., Doyle, J., & Waters, E. (2011). Cochrane Update. 'Scoping the scope' of a cochrane review. *Journal of Public Health, 33*(1), 147–50. https://doi.org/10.1093/pubmed/fdr015.

BALEAP. (2022). *BALEAP Accreditation Scheme (BAS) for EAP courses.* https://www.baleap.org/accreditation/institutions

Benito, Á., Yenisey, K. D., Khanna, K., Masis, M. F., Monge, R. M., Tugtan, M. A., Araya, L. D. V., & Vig, R. (2021). Changes that should remain in higher education post COVID-19: A mixed-methods analysis of the experiences at three universities. *Higher Learning Research Communications, 11*, 51–75. https://doi.org/10.18870/hlrc.v11i0.1195

Bernstein, A. G., & Issac, C. (2018). Critical thinking criteria for evaluating online discussion. *International Journal for the Scholarship of Teaching and Learning, 12*(2), 1–8. https://doi.org/10.20429/ijsotl.2018.120211

Boland, A., Cherry, M. G., & Dickson, R. (2014). *Doing a systematic review.* Sage Publication.

Bond, M., Buntins, K., Bedenlier, S., Zawacki-Richter, O., & Kerres, M. (2021). Mapping research in student engagement and educational technology in higher education: A systematic evidence map. *International Journal of Educational Technology in Higher Education, 17*(2). https://doi.org/10.1186/s41239-019-0176-8

Bozkurt, A., Jung, I., Xiao, J., Vladimirschi, V., Schuwer, R., Egorov, G., Lambert, S. R., Al-Freih, M., Pete, J., Olcott, D., Jr., Rodes, V., Aranciaga, I., Bali, M., Alvarez, A. V., Jr., Roberts, J., Pazurek, A., Raffaghelli, J. E.,

Panagiotou, N., de Coëtlogon, P., Shahadu, S., Brown, M., Asino, T. I., Tumwesige, J., Ramirez Reyes, T., Barrios Ipenza, E., Ossiannilsson, E., Bond, M., Belhamel, K., Irvine, V., Sharma, R. C., Adam, T., Janssen, B., Sklyarova, T., Olcott, N., Ambrosino, A., Lazou, C., Mocqet, B., Mano, M., & Paskevicius, M. (2020). A global outlook to the interruption of education due to COVID-19 pandemic: Navigating in a time of uncertainty and crisis. *Asian Journal of Distance Education, 15*(1), 1–126. https://doi.org/10.5281/zenodo.3878572

Eden, B. L. (2016). Game it up! Using gamification to incentivize your library. *Journal of Electronic Resources Librarianship, 28*(2), 135–135. https://doi.org/10.1080/1941126X.2016.1167554

Feijóo, J. C. M., Suárez, F., Chiyón, I., & Alberti, M. G. (2021). Some web-based experiences from flipped classroom techniques in AEC modules during the Covid-19 lockdown. *Education Sciences, 11*(5). https://doi.org/10.3390/educsci11050211

Giray, G. (2021). An assessment of student satisfaction with e-learning: An empirical study with computer and software engineering undergraduate students in turkey under pandemic conditions. *Education and Information Technologies, 26*(6), 6651–6673. https://doi.org/10.1007/s10639-021-10454-x

Google. (2022). *Communicate flexibly with Google Workspace for education.* https://edu.google.com/intl/ALL_uk/products/workspace-for-education/education-fundamentals/

Gupta, S. B., & Gupta, M. (2020). Technology and e-learning in higher education. *International Journal of Advanced Science and Technology, 29*(4), 1320–1325.

Heliporn, G., Lakhal, S., & Bélisle, M. (2021). An examination of teachers' strategies to foster student engagement in blended learning in higher education. *International Journal of Educational Technology in Higher Education, 18*(25). https://doi.org/10.1186/s41239-021-00260-3

Joshi, N., Lau, S. K., Pang, M. F., & Lau, S. S. Y. (2021). Clickers in class: fostering higher cognitive thinking using concepts tests in a large undergraduate class. *The Asia-Pacific Education Researcher, 30*, 375–394. https://doi.org/10.1007/s40299-020-00525-x

Kohnke, L., & Moorhouse, B. L. (2021). Adopting HyFlex in higher education in response to COVID-19: Students' perspectives. *Open Learning, 36*(3), 231–244. https://doi.org/10.1080/02680513.2021.1906641

Lapitan, L. D., Tiangco, C. E., Sumalinog, D. A. G., Sabarillo, N. S., & Diaz, J. M. (2021). An effective blended online teaching and learning strategy during the COVID-19 pandemic. *Education for Chemical Engineers, 35*, 116–131. https://doi.org/10.1016/j.ece.2021.01.012

Lasserson, T. J., Thomas, J., & Higgins, J. P. T. (2022). Chapter 1: Starting a review. In J. P. T. Higgins, J. Thomas, J. Chandler, M. Cumpston, T. Li, M. J. Page, & V. A. Welch (Eds.), *Cochrane handbook for systematic reviews of interventions: Version 6.3*. Cochrane Collaboration. www.training.cochrane.org/handbook

Latorre-Cosculluela, C., Suárez, C., Quiroga, S., Sobradiel-Sierra, N., Lozano-Blasco, R., & Rodríguez-Martínez, A. (2021). Flipped classroom model before and during COVID-19: Using technology to develop 21st century skills. *Interactive Technology and Smart Education, 18*(2), 189–204. https://doi.org/10.1108/ITSE-08-2020-0137

Lytvyn, V., Akimova, O., Kuznetsova, H., Zenchenko, T., Stepanenko, O., & Koreneva, I. (2021). The use of synchronous and asynchronous teaching methods in pedagogical education in COVID-19 terms. *International Journal of Health Sciences, 5*(3), 617–629. https://doi.org/10.53730/ijhs.v5n3.2681

Microsoft. (2022). *Office 365 Education*. https://docs.microsoft.com/en-us/office365/servicedescriptions/office-365-platform-service-description/office-365-education

Muñoz, M., Hernández, L., Mejia, J., Gasca-Hurtado, G. P., & Gómez-Alvarez, M. C. (2017). State of the use of gamification elements in software development teams. *Proceedings of the European Conference on Software Process Improvement*, pp. 249–258. https://doi.org/10.1007/978-3-319-64218-5_20

Neimann Rasmussen, L., & Montgomery, P. (2018). The prevalence of and factors associated with inclusion of non-English language studies in Campbell systematic reviews: a survey and meta-epidemiological study. *Systematic Reviews, 7*, 129. https://doi.org/10.1186/s13643-018-0786-6

Nerantzi, C. (2020). The use of peer instruction and flipped learning to support flexible blended learning during and after the COVID-19 pandemic. *International Journal of Management and Applied Research, 7*(2), 184–195. https://doi.org/10.18646/2056.72.20-013

Nieto-Escamez, F. A., & Roldán-Tapia, M. D. (2021). Gamification as online teaching strategy during COVID-19: A mini-review. *Frontiers in Psychology*. https://doi.org/10.3389/fpsyg.2021.648552

Nimmo, F. (2022). *The use of an assessed asynchronous online discussion forum to help foster deep learning*. EAP in the North: Life online and beyond. https://www.baleap.org/event/eap-in-the-north-life-online-and-beyond

Notion Labs, Inc. (2021). *Notion*. https://www.notion.so/product

Oraif, I., & Elyas, T. (2021). The impact of COVID-19 on learning: Investigating EFL learners' engagement in online courses in Saudi Arabia. *Education Science, 11*(3), 99. https://doi.org/10.3390/educsci11030099

Ożadowicz, A. (2020). Modified blended learning in engineering higher education during the COVID-19 lockdown-building automation courses case study. *Education Sciences, 10*(10), 1–20. https://doi.org/10.3390/educsci10100292

Page, M. J., McKenzie, J. E., Bossuyt, P. M., et al. (2021). The PRISMA 2020 statement: An updated guideline for reporting systematic reviews. *Systematic Reviews, 10*, 89. https://doi.org/10.1186/s13643-021-01626-4

Pichardo, J. I., López-Medina, E. F., Mancha-Cáceres, O., González-Enríquez, I., Hernández-Melián, A., Blázquez-Rodríguez, M., et al. (2021). Students and teachers using Mentimeter: Technological innovation to face the challenges of the COVID-19 pandemic and post-pandemic in higher education. *Education Sciences, 11*(11), 667. https://doi.org/10.3390/educsci11110667

Pinho, C., Franco, M., & Mendes, L. (2018). Web portals as tools to support information management in higher education institutions: A systematic literature review. *International Journal of Information Management, 41*, 80–92. https://doi.org/10.1016/j.ijinfomgt.2018.04.002

Quality Assurance Agency for Higher Education. (2020). *Building a taxonomy for digital learning*. https://www.qaa.ac.uk/docs/qaa/guidance/building-a-taxonomy-for-digital-learning.pdf

Rebelo Da Silva, N., Zaranyika, H., Langer, L., Randall, N., Muchiri, E., & Stewart, R. (2017). Making the most of what we already know: A three-stage approach to systematic reviewing. *Evaluation Review, 41*(2), 155–172. https://doi.org/10.1177/0193841X16666363

Royal Society for Public Health. (2021). *Disparity begins at home: How home working is impacting the public's health*. https://www.rsph.org.uk/our-work/policy/wellbeing/disparity-begins-at-home.html#:~:text=The%20report%20includes%20a%20snapshot,a%20better%20work%2Flife%20balance

Saikat, S., Dhillon, J. S., Wan Ahmad, W. F., & Jamaluddin, R. A. (2021). A systematic review of the benefits and challenges of mobile learning during the COVID-19 pandemic. *Education Sciences, 11*(9), 459.

Sun, A., & Chen, X. (2016). Online education and its effective practice: A research review. *Journal of Information Technology Education, 15,* 157–190. https://doi.org/10.28945/3502

Wang, Y., Stein, D., & Shen, S. (2021). Students' and teachers' perceived teaching presence in online courses. *Distance Education, 42*(3), 373–390. https://doi.org/10.1080/01587919.2021.1956304

Wichanpricha, T. (2021). Synchronous online learning through Microsoft teams at tertiary level: Academic English course. *Journal of Educational and Social Research, 11*(5), 123–140. https://doi.org/10.36941/jesr-2021-0111

Wollmann, T., Abtahi, F., Eghdam, A., Seoane, F., Lindecrantz, K., Haag, M., & Koch, S. (2016). User-centred design and usability evaluation of a heart rate variability biofeedback game. *IEEE Access, 4,* 5531–5539.

Yatigammana, K., & Wijayarathna, G. (2021). Students' perceptions of online lecture delivery modes: Higher education during COVID-19 pandemic and beyond. *International Journal of Emerging Technologies in Learning, 16*(21), 58–73. https://doi.org/10.3991/ijet.v16i21.25305

Assessing Doctorateness in the Professional Doctorate Portfolio for Language Practitioners: From Publishability to Impact

Mark Carver

1 TESOL Doctorate Innovations in the UK

In the UK, the Quality Assurance Agency's doctoral characteristics statement helps to benchmark standards across different types of doctorate, whether the traditional PhD, PhD by publication, EdD, DProf, ProfDoc, or any number of equivalent awards (Quality Assurance Agency, 2020). Among these doctoral characteristics, perhaps the best known is the original contribution to knowledge as the hallmark of doctoral-level work globally. Other characteristics are a matter of definition: doctorates are specified as the highest earned degree awarded by any university, thereby implying the highest levels of rigour and status. Creating a new qualification at this level therefore requires demonstrations of parity and status

M. Carver (✉)
International Education and Lifelong Learning Institute,
University of St Andrews, St Andrews, UK
e-mail: mac32@st-andrews.ac.uk

© The Author(s), under exclusive license to Springer Nature Switzerland AG 2024
S. W. Chong, H. Reinders (eds.), *Innovation in Language Learning and Teaching*, New Language Learning and Teaching Environments,
https://doi.org/10.1007/978-3-031-66241-6_9

which, if extended to mimicry, can risk stifling innovation. Nevertheless, new and innovative doctorates have been developed in recent years, particularly those designed to serve non-traditional doctoral candidates or subject areas (Willems, 2010).

One recent innovation is the named award in English Language Teaching (ELT) or Teaching English to Speakers of Other Languages (TESOL) rather than doctoral qualifications in education or educational research used as a vehicle for a thesis in ELT. Nevertheless, the more established postgraduate domains of education or applied linguistics are still used as inspiration for the design of PhDs in TESOL such as those at the Universities of York and Stirling. This is in part because there is less of a bottom-up development of TESOL from undergraduate through to postgraduate taught and postgraduate research degrees. As a named subject, TESOL's presence in university qualifications is only recorded in the last 40 years (Carver, 2020), with doctoral-level study being sufficiently rare that master's level is typically regarded as "the standard terminal degree" in TESOL (Stapleton & Shao, 2018, p. 12).

At the same time, the EdD has developed with a shift in emphasis from training of the individual doctoral candidate to the impact they can have on practice, and perhaps even the growing expectation that doctoral learning should be change-oriented (Becton et al., 2020). This is evident in the recruitment of candidates in senior or mid-career professional roles, the marketing of programmes, module choices, and expectations for the kinds of research undertaken by EdD candidates. Thus, innovations in TESOL at the doctoral level can be helpfully thought of as following two tracks: one of building legitimacy through conforming to traditional expectations of a PhD programme, and one of more radical design which relies on demonstrating equivalent rigour and prestige. Rather than debating whether this is a spectrum or dichotomy, Wellington's use of Wittgenstein's "family resemblance" applied to doctoral qualifications (Wellington, 2013, p. 1501) is useful in identifying innovation at different levels, whether innovating 'within' the wrapper of an established qualification or 'outwith' its confines and expectations. Running throughout these levels of innovation is the unifying concept of doctorateness as both enabling and constraining innovation.

2 Doctorateness as Instructive for Innovation

The concept of doctorateness can offer a guide for the norms and the limits of acceptability within doctoral programmes. The term came from broader discussions in the UK about 'graduateness' (hence 'doctorateness' rather than 'doctoralness') and so originally referred to the personal attributes of graduates of doctoral programmes, built particularly around the idea of a transformative learning experience (Trafford & Leshem, 2009). As discussion developed around how to assess such attributes, the term expanded to consider the range of impacts and outputs of a doctoral programme beyond the individual graduate. More recent conceptual development emphasises outputs for a range of stakeholders in doctoral programmes, fitting with the broader discussions around impact of research (Yazdani & Shokooh, 2018). Expanding further to use the concept to guide innovation, doctorateness helps to focus on the key features of doctoral programmes and where variance occurs within different designs.

Yazdani and Shokooh (2018) are particularly helpful in drawing out the definitional features of a doctorate as distinct from convention. For example, that doctorates are the highest level of award is foundational: creating a new programme above master's level but not awarded at doctoral would simply not be regarded as a doctorate. Likewise, it would be exceptionally rare for a doctorate to not involve a viva voce exam. Other matters can play with the notion of a family resemblance (Wellington, 2013), especially when considering the outputs of a doctorate; to what extent a portfolio is like a thesis or an arts performance is like a journal article. Provision for students shows even more flexibility, with some doctorates mirroring the traditional master/apprentice model while others emphasise taught provision or broader research skills (Taylor, 2012).

The flexibility of doctorateness can also be useful in framing historical innovations in doctorates as the number of doctoral students has dramatically expanded, highlighting moves from the mediaeval emphasis on mastery through to the nineteenth century focus on generation of new research, the integration and application of knowledge to practical contexts in the mid-twentieth century, and through to a contemporary move away from traditional career expectations and a commensurate emphasis on transferable skills and competencies. Doctorateness also highlights the risk of conservatism in doctoral innovation where developments are built upon each other, such that expectations continue to rise over each iteration of doctoral qualification rather than one innovation supplanting another part of the provision. This might cynically be seen as part of the ever-increasing demand for credentials symptomatic of the diploma disease, but is more charitably an indication of inter-generational parity aiming to protect the status of what has persisted over the centuries as the highest level of qualification.

One risk in using doctorateness to establish parity is bloating the expectations of programme outputs, especially with innovations where there is some anxiety about the status of a new qualification type or discipline area. Thus, an EdD might be designed with published outputs and taught modules but still require a substantial thesis and viva voce. In the UK, even where university regulations give a nominal credit weighting to a doctorate of 540 credits, the completion of several 15-credit taught modules is unlikely to lead to a proportionate reduction in thesis expectations.

As an overarching concept, doctorateness offers a route through such tensions by offering ways to assess synergy across different parts of the thesis or different assessed outputs. This can be used to evaluate innovations by ensuring that a programme still delivers on core competences such as clarity of presentation as evidence of professional skills or a sound conceptual framework (Leshem, 2020; Trafford & Leshem, 2009). When this interpretation of doctorateness as a tacit construct is combined with programme-focused approaches to assessment, a doctoral programme can focus on creating an argument that doctorateness has been demonstrated across the range of outputs rather than forcing a pretence of evidencing that discrete learning outcomes have been met for each assessed item. Innovation is therefore supported by doctoral assessment focused on doctorateness as a claim made throughout all doctoral outputs, which contrasts against more conventional assessment approaches based on constructive alignment.

Different aspects of doctorateness can also be prioritised for a particular scholarly output or to structure student development at different points of the doctoral journey. For instance, Sanganyado et al. (2022, p. 930) discuss how supervisors can enable doctorateness incrementally as "the transition from knowledge consumption to knowledge creation, original scholarly contribution, and research integrity". Such an approach is helpful for designing a programme which moves from a taught phase to an independent research phase, and for planning annual progress review benchmarks. Sanganyado et al.'s work also creates a useful pathway for considering how doctorateness as a developing characteristic can integrate with practitioner values. Indeed, the example of using doctorateness to develop innovation in this chapter advances an argument that doctorateness as a broad concept is necessarily tacit, but also that it can be grounded in a social and professional context. By borrowing the expectation that practitioner identity development should be part of the EdD process (e.g. Tupling & Outhwaite, 2017), a bridge is created so that the established literature on teacher professionalisation can inform what the gradual development of doctorateness may look like in the specific context of a TESOL professional.

Having established some of the parameters for innovation under the protection of 'doctorateness', professional values needed to be articulated that would justify and drive innovation. For the Professional Doctorate (DProf) TESOL, these were practitioner values of principled eclecticism (Mellow, 2002), moral and social practice (Goodson, 2000), being a doctoral practitioner (Hughes et al., 1998; Robinson, 2018; Yazdani & Shokooh, 2018), reflective practice for language teachers (Farrell, 2022), and the doctoral journey as one of professional learning requiring autonomy, disturbance, and dialogue (Hall & Wall, 2019). As a very basic overview of how these concepts are embedded in the DProf programme, principled eclecticism refers to a pluralistic approach to pedagogy where no single method is unquestioningly followed and an evidence-based rationale can be given for a teacher's pedagogical choices. Moral and social practice is taken from Goodson's larger piece on the obligations for professionals to have both opportunities and expectations that they will engage with moral and social aspects of their practice, including both the opportunity and responsibility for exercising discretionary judgement, working collaboratively, and having genuine care for their students. The various sources used to construct the concept of a doctoral practitioner are represented together as a requirement for DProf students to meet the needs of a stakeholder other than the university (i.e. having an impact on practice), including developing the long-term skills and dispositions that will sustain a scholarly approach to practice in the long-term as part of a student's professional identity and development of their own capital. There is still some debate regarding if the programme should specifically expect students to have a transformational experience, or if establishing that direct aim might make such an outcome less likely. Reflective practice draws explicitly on Farrell's (2017) work as opposed to the more general teacher reflection models from Gibbs (1988) or Schön (1995) because his work is more specific to language teachers and has the advantage of reflecting on contextual factors, an element of doctorateness that Gibbs and Schön do not address. Finally, the concepts of autonomy, disturbance, and dialogue from Hall and Wall (2019) are used to great effect in Wall's own professional doctorate at the University of Strathclyde. The concepts are used here to assert the practitioner's unique insights into what satisfactory impact would look like in their context (autonomy), the need to engage with complexity and take greater risks in asking difficult questions (disturbance), and the requirement to communicate research across different contexts, including where it has not 'worked' (dialogue). These values are perhaps most obvious in the 'outputs not articles' innovation in example 2, where removing the requirement that every output be published in a journal increases the scope to take more risks with research or to include 'failed' studies in the portfolio without worrying about the 'success narrative' norm in academic publishing.

While this seems a long list of influences to try weave throughout a programme, as summarised in Table 1, it is important to note that DProf TESOL is a part-time only programme, so the doctoral journey is mapped over five or six years. An example of how these concepts are enacted at the start of the DProf programme is given below in the 'Being a doctoral practitioner' section.

Table 1 Expansion of the concept of doctorateness to incorporate professional values relevant to DProf TESOL

Source	Concepts/criteria of doctorateness
Trafford and Leshem (2008)	Contribution to knowledge; stated gap in knowledge; explicit research questions; conceptual framework; explicit research design; appropriate methodology; 'correct' data collection; clear/precise presentation; full engagement with theory; cogent argument throughout; research questions answered; conceptual conclusions.
Yazdani and Shokooh (2018)	Formal process; lengthy process; apprenticeship; development and change; professional experience; socialisation; doctoral identity; research competence; higher order thinking skills; mastery of discipline knowledge; teaching competence; wisdom; original contribution; sizeable written product; peer-examined work; publishable work; concept utilisation; highest level of award; scholarship to and stewardship of the discipline; position in a scientific community; personal growth; impact on knowledge society or economic growth; impact on human capital development.
Sanganyado et al. (2022)	Knowledge creation; original scholarly contribution; research integrity.
Tupling and Outhwaite (2017)	Identity development as a practitioner.
Mellow (2002)	Pluralistic approach to pedagogy; ability to critique research base of pedagogical innovations.
Goodson (2000)	Engagement with moral and social aspects of practice; expectation to use professional judgement; using authority or status to facilitate collaboration.
Robinson (2018)	Impact on practice; sustained scholarly approach to practice; identity development as a scholarly practitioner.
(Farrell, 2022)	Reflection as habitual practice; reflection on the practitioner's assumptions and beliefs; reflection on the moral, political, emotional, ethical, and community/social issues of practice.
Hall and Wall (2019)	Explicit claim to what impact should look like in a specified area of practice; engaged with complexity and risk-taking; communicating across contexts.

3   Innovations Within DProf TESOL

At the time of creating DProf TESOL, the University of St Andrews already had a DProf in International Relations, offered in parallel to a PhD in the same school but recruiting from those working full-time, such as in government or security services. The appeal was a qualification that did not require substantial time away from work, require a large thesis, or even require substantial publications, but rather focused on developing the student and their impact in practice. Following this model, but recognising that teachers do not have the same impediments to publication as those working in counter-terrorism, DProf TESOL was planned to continue from the relatively new MSc TESOL (replacing MLitt ELT in 2018) as a way to structure and recognise the professional learning of senior practitioners. The first DProf TESOL cohort started in 2021, with 4 students, with enrolment at 40 students as of January 2024. It is delivered entirely remotely, using Teams and Moodle, and has students based all over the world. Most students are mid-career, at associate lecturer or equivalent level, and all are either teaching or leading teams of teachers.

Example 1: Being a Doctoral Practitioner

Students begin with a doctoral-only module called 'Being a doctoral practitioner'. Its learning outcomes are:

1. Articulate a context-relevant overview of what a doctoral practitioner does
2. Critically engage with current debates and trends in TESOL and ELT
3. Critique the use of evidence in a professional or academic setting
4. Reflect upon professional values in TESOL and ELT

Thus, the assessment for Being a Doctoral Practitioner is the first step in preparing for the portfolio and viva because the student starts building their argument for what doctorateness should look like in their professional context, with the remaining four or five years spent developing and demonstrating such. Assessment for the module can therefore be negotiated to fit a student's professional context, but most tasks focus on the integration of theory and practice in their workplaces by using one of four recommended titles:

1. Critique any two related articles from a practitioner research journal and suggest a theoretical framework that could strengthen their contribution to the literature.
2. Conduct a cultural audit of how evidence is used in your workplace and make recommendations for developing the scholarly community therein.
3. Discuss the evidence base behind a theory or technique that is popular in your workplace—to what extent is this practice evidence-informed?
4. A reflective essay on the professional status of language teachers in your local context. To what extent does local understanding of a leading practitioner in your field align with the concept of 'doctorateness'?

Task 1 has not been chosen or adapted by any candidate in the four years of the programme, but was included as an option for those in a new professional context or who were not yet comfortable critiquing practice in their own workplace. The task is not innovative other than in offering students a free choice of article, but it at least aligns with the emphasis on theoretical frameworks in doctoral-level work (Trafford & Leshem, 2009). Task 2 is almost as unpopular and will likely be removed from the module in its 2026 update, but was designed around the ideas of principled eclecticism (Mellow, 2002) and the well-established problems of teachers being able to exercise professional judgement in how they integrate or resist new trends (Goodson, 2000; Kerr, 2022).

Task 3 is more popular and is a guide for evaluating impact and the exercise of professional discretion as students explain why their chosen approach is popular in their context and then critique both the literature-based rationale for adopting the approach and a practice-based reflection in its appropriateness for their particular context. However, when looking at how students go on to develop their portfolio in later years, future versions of this assessment will likely build towards a research synthesis as another way of achieving the same kinds of reflection but also supporting a methodology which is quickly becoming a signature output of the DProf for its potential in facilitating dialogue between research and pedagogy (Chong, 2022). Students on this module might, in future, be asked to create a research synthesis protocol and reflect on what would help it to have impact on practice in their own context, thus replacing tasks two and three.

By far the most popular is task 4, with more than 80% of students choosing or adapting this option. This gives the opportunity to reflect on debates around professional status and identity (e.g. Ding et al., 2019), while also highlighting the value of reflective writing as a genre. The innovation intended here is that 'leading practitioner' can be interpreted in a range of context-specific ways based on the student's current or intended role, but that this must be critiqued through the lens of doctorateness. For students at the start of their doctoral journey, such a reflection may be a disruptive experience, but ultimately is a disruption that begins the discussion towards what doctorateness should look like as the student goes on to acquire and embody this in their own work, expressed in the use of 'being' in the module title from Craig's metaphors of learning teaching (Craig, 2018).

Weekly seminars also intend to be disruptive in their tasks and required reading, the latest version of which can be seen at https://sta.rl.talis.com/programmes/tesol.html. The first week invites critique of papers from a practitioner-focused journal, challenging students to articulate the extent to which they could rely on the articles. This will be important for judging research quality in general, and especially for those who go on to conduct a research synthesis, but also sets the scene for reflecting on the necessary compromises in research and how students might need to defend the flaws in their own portfolio. This sets up the more critical literature in week 2, such as Medgyes (2017) and Sato and Loewen (2019), where students are confronted with the reality that publishing research and having an impact on practice are weakly related at best. For a programme designed around the latter (Carver, 2023), this is an important disruption to conventional thinking.

Week 3 models a critique of task-based language teaching, providing a ready example of the kind of critique expected for assessment choice 3 as well as challenging students to think about what counts as 'state of the art' and how innovations in pedagogy need to be understood in a broader historical and cultural context. In the same spirit, week 4 is linked with assessment choice 4 in contrasting the training/development and impact of teachers in two different roles: volunteer teachers working with hill tribes in Thailand (Bernstein & Woosnam, 2019) and EAP teachers working in British universities (Ding & Bruce, 2017). The challenge here is to consider language teacher professionalism as context-bound rather than just on a spectrum and how professionals need to accrue cultural capital in order to have an impact on practice. In this week, the volunteer teachers provide a tragic example of well-intentioned teachers having very little impact due to constraints of context and low status, pushing DProf students to consider impact not just beyond publishing but beyond the in-the-moment impact of a teacher on a group of learners and into something more enduring. Week 5 concludes this line of thought with the somewhat disheartening example from Poole et al. (2021) exploring barriers to impact for teachers working in a context which is seemingly ideal for translating research into practice and vice versa. While intended as a model to the unpopular assessment choice 2, the use of Poole's work concludes a module in which knowledge is presented as problematic, contested, and bound by context.

Example 2: Doctoral Portfolio Outputs

Perhaps the most innovative feature of DProf TESOL is its rejection of publishability as a defining indicator of doctorateness (Carver, 2023). This decision was mostly based on the status of EAP practitioners in the academy (Ding et al., 2019) and how some journal editors consider TESOL contexts to be peripheral (Yuan et al., 2022), so it would be unfair if journal editors could become de facto gatekeepers to the award of a doctoral degree. This is all the more persuasive when considered alongside the broader social justice argument that academic publishing perpetuates Anglo-centric norms and other problematic norms around race and gender which are all the more acute in TESOL (R'boul, 2023). There is also a practical advantage that graduation will not be delayed by slow peer review or editorial processes, or that students will choose journals based on their turnaround times rather than the intended audience. Here there is a clear advantage to the programme being run at a high-status ancient university; just as it is a matter of definition that a doctoral degree is the highest level of award from any university, it can be reasoned that a doctoral degree does not require the approval of academic journals because the awarding university asserts it as the highest award.

Instead of relying on journal rank or other status markers to indicate quality, students will need to use their portfolio critical commentary to justify their choice of outlet. This helps to shift the emphasis away from what can be published to the intended impact of an output. A traditional, high-status journal might be needed if the student is working at a more conceptual level and needs the space and forum to theorise, but more niche and practitioner-focused journals are expected to be the norm.

In keeping with the latter emphasis of transferable skills within doctorateness, collaboration is also encouraged. Indeed, if following the programme's recommended research synthesis approach (Chong & Plonsky, 2021), collaboration is necessary. Here there is a practical restriction that the portfolio items must have the student as first author and evidence that the student was involved in every part of the output and any revisions process, but the explicit encouraging of collaboration with peers and supervisors is intended as an innovation that adds more authenticity to the DProf assessment regime. The portfolio also takes great care to require outputs rather than articles, again based on the idea that innovation is justified in the accompanying critical commentary. Named examples of outputs include a policy paper for the student's workplace, a redesigned test for students, or materials for a staff development workshop. This is intended as an invitation to innovate in what the student wishes to create and put forward as evidence of their doctorateness, while also challenging students to explain synergy or 'embeddedness' (Hall & Wall, 2019) between their outputs.

Example 3: Module Re-assessment

Based on a long-standing frustration that re-assessment practices are a missed opportunity for dialogic feedback (Carver, 2017), the convention that module grades for doctoral students are only recorded as pass or fail presented an opportunity since capped marks would not be a problem because there is no GPA to be concerned about. The aim of innovation here was to model the normal expectation that academic work will be revised based on feedback, with the task given as:

> Write a 2000-word reflective essay on feedback from your assessment indicating where you will be able to turn this into feedforward. As an appendix, include your originally-submitted [5000 word] assignment, the feedback from your lecturer, and examples of revisions and corrections you are able to make using 'tracked changes' in Word.

Even though re-assessment feedback is only given from one assessor (rather than two peer reviewers and an editor as in journal peer review), the resubmission task is designed so that the student needs to reflect on what are simple corrections to improve the current piece of work and which feedback should be taken forward to future tasks as feedforward or the basis for further dialogue with their supervisor. This innovation also recognises that the traditional approach of students making corrections and then resubmitting work at the end of the process can be emotionally damaging (Mitchell et al., 2023). This change to dialogic feedback and removing the need to make multiple minor corrections might therefore support a more collaborative ethos in supervision. Moreover, it recognises that resubmission only serves a pedagogical purpose when students are supported to make their best efforts rather than seeing it as "a bar to jump over" (Proud, 2015, p. 681). While a fairly minor shift in emphasis, this change to assessment is innovative given that resubmission practices are rarely given much consideration, particularly at postgraduate level. The innovation therefore allows the DProf programme to model its own values of disturbance and collaboration as well as modelling how a professional engages with feedback.

4   Building on the Innovations

This chapter has outlined innovations in a new professional doctorate and how innovations were facilitated and guided by doctorateness as an overarching concept which allowed the integration of professional learning values into the doctoral journey. Innovations were also supported by mimicry of existing 'gold standards' of doctoral provision, showing where it is important to maintain the 'family resemblance' of doctoral programmes. The most obvious example of this in assessment is the use of the viva voce, an approximately three-hour oral exam led by an established external academic which can include both broad and forensic questioning on any part of the doctoral journey and its outputs and is still considered the defining feature of a doctoral programme and a rite of passage for new academics (Bitzer et al., 2018). Quality assurance anxieties can likewise be eased by outlining the values and skills of a doctoral practitioner which can be mapped against more established standards used in other doctoral programmes. Thus, the programme includes the university-wide 'Gradskills' provision which aligns with Vitae's Researcher Development Framework, while students are also supported through achieving professional recognition through the BALEAP fellowship standards or the parallel Advance HE fellowship levels, either as a direct application or through enrolling on a PGCert in academic practice. With this external recognition, an experienced external examiner, output publication, and a viva, the programme as a whole has a robust claim to being a doctoral-level programme, but there is still a need to reflect on the value of the innovations outlined in this chapter.

The main challenge is deciding a standard for success. Part-time, online, professional doctorates might reasonably expect a lower completion rate than full-time, on-campus, funded PhDs. By the same token, the students admitted to a highly selective programme and university might be expected to achieve publication and success even with a mediocre doctoral provision. The candidates selected onto the programme therefore make it challenging to attribute programme shortcomings when there are myriad ways in which life gets in the way of successful study, while it is equally challenging to attribute programme success where candidates might still be successful with minimal babysitting from a supervisor.

Returning to the practitioner values outlined at the start of the chapter, Table 2 summarises where each example of innovation is guided by one or more value. While a necessarily reductive representation, it helpfully shows the DProf's developing identity and mission.

Table 2 Key guiding values for innovations

Principle	Being a doctoral practitioner module	Outputs, not articles	Portfolio narrative	Dialogic resubmission practices
Pluralistic approach to pedagogy rather than a single 'best practice'	✔	✔		
Engages with the moral and social aspects of professional work	✔		✔	
Works collaboratively, including with peers and learners		✔		✔
Meets the needs of a stakeholder other than St Andrews		✔		
Develops long-term skills and an identity as a scholarly practitioner	✔	✔	✔	
Demonstrates synergy or embeddedness			✔	
Reflects on contextual factors related to practice	✔		✔	
Creates an authoritative argument for what success looks like in a given context			✔	
Engages with complexity and risk, learning from 'failure'		✔		✔

From this, future developments have already been identified ahead of a programme and module refresh in 2026, including ways in which stakeholders from students' professional contexts can be more involved in the DProf. The most significant development is the popularity among students of a research synthesis as their second portfolio output. It will need to be carefully considered how to balance this with flexibility, but if there is a 'normal' pathway of outputs that start with a revised version of the 'Being a Doctoral Practitioner' assessment and then a related research synthesis, then the programme may be able to structure support for this progression. A research synthesis may also address the need for students to navigate a research landscape where the rigour and relevance of research is increasingly called into question. Research syntheses are both valuable and innovative in TESOL, so future changes to the DProf will consider how to promote this as a 'signature' output without restricting students who wish to evidence their understanding of research quality and relevance in another way.

Future developments of the DProf will also need to consider how the qualification fits into the broader qualification landscape, being aware of how the development of innovative programmes can be supported or resisted in the political, professional, and university spaces (Kennedy, 2018). Some governments still do not recognise distance doctorates, and there is a persistent snobbery around the PhD brand that is only partly mitigated by snobbery around the St Andrews brand. It is unlikely that journal articles will lead to changes in these political spaces, so retaining a policy paper or critique as an example of a portfolio output will be useful for encouraging DProf students to engage in this kind of work, as does an emphasis on Goodson's (2000) moral imperative for teachers as professionals. The professional space seems the area where the DProf can have the most impact, since an impact on practice is integrated throughout the programme and required for the degree award. It is also pleasing to see a positive reception within the university space as more disciplines consider adding a DProf alongside their PhDs as a more flexible and practice-focused option. Kennedy (2018) shows how paying attention to these three spaces helps to guide a programme to have a transformational impact on the profession, building on her earlier work on transformative professional learning at the individual level. This is exactly the kind of challenge that a DProf needs to guide its development and force it to continue to innovate, accepting nothing less than a transformation in the professional landscape for the doctoral practitioners it produces.

Impact of Professional Doctorates on Innovating Language Teaching

Just as the DProf TESOL requires its graduates to evidence the impact of their innovations on their practice, so too must the programme itself have an impact on the profession. The online-only and practice-based innovation opens doctoral-level study to students who might otherwise never be able to take a traditional PhD due to work or personal commitments. The part-time-only design also makes for a more gradual transition from practitioner to leader, in a way that hopefully mitigates the concern that TESOL practitioners can lose sight of their professional values and funds of knowledge when they move into more senior roles (Ding & Bruce, 2017). The portfolio assessment is a partial remedy to the pressure to publish, challenging students to think about the best medium in which to communicate to have the desired impact rather than chasing a specific journal metric. The use of remote-only staff and external supervisors also broadens the reach of the programme, helping to challenge the 'guest from the west' trope and increasing opportunities to support and examine doctoral-level work to academics who might otherwise be unwilling or unable to be physically in St Andrews. Finally, as the programme develops its signature outputs, it is hoped that the DProf TESOL structure might offer a blueprint for early career professional development in TESOL that will be valuable more broadly, even to those not studying for a doctorate, as they consider how to move from critiquing and synthesising the evidence base through to designing, conducting, and communicating research that engages with professional values and stewardship of the discipline.

References

Becton, Y. J., Bogiages, C., D'Amico, L., Lilly, T., Currin, E., Jeffries, R., & Tamim, S. (2020). An emerging framework for the EdD activist. *Impacting Education: Journal on Transforming Professional Practice, 5*(2), 43–54.
Bernstein, J. D., & Woosnam, K. M. (2019). Same same but different: Distinguishing what it means to teach English as a foreign language within the context of volunteer tourism. *Tourism Management, 72*, 427–436.

Bitzer, E., Trafford, V., & Leshem, S. (2018). The doctoral viva voce as a rite of passage into academia. In *A scholarship of doctoral education–On becoming a researcher* (pp. 229–248). Sun Press.

Carver, M. (2017). Limitations of corrective feedforward: A call for resubmission practices to become learning-oriented. *Journal of Academic Writing*.

Carver, M. (2020). English language teacher preparation. In R. Shanks (Ed.), *Teacher preparation in Scotland* (pp. 187–199). Emerald Publishing Limited.

Carver, M. (2023). Why do a doctorate? From 'PhD by publication' to 'PhD by impact'. *Research Intelligence, 155*, 34–35.

Chong, S. W. (2022). Research synthesis in applied linguistics: Facilitating research-pedagogy dialogue. *Language Teaching, 55*(1), 142–144.

Chong, S. W., & Plonsky, L. (2021). A primer on qualitative research synthesis in TESOL. *TESOL Quarterly, 55*(3), 1024–1034.

Craig, C. J. (2018). Metaphors of knowing, doing and being: Capturing experience in teaching and teacher education. *Teaching and Teacher Education, 69*, 300–311.

Ding, A., & Bruce, I. (2017). Developing EAP practitioners. In *The English for academic purposes practitioner: Operating on the edge of academia* (pp. 117–177). Springer.

Ding, A., Hyland, K., & Wong, L. (2019). EAP practitioner identity. In *Specialised English: New directions in ESP and EAP research and practice* (pp. 63–75). Routledge.

Farrell, T. S. (2017). *Research on reflective practice in TESOL*. Routledge.

Farrell, T. S. (2022). *Reflective practice in language teaching*. Cambridge University Press.

Gibbs, G. (1988). *Learning by doing*. Oxford Polytechnic University.

Goodson, I. F. (2000). The principled professional. *Prospects, 30*(2), 181–188.

Hall, E., & Wall, K. (2019). *Research methods for understanding professional learning*. Bloomsbury.

Hughes, J., Denley, P., & Whitehead, J. (1998). How do we make sense of the process of legitimising an educational action research thesis for the award of a PhD degree? A contribution to educational theory. *Educational Action Research, 6*(3), 427–451.

Kennedy, A. (2018). Developing a new ITE programme: A story of compliant and disruptive narratives across different cultural spaces. *European Journal of Teacher Education, 41*(5), 638–653.

Kerr, P. (2022). *30 trends in ELT*. Cambridge University Press.

Leshem, S. (2020). Identity formations of doctoral students on the route to achieving their doctorate. *Issues in Educational Research, 30*(1), 169–186.

Medgyes, P. (2017). The (ir) relevance of academic research for the language teacher. *ELT Journal, 71*(4), 491–498.

Mellow, J. D. (2002). Towards principled eclecticism in language teaching: The two-dimensional model and the centering principle. *TESL-EJ, 5*(4), 1–18.

Mitchell, V., Borgstrom, E., Murphy, S., Campbell, C., Sieminski, S., & Fraser, S. (2023). Exploring the experiences of distance learning students being supported to resubmit a final assignment following a fail result. *Assessment & Evaluation in Higher Education.* https://doi.org/10.1080/02602938.2023.2199953

Poole, A., Yue, S., & Liujinya, Y. (2021). 'We have the DNA of a university': Chinese english teachers' conceptions of classroom research. *Professional Development in Education.*

Proud, S. (2015). Resits in higher education: Merely a bar to jump over, or do they give a pedagogical 'leg up'? *Assessment & Evaluation in Higher Education, 40*(5), 681–697.

Quality Assurance Agency. (2020). *Characteristics statement: Doctoral degree.* https://www.qaa.ac.uk/docs/qaa/quality-code/doctoral-degree-characteristics-statement-2020.pdf

R'boul, H. (2023). *Postcolonial challenges to theory and practice in ELT and TESOL: Geopolitics of knowledge and epistemologies of the South.* Taylor & Francis.

Robinson, C. (2018). The landscape of professional doctorate provision in English higher education institutions: Inconsistencies, tensions and unsustainability. *London Review of Education, 16*(1), 90–103.

Sanganyado, E., Nunu, W. N., & Sanganyado, S. (2022). Towards a framework for embedding doctorateness in research proposals. *Innovations in Education and Teaching International.* https://doi.org/10.1080/14703297.2022.2124186

Sato, M., & Loewen, S. (2019). Do teachers care about research? The research–pedagogy dialogue. *ELT Journal, 73*(1), 1–10.

Schön, D. A. (1995). Knowing-in-action: The new scholarship requires a new epistemology. *Change: The Magazine of Higher Learning, 27*(6), 27–34.

Stapleton, P., & Shao, Q. (2018). A worldwide survey of MATESOL programs in 2014: Patterns and perspectives. *Language Teaching Research, 22*(1), 10–28.

Taylor, S. E. (2012). Changes in doctoral education: Implications for supervisors in developing early career researchers. *International Journal for Researcher Development, 3*(2), 118–138.

Trafford, V., & Leshem, S. (2008). *Stepping stones to achieving your doctorate.* McGraw-Hill.

Trafford, V., & Leshem, S. (2009). Doctorateness as a threshold concept. *Innovations in Education and Teaching International, 46*(3), 305–316.

Tupling, C. L., & Outhwaite, D. (2017). Developing an identity as an EdD leader: A reflexive narrative account. *Management in Education, 31*(4), 153–158.

Wellington, J. (2013). Searching for 'doctorateness'. *Studies in Higher Education, 38*(10), 1490–1503.

Willems, C. (2010). But what makes it doctoral? Taking on the traditionalists: Interdisciplinary, practice-led doctoral research in the creative industries-a case study in academic politics, research, rigour and relevance. *The International Journal of Interdisciplinary Social Sciences, 5*(7), 331–346.

Yazdani, S., & Shokooh, F. (2018). Defining doctorateness: A concept analysis. *International Journal of Doctoral Studies, 13*, 31.

Yuan, R., Lee, I., De Costa, P. I., Yang, M., & Liu, S. (2022). TESOL teacher educators in higher education: A review of studies from 2010 to 2020. *Language Teaching.*

To Test or Not to Test? Assessing the English Proficiency of International Applicants to a Scottish University with Reference to Educational Background

Eoin Jordan

1 Introduction

With a trend of increasing numbers of international students studying in UK higher education (HE) over the past 30 years,[1] the assessment at scale of international applicants' English language ability has become an important challenge for UK Higher Education Institutions (HEIs). While asking applicants to provide an English language test score to evidence their ability is one option open to institutions, careful consideration needs to be given to which tests and scores should be considered acceptable for each course. A significant number of applicants may also

---

[1] https://migrationobservatory.ox.ac.uk/resources/briefings/student-migration-to-the-uk/

E. Jordan (✉)
University of St Andrews, St Andrews, UK
e-mail: epj2@st-andrews.ac.uk

have English-medium study experience, and judgements need to be made regarding when this should or should not be considered sufficient evidence of English language ability for academic study.

With relevance to the issues noted in the previous paragraph, in this chapter I have detailed the development of procedures and online guidance to assess whether applicants for degree programmes at a Scottish HEI (University of St Andrews) possessed threshold English language proficiency for academic study based on their educational backgrounds, as well as related developments in how different English language test scores were used to evaluate proficiency at point of entry. The chapter begins with a detailed description of the context of the innovation, noting the complexities and different stakeholders involved in evaluating English language ability for entry onto degree programmes at the University of St Andrews (hereafter, St Andrews), as well as the decision-making body for published admissions requirements. The remainder of the chapter presents a chronological and reflective account of the development of English language entry requirements at St Andrews from 2019 onwards.

Defining Innovation

The term "innovation" is defined in this chapter as "the implementation of a new or significantly improved product (good or service) or process, a new marketing method, or a new organisational method in business practices, workplace organisation or external relations", in line with Vincent-Lancrin et al. (2017, p. 7). In this instance, the innovation detailed constitutes significantly improved processes and practice in evaluating English language ability.

The developments described in this chapter were innovative in adopting a transparent, holistic, and inclusive approach to evaluating English language proficiency for large numbers of international applicants, and in aiming to ensure that, to the greatest extent possible, applicants with significant and successful English-medium educational experience were not asked to obtain additional English language proficiency test scores to evidence their ability. They were also innovative in working within the constraints of immigration requirements and guidance from UK Visas and Immigration (UKVI) regarding how HEIs are able to assess English language ability for international students who require a visa to study in the UK.

The definition of innovation employed here focuses on organisational change, which contrasts with some other definitions seen in language education literature that have a stronger pedagogical focus. For instance, Carless (2013) defines innovation as "an attempt to bring about educational improvement by doing something which is perceived by implementers as new" (p. 1). More recently, East (2022) focuses specifically on pedagogical innovation. The innovation described in this chapter also fits to some extent with the Carless definition, given that better assessment of English language ability at point of entry for students seems likely to have educational benefits, by ensuring students have a level of ability to engage meaningfully in their studies. However, this chapter primarily aims to draw readers' attention to innovation that extends beyond the purely pedagogical, while still having an important impact on learning and teaching.

My Role in This Innovation

As Director of the International Education Institute, I lead the part of the university that houses expertise on English language teaching and assessment, and I also have expertise in this area myself. Based on this positioning within the institution, I proposed and led the implementation of the innovations described in this chapter, in collaboration and consultation with the key stakeholders described in later sections.

Ethical Considerations

The online information about English language entry requirements for University of St Andrews, which is the focal point of this chapter, is in the public domain, and therefore institutional identity has not been masked. Internal institutional information that is not in the public domain has not been shared, and the identities of individual stakeholders other than the author himself have been masked. The text of the chapter, which has been written as an individual reflective account by the author, was also shared for comment by key internal stakeholders prior to publication.

2 Why Is English Language Entry Assessment Important for St Andrews and Other UK HEIs?

The assessment of applicants' English language ability prior to them being issued with an unconditional offer to study at a university in the UK, such as St Andrews, is important to a wide range of stakeholders. I have outlined the key external and internal stakeholders in the case of St Andrews in the following subsections, to illustrate the range of considerations that influence how English language proficiency is assessed. It should be noted that the analysis below gives primary focus to the sometimes conflicting interests of different parts of the university, rather than treating the institution as a single entity. However, ultimately these different interests feed in to global decision-making by university senior leadership, who need to balance international student recruitment requirements (to ensure both a beneficial international community and adequate income to finance activities) against the possibility of reputational damage (e.g. from students not having adequate English language ability to succeed on their programmes), and potentially even the risk of having the institution's licence to sponsor international students revoked by UKVI.

Finally, in addition to the key stakeholders listed below, it is worth noting the interest that language testing organisations, who benefit financially from students being required to take English language proficiency tests, have in their tests being recognised as suitable evidence of English language ability by individual institutions. While these organisations were not considered to be "key stakeholders" for decision-making by the university, the competitive market of language testing options for university applicants is a feature of the broader landscape in UK higher education (HE).

Key External Stakeholders: Prospective Students

Prospective students who wish to enrol on a course at St Andrews need to meet specified English language entry requirements, alongside other academic requirements. In addition to having a role in managing overall student numbers, the primary purpose of these requirements is to make as transparent as possible to prospective students the level of ability, or at least previous performance, that is needed to succeed on a course. While English language test score requirements may be presented in a fairly straightforward manner, a considerable amount of qualitative detail is needed for a prospective applicant to understand whether their individual educational background may meet English language requirements.

Given the gatekeeping role of English language requirements (i.e. entry to a university is only typically possible if these are met) for prospective students, the setting of slightly higher or lower English language test scores as entry requirements for degree programmes may influence whether prospective students choose to apply for the programme or not. For someone who feels they may struggle to achieve a higher English language test score, programmes that require lower test scores may appear a safer option. On the other hand, some prospective applicants may view higher English language test score requirements as an indicator of a higher quality or more in-demand course.

Key External Stakeholders: Student Recruitment Agents and High School Counsellors

Both student recruitment agents (for all levels of study) and high school counsellors (for undergraduate study) are involved in advising students about possible HE study options, so need clear information about what English language entry requirements are. These groups are likely to be motivated to provide their clients with the most favourable offers of study possible from HEIs, in terms of both academic and English language requirements.

Key External Stakeholder: UK Visas and Immigration (UKVI)

As compliance with UKVI guidance and regulations is a necessity for all HEIs if they wish to continue to be able to sponsor visas for international students, the framework that UKVI's policy documentation provides can be seen as an essential underlying framework on which St Andrews and other institutions develop their own individual English language requirements. Details about current UKVI requirements and guidance can be found online[2] (also see Home Office (2024)). It should be noted that documentation in this area is constantly evolving, and that some aspects of the requirements have changed since the innovations reported on here were first implemented in summer 2019. Statements of changes to immigration rules over time are available online.[3] In the subsections below, I have highlighted two components of the overall UKVI framework that are of particular relevance to the design of English language entry requirements.

Specification of a Minimum Level of English Language Ability

UKVI documentation indicates that all students studying on degree programmes in HE in the UK should demonstrate that they have a level of English language ability that corresponds to at least B2 on the Common European Framework of Reference for Languages (CEFR) (Council of Europe, 2024) across the four skills of reading, writing, speaking, and listening. For students studying on "pre-degree" courses, which provide a pathway onto degree programmes, the minimum requirement is at least B1. CEFR is a framework that was developed by the Council of Europe to describe levels of ability in any language. It consists of "can do"

---

[2] https://www.gov.uk/student-visa/knowledge-of-english
[3] https://www.gov.uk/government/collections/immigration-rules-statement-of-changes

statements in a wide range of domains, as well as overall descriptors for each level. On the scale, B2 represents the third highest level. This is a substantial level of ability that is likely only to be achieved after many years of study. No specific rationale is provided as to why UKVI felt that B2 is an appropriate level for academic study on degree programmes in HE; however, can-do descriptors at this level describe engagement with complex text and abstract topics, which appears appropriate to academic study at degree level in English.

Nationality Exemptions

Public-facing web information[4] indicates that nationals of the following countries do not need to provide evidence of English language ability for visa application purposes:

- Antigua and Barbuda
- Australia
- the Bahamas
- Barbados
- Belize
- The British overseas territories
- Canada
- Dominica
- Grenada
- Guyana
- Ireland
- Jamaica
- Malta
- New Zealand
- St Kitts and Nevis
- St Lucia
- St Vincent and the Grenadines
- Trinidad and Tobago

---

[4] https://www.gov.uk/student-visa/knowledge-of-english

- UK
- USA

In UKVI's guidance document (Home Office, 2024), reference is made to nationals of a "majority English speaking country" (p. 11). While the list of countries is redacted in the guidance document, it seems likely that the countries considered to be majority English speaking are the ones listed above. The list excludes many countries and territories where English has official status.

Key Internal Stakeholder: The Receiving School/Department/Institute

The schools/departments/institutes that teach students are important stakeholders in setting English language entry requirements. In general, my own interactions with academic teaching staff indicate that a primary concern on their part is that students who join degree programmes have an adequate level of English language ability to cope with their course. If a student struggles with English, as well as being a challenge for the student themselves, this may also result in additional school/department/institute resources being committed to support the student. A further concern here is the difficulty of managing a student who is failing on a course, if this is on account of their language ability. Counterbalanced against these concerns is the need to ensure that courses have sufficient numbers of students to make them viable, which is a potential motivator for wanting requirements not to be too high, or too difficult to evidence.

Key Internal Stakeholder: Registry Office

The Registry Office has multiple functions within St Andrews, one of which is managing visa compliance for international students. This function may sit elsewhere in other UK HEIs, but each institution should have a primary point of contact with UKVI, and some mechanism for ensuring that visa compliance considerations are taken into account with regard to admissions decision-making. In the St Andrews context, Registry's "voice" within discussions about admissions processes is influenced significantly by considerations about the efficiency and accuracy of application processing (an important consideration for an institution that receives a high volume of applications), as well as ensuring that admissions decision-making is compliant with the most up to date visa guidance from UKVI, and communications from UKVI received via other channels (e.g. audits).

The concern with UKVI requirements is motivated by the understanding that UKVI has the power to remove an HEI's right to sponsor visas for international students if it believes practice at the institution to be problematic. Indeed, it has previously used these powers with other institutions (e.g. Batty, 2012).

Key Internal Stakeholder: Admissions Office

As a selective HEI, St Andrews receives a high volume of applications relative to total available places. However, there is still significant competition between selective institutions to recruit and convert the most able students. It is also the case that not all programmes and levels of study are equally popular, and so in some areas there is a greater need to invest in converting applicants into students than in others.

These considerations mean that the Admissions Office has a strong focus on both ensuring that the application to enrolment journey for suitably qualified applicants is as smooth as possible, and maintaining positive relationships with student recruitment agents and high school counsellors to ensure that they continue to support prospective students in applying to St Andrews. Both of these areas of focus are influenced by the English language entry requirements set for degree programmes. If these are set too high, are inappropriate, or are difficult to navigate, then this will make the application to enrolment journey less smooth, and may result in some strong applicants dropping out of the process. Additionally, high school counsellors based at English-medium international schools may feel that education at their school should be adequate evidence of English language ability, and may consider it inappropriate for their students to be asked to provide an English language test score in addition to evidence of their high school education in order to enrol. They may also find that their students are asked to provide English language test scores for some HEIs but not others, as each institution sets its own requirements. For recruitment agents too, if they are dealing with prospective students who have attended English-medium schools, they may not look favourably on these students being asked to provide additional evidence of English language ability, particularly if competitor institutions do not require this.

Key Internal Stakeholder: International Education Institute

In my role as Director of the International Education Institute, there are several ways in which the English language requirements set across the university impact on the work of the institute that I lead. Firstly, some of these requirements apply to courses that the institute delivers, and so the concerns outlined in the section titled "Key Internal Stakeholder: The Receiving School/Department/Institute" apply.

Secondly, prior to the innovation described in this chapter, I and other colleagues in the institute were regularly consulted on individual applicant cases regarding whether different types of evidence of English language ability were appropriate or not. These consultations originated variously from other schools/departments, the Registry Office, and the Admissions Office, and were brought to us on the basis that the institute was a centre of expertise within the university on English language teaching and assessment.

Thirdly, the institute runs a service, currently titled "Academic English Service (AES)", that supports degree programme students who are users of English as an additional language with developing their academic English skills. If English language entry requirements were to be set in a manner that allowed a large number of students with inadequate English language ability to enter the university, the service would potentially not be able to meet the needs of these students without significant additional resources.

Finally, the institute delivers pre-sessional courses for international students who are users of English as an additional language, which are primarily utilised by offer-holders who have narrowly failed to achieve the English language test scores they require to enter their degree programmes in schools/departments. If these offer-holders perform successfully on their assessments at the end of their pre-sessional course, they are able to use this as evidence of English language ability to meet the English language condition on their degree programme offer. As the pre-sessional courses offer a route to meeting English language requirements for a wide variety of degree programmes, the English language entry requirements for the pre-sessional courses need to be carefully aligned with those of the destination degree programmes, to ensure that entry and exit levels of English language ability for pre-sessional students are not too far apart.

3   Decision-Making Committee for Admissions Requirements

The university's designated committee for deciding on changes to admissions requirements of any kind, including English language requirements, is the "Qualifications Group". This committee meets several times in the academic year, and may additionally consider proposed changes via asynchronous online discussion between meetings. It includes representation of academic staff, as well as representatives from the Admissions and Registry Offices.

4   English Language Entry Requirements and Evaluation Process Prior to the 2019–2020 Academic Year

Prior to the 2019–2020 academic year, a set of English language requirements that had previously been approved by the Qualifications Group were published on the university website. These requirements were developed prior to me joining the university in February 2018. The English language entry requirements webpages provided sets of language test scores that could be used to evidence ability for entry onto degree programmes at the university. However, there were several issues that had become evident to me by the summer of 2019.

One issue was that while required International English Language Testing System (IELTS) (IELTS, 2024) overall scores and scores in each of the four language skills of reading, writing, speaking, and listening were stated for each programme of study, this level of detail was not available for other tests. Indeed, the web information was organised around IELTS scores, as the most submitted test score, rather than CEFR levels of ability. A benchmarking table for IELTS was provided, but this focused only on overall scores. While component skill scores follow the same scale for some tests listed (e.g. Pearson Test of English/PTE), they do not for others (e.g. TOEFL iBT), meaning that it was not possible to work out what score was required in each skill for each test. In general, the focus also appeared to be on looking at overall scores, rather than individual skill component scores.

The exact score requirements for different areas and levels of study had also evolved to include a significant number of minor differences in both overall and skill component scores. This reflected different priorities in different disciplines and levels of study, but also meant that the information presented appeared quite complex.

Information presented about whether previous English-medium study experience would count as acceptable evidence of English language ability was limited in detail, which prompted enquiries from applicants, but offered no clear guidance on which to base decisions. It also meant that some applicants were asked to provide English language test scores to evidence their language ability, despite having graduated from English-medium degree programmes at internationally high-ranking institutions where English was clearly the medium of instruction.

Additionally, a range of high school English language qualifications, mainly from national curricula in European Union countries, were listed as being acceptable evidence of English language ability, even though benchmarking for most of these qualifications suggested a level of ability that was lower than that indicated by IELTS scores required for degree programmes.

A further issue in terms of process was that it was not clear to me exactly where final decision-making power lay for cases where I was consulted about applicant documentation to evidence English language ability. In cases where disagreements arose between myself and an academic member of staff in the receiving School for a programme, it was unclear whose judgement would ultimately be followed.

Overall, while the published English language requirements in place prior to September 2019 did cover the majority of applications received, and consultation did consistently occur on cases where the evidence of English language ability presented by an applicant did not meet published requirements, there was scope for enhancement in terms of the detailed benchmarking of the English language test scores required, and explanation of the conditions under which an applicant might use previous educational experience as evidence of their English language ability.

5 Initial Changes to Requirements and Process in the 2019–2020 Academic Year

Introduction of CEFR-Benchmarked Language Test Profiles Covering Four Skills

To improve the presentation of information about scores on different English language tests that were required for each course, I worked with colleagues in the institute to develop a set of language "profiles" benchmarked to CEFR. The starting point for this benchmarking was a recognition that historical English language requirements at St Andrews had been presented primarily in terms of IELTS scores, and therefore the CEFR scale developed for the language profiles needed to have good alignment with the increments of the IELTS evaluation scale. The scale incorporated plus/minus notification at each CEFR level to achieve this goal, resulting in the scale and IELTS alignment shown in Table 1. Existing overall and component IELTS test score entry requirements for courses ranged from 5.0 to 8.0, so the CEFR scale only covered this range.

Table 1 CEFR scale for language profiles with IELTS alignment

CEFR level	IELTS score equivalent
C1+	8.0
C1	7.5
C1-	7.0
B2+	6.5
B2	6.0
B2-	5.5
B1+	5.0

Each language profile created consisted of specific configurations of an overall CEFR level and CEFR levels on each of the four skills of listening, reading, speaking, and writing. Two variants of each profile were also developed—one variant that only listed Secure English Language Test (SELT) scores, and another that allowed for a wider range of English language tests. SELTs are UKVI-endorsed tests that can be used for immigration purposes.[5] The SELT-only profiles needed to be used for pre-degree programmes, for which SELT provision is a visa requirement for almost all students, while the profiles allowing for a wider range of tests were to be used for degree programmes, for which a wider range of tests were acceptable.

Scores for all acceptable tests were then benchmarked against the different CEFR levels, with reference to each test's own publicly available benchmarking, and UKVI's published benchmarking for SELTs (see footnote 4). Once this alignment work was complete, a set of profiles was created in the format shown in Figs. 1 (a) and (b), allowing all equivalent acceptable test scores to be presented together in a single table. Profiles were labelled by number (with the lowest number representing the highest requirement), and with the letter "S" for SELT, "D" for Degree Programme (with "D" profiles allowing a wider range of non-SELT tests), and "M" for BSc Medicine requirements, which only allowed for an IELTS test score to be submitted. This gave an overall total of 20 profiles, although some of these represented the same CEFR levels in "D" and "S" variants. The list of profiles with associated CEFR thresholds is shown in

---

[5] https://www.gov.uk/guidance/prove-your-english-language-abilities-with-a-secure-english-language-test-selt

Profile 7-D (Direct entry)

The table below includes all approved English language tests and scores for Profile 7-D (Direct entry).

All tests listed below are in-person tests.

Test	Minimum component scores (Listening, Reading, Writing, Speaking)	Minimum overall score
Cambridge English Qualifications	169	176
IELTS (Academic)	6.0	6.5
LanguageCert International ESOL B2 (Listening, Reading, Writing, Speaking)	66% (or 66% at C1 level)	76% (or 66% at C1 level)
PSI Skills for English UKVI 4SC1	Pass	Pass
PTE Academic	50	58
TOEFL iBT	Listening: 12 Reading: 13 Writing: 21 Speaking: 18	79
Trinity Integrated Skills in English (ISE) II	Merit (or Pass at level III)	Distinction (or Pass at level III)
Pre-sessional/AEQC	7	11

Profile 7-S (SELT)

The table below includes all approved English language tests and scores for Profile 7-S (SELT).

All tests listed below are in-person tests.

Test	Minimum component scores (Listening, Reading, Writing, Speaking)	Minimum overall score
IELTS for UKVI (Academic)	6.0	6.5
LanguageCert International ESOL SELT B2 (Listening, Reading, Writing, Speaking)	66% (or 66% at C1 level)	76% (or 66% at C1 level)
PSI Skills for English UKVI 4SC1	Pass	Pass
PTE Academic UKVI	50	58
Trinity Integrated Skills in English (ISE) SELT II	Merit (or Pass at level III SELT)	Distinction (or Pass at level III SELT)

Fig. 1 (a) Sample language profile (Retrieved from https://www.st-andrews.ac.uk/subjects/entry/language-requirements/profiles/7-d/); (b) Sample language profile (Retrieved from https://www.st-andrews.ac.uk/subjects/entry/language-requirements/profiles/7-s/)

Fig. 2. Each degree programme (or faculty at undergraduate level) was then assigned a profile equivalent to the IELTS scores they required at the time of development.

These new profiles enabled a range of different tests, including all approved SELTs, to be displayed on equal footing, rather than privileging one test (IELTS) and treating others as "alternatives". The profiles also meant that each degree programme had minimum score requirements listed explicitly for all acceptable English language tests, rather than requiring users to try to work out what they might need on tests other than IELTs via a benchmarking table.

CEFR levels for each English language test profile

Profile	Listening	Reading	Writing	Speaking	Overall score
1-D	C1+	C1+	C1+	C1+	C1+
2-M	C1-	C1-	C1-	C1-	C1-
3-D or 3-S	B2+	B2+	B2+	B2+	C1-
4-D or 4-S	B2	B2	C1-	B2	C1-
5-D or 5-S	B2	B2	B2	B2	C1-
6-D or 6-S	B2	B2	B2+	B2	B2+
7-D or 7-S	B2	B2	B2	B2	B2+
8-S	B2-	B2-	B2+	B2-	B2+
9-S	B2-	B2-	B2-	B2-	B2+
10-S	B2-	B2-	B2	B2-	B2
11-S	B2-	B2-	B2-	B2-	B2
12-S	B1+	B1+	B2	B1+	B2
13-S	B1+	B1+	B1+	B1+	B2
14-S	B1+	B1+	B2-	B1+	B2-
15-S	B1+	B1+	B1+	B1+	B2-

Fig. 2 List of language profiles with associated CEFR thresholds (Retrieved from https://www.st-andrews.ac.uk/subjects/entry/language-requirements/profiles/reference-tables/)

Guidance on When Educational Background Can Be Used to Evidence English Language Requirements at Undergraduate Level

Based on reflection on queries received in the preceding year regarding whether applicants who attended various English-medium high schools should be required to provide a test score to evidence their English language ability or not, I liaised with colleagues to develop text that could be used to inform decisions. This text was intended to provide guidance for both applicants and staff. Ultimately, the following text was approved by the Qualifications Group for all degree programmes other than Medicine (which required different arrangements) and published online[6]:

You should not need to provide an English language test score to evidence your English language ability if one of the following applies:

- *You are a national of the UK, Canada or one of the countries considered by UKVI to be a majority English-speaking country.*
- *You have a secondary/high school leaving qualification that:*
  - *Was taken at a school with a substantial English language educational environment, as evidenced by an appropriate online presence, and at which you were registered as a student for at least the final two years of your secondary/high school education.*
  - *Includes at least one subject with a substantial component of writing in English.*

In the case that an applicant was studying at a school with a substantial English language educational environment, it appeared highly likely that they would have practised extensively their English language reading, listening, and speaking skills; however, if they were studying only quantitative subjects (e.g. A-levels in Mathematics, Further Mathematics and Physics), then it may not have been the case that they had benefited from extensive experience in writing in English. Given the need to be

---

[6] https://web.archive.org/web/20200929080832/https://www.st-andrews.ac.uk/subjects/entry/language-requirements/undergraduate/.

confident that students had appropriate levels of ability across all four skills, and the considerable amount of university assessment that requires students to write in English, it seemed appropriate to include the latter part of the requirements.

Only accepting qualifications from high schools with a "substantial English language educational environment" was in recognition of the fact that English-medium study can describe a wide variety of educational experiences, some of which might involve limited usage of English outside of scheduled classes and/or not all classes being taught in English. The two-year period of enrolment required was set in line with the typical two-year duration of study for high school qualifications such as A-levels.

The bullet point relating to nationality was included to allow continuity of practice from the previous year, as there were concerns that making changes to requirements for these nationalities would be operationally problematic.

Guidance on When Educational Background Can Be Used to Evidence English Language Requirements at Postgraduate Level

At postgraduate level, a lack of clear guidance about when English-medium undergraduate study could be used to evidence English language ability had previously resulted in many applicants with undergraduate English-medium degrees being asked to submit English language tests. In some cases, these applicants were graduates of very highly ranked international universities, and there appeared to be a risk of reputational damage in not recognising this as legitimate evidence of English language ability. It was also the case that applicants from countries where English has official status, at least in part as a legacy of British colonialism, who presented with English-medium degrees from that country were often asked to provide an English language test to evidence their ability. This position seemed problematic in that it appeared to assert the superiority of English in some contexts (e.g. the UK, the USA) over others (e.g. Singapore, Zimbabwe).

Kachru's three circles model (Kachru, 1991) seemed an appropriate "lens" through which to consider how postgraduate applicants' educational background could be used to evidence English language ability. Rather than there being a single "English", the model recognises that multiple varieties of English exist globally, and categorises the contexts of these varieties into "inner circle", "outer circle", and "expanding outer circle" countries. Inner circle countries are those where English is the first or native language for the majority of inhabitants—examples would be the UK, the USA, Australia, and New Zealand. Outer circle countries are those where English has official status and may be used as the main language of internal communication in particular domains (e.g. schools, courts), usually for historical reasons related to British colonialism, but it is not the primary language of day-to-day communication for the majority of the population. Examples of outer circle countries are Malaysia and Zimbabwe. Finally, expanding outer circle countries are those where English has no official role, but may still be studied in schools and used for communication with people from other countries. Japan and China are examples of expanding outer circle countries.

In developing guidance based on the three circles framework, I started by considering UKVI's list of majority English-speaking countries, together with the UK, to be broadly representative of the inner circle countries. I then considered all countries where English has official status in some form to be representative of the outer circle countries, and all remaining countries to constitute the expanding outer circle. I then developed guidance text to indicate that English-medium degrees from legitimate HE institutions in inner circle and outer circle countries should be considered suitable evidence of English language ability. Within expanding outer circle countries, only English-medium degrees from institutions that offer a substantial number of English-medium degree programmes, and also that are highly ranked internationally, would be considered suitable evidence of language ability. The requirement for the institution to have a substantial number of English-medium degree programmes was intended as an indicator of confidence that investment had been made in infrastructure and support for English language delivery, while the ranking requirement was intended as an indicator that the institution held itself to high international standards.

One particular challenge was compiling a list of outer circle countries to share on the website. English having "official status" can cover a range of different scenarios, not just having English listed as an official language—for example, it may be the primary language of instruction in schools, but not an official language. To compile an accurate and inclusive list, I triangulated information from multiple sources. I started with a list of countries where English has official status on Wikipedia,[7] and then attempted to verify whether other sources such as the CIA World Factbook[8] also supported the claim. I also separately researched candidate outer circle countries that were missing from the Wikipedia list (e.g. India) to consider whether they should be included or not. After compiling a list of countries/territories, for smaller entities, I then searched online to see if there was any evidence that an HEI existed there, as it would not have been meaningful to include countries on the list that did not have any HE institutions based locally. After excluding a small number of locations on this basis, I finalised the list.

After consultation with colleagues internally, and in consideration of UKVI guidance, it was decided that information would most effectively be displayed with a slight deviation from the three circles model. Information for applicants with degrees from the UK was positioned first, followed by information for applicants with degrees from remaining inner circle and outer circle countries combined. Information for applicants with degrees from expanding outer circle countries was placed after this. The following text was ultimately approved by the Qualifications Group and published online[9]:

You should not need to provide an English language test score to evidence your English language ability if one of the following applies:

- *You have completed a UK undergraduate degree with at least the final two years taught in the UK, or you have completed a UK postgraduate degree that was taught entirely in the UK.*

---

[7] https://en.wikipedia.org/wiki/List_of_countries_and_territories_where_English_is_an_official_language.

[8] https://www.cia.gov/the-world-factbook/.

[9] https://web.archive.org/web/20201028152332/https://www.st-andrews.ac.uk/subjects/entry/language-requirements/postgraduate/.

- *You have completed a qualification equivalent to a UK undergraduate or postgraduate degree taught entirely in English at a nationally accredited English-medium university (as evidenced by its web presence) in one of the following countries/territories where English has official status:*
- *Anguilla*
- *Antigua and Barbuda*
- *Australia*
- *Barbados*
- *Belize*
- *Botswana*
- *British Virgin Islands*
- *Cameroon*
- *Canada*
- *Cayman Islands*
- *Cook Islands*
- *Dominica*
- *Fiji*
- *Ghana*
- *Grenada*
- *Guyana*
- *Hong Kong*
- *India*
- *Ireland*
- *Jamaica*
- *Kenya*
- *Kiribati*
- *Lesotho*
- *Liberia*
- *Malawi*
- *Malta*
- *Marshall Islands*
- *Mauritius*
- *Montserrat*
- *Namibia*
- *New Zealand*
- *Nigeria*

- *Pakistan*
- *Papua New Guinea*
- *Philippines*
- *Rwanda*
- *Seychelles*
- *Sierra Leone*
- *Singapore*
- *Solomon Islands*
- *South Africa*
- *South Sudan*
- *St Kitts and Nevis*
- *St Lucia*
- *St Vincent and the Grenadines*
- *Sudan*
- *Swaziland*
- *Tanzania*
- *The Bahamas*
- *The Gambia*
- *Tonga*
- *Trinidad and Tobago*
- *Turks and Caicos Islands*
- *Uganda*
- *United States of America*
- *Vanuatu*
- *Zambia*
- *Zimbabwe*

Undergraduate or postgraduate degrees taught through the medium of English from countries which are not listed above may also be considered as evidence of English language ability if both of the following conditions are met:

- *The web presence of the awarding institution clearly evidences a substantial number of degree programmes taught through the medium of English.*

- The awarding institution is prominent in international university rankings (typically, the institution should feature in the top 300 of current QS university rankings).

The three circles model was not as useful for informing undergraduate English language entry requirements, as a large proportion of international undergraduate applicants have followed an international high school curriculum/qualification (e.g. International Baccalaureate), rather than a national one. In fact, many of the national high school qualifications from outer circle countries (e.g. Malaysia, Kenya, Nigeria) are not currently acceptable qualifications to apply directly for undergraduate programmes at St Andrews, and so students who have taken these need to apply for a pre-degree programme, and would therefore be required to submit a SELT to evidence their language ability under UKVI rules.

Developing a Clear Decision-Making Process

To operationalise the new guidelines, it was agreed that decisions on whether English language conditions should be applied to offers would be made by Registry staff, rather than the offer-makers in schools, or the Admissions Office (although offer-makers could still make recommendations, and include a rationale for any unusual cases). Registry staff would then apply English conditions to offers for applicants who did not currently meet the English language requirements published on the university website. For postgraduate applicants, decisions were taken entirely based on publicly available information on the university website. However, for undergraduate applicants one area where further internal guidance was needed was on what could be considered as a "subject with a substantial component of writing in English". An internal-only list of examples was developed for different international and national qualifications, to ensure consistency in decision-making in this area. If Registry staff were unsure about any cases, these were escalated via a spreadsheet where both I (from a language ability perspective) and a senior Registry colleague (from a visa compliance perspective) reviewed cases and left comments. A final decision was then made by the senior Registry colleague on whether an English language condition needed to be applied. In principle, if the applicant did not require a visa for study, the decision was based on my recommendation alone.

6   Further Changes to Requirements in 2021–2022

Development of Requirement for a Minimum Grade in a Subject with a Substantial Component of Writing for Undergraduate Applicants with English-Medium Education

Following discussions during the 2020–2021 academic year, a minimum score requirement was introduced on the "subject with a substantial component of writing in English" for undergraduate applicants who wished to evidence their English language ability via their educational background. The new requirement was that such applicants needed to have a grade equivalent to a B or higher on this subject. While undergraduate offers would typically require grades at this level or higher anyway, it was noted that applicants may receive offers that ask for a certain number of subject grades, and that it might sometimes be possible to meet the offer conditions with subjects that did not require a great deal of writing in English, but perform poorly on other subjects which required more writing in English. The previous internal guidance document was developed further to indicate what grades would be required on different subjects in different national and international high school qualifications.

Making Internal Guidance External

A further enhancement in this cycle was to publish the guidance that was previously internal-only on the university website, to allow for greater transparency for applicants. The information now available lists different high school qualifications and grades that can be used to meet the "subject with a substantial component of writing in English" requirement at undergraduate level.

7 Further Changes to Requirements in 2023–2024

Additional Documentation Required from Postgraduate Applicants for English-Medium Degrees from Countries Not on the UKVI Majority English-Speaking Country List

In response to UK-wide concerns about fraudulent applications from a number of regions globally, a senior member of Registry staff and I discussed measures we could take to guard against this possibility. An outcome of this discussion was that the Registry Office proposed to the Qualifications Group that an additional English language proficiency statement from Education Counseling and Credit Transfer Information Service[10] (ECCTIS) should accompany all degree programme certificates and transcripts used to evidence English language ability from countries that are not on UKVI's majority English-speaking country list. These statements from ECCTIS, which may also be used for other immigration purposes, represent a further check regarding whether documentation submitted was genuine, but still allow applicants to use their educational experience to evidence their English language ability. The proposal was approved, and web information was updated accordingly for the 2023–2024 student recruitment cycle. For easy reference, Fig. 3 summarises all key developments in English language requirements over time from prior to 2019 through to 2024.

---

[10] https://www.ecctis.com/visasandnationality.

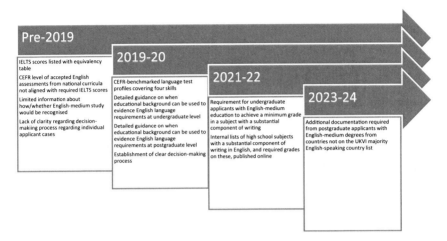

Fig. 3 Timeline of English language entry requirement developments (pre-2019 to 2024)

8 What Has Worked Well

More Consistent Decision-Making

The development of extensive guidance, as well as clarification of the decision-making process, has resulted in more consistent decision-making across similar programmes, while still allowing for differences between programmes where this is intentional. This increase in consistency has particularly been the case for postgraduate programmes, where offer-making has historically been more decentralised than for undergraduate programmes, where the Admissions Office plays a greater central role.

More Inclusive and Nuanced Approach to Evidencing English Language Ability

In general, the changes made have been successful in ensuring that English language test scores are requested from applicants in cases where there is a significant risk that they do not have a level of language ability to enable success on their degree programme, but that test scores are not requested by default in most cases where an applicant has engaged in extensive English-medium study experience in a substantial English language environment. This more nuanced approach has been beneficial in maintaining positive relationships with many good-quality English-medium high schools, which could interpret a request for their graduates to provide a language test score to enter the university as a comment on the quality of the education that they provide. At postgraduate level too, the new guidelines allow for recognition of an increased range of English-medium degree programmes to be used as evidence of English language ability, while still limiting this possibility to institutions where a substantial English language educational environment exists. The way in which the requirements have been presented also strikes a more welcoming stance to applicants than previous information. This is particularly the case for applicants from outer circle countries, for whom the guidelines represent an explicit acknowledgement of the value and legitimacy of English used in those contexts.

Clearer and More Even-Handed Information about English Language Tests

For students who do need to take an English language proficiency test, the new profiles provide all the information they need in one place, in a way that does not privilege any one test over another. This allows applicants to see clearly what scores they need to achieve on each test side by side, without needing to refer to any additional benchmarking tables. The format of the profiles has also made it easier to incorporate information from new SELTs, as they are approved.

9 Ongoing Issues and Lessons Learned

While some improvements have been made to the presentation of information online, the complex nature of English language entry requirements would benefit from more dynamic online presentation. For example, the inclusion of drop-down menus to filter only details that are relevant to the user would make this information much easier to engage with for prospective students. This has not yet been implemented at St Andrews owing to web development resource constraints.

A further ongoing issue has been changes to score benchmarking between test providers, and lack of alignment between test-provider benchmarking and the benchmarking published by UKVI. This has resulted in a need to make some minor adjustments to threshold test scores over the past few years. Changes to tests, or the introduction of new tests by currently recognised providers, also require analysis and potential changes to published information about acceptable tests and scores.

Through the process of working with colleagues to develop English language entry requirements at St Andrews, an important lesson I learned was that highly specific guidance is needed for both staff involved with application processing and prospective students. When detailed and specific information is not available, this can lead to significant numbers of queries arising, given the large number of applicants, and risks inconsistent evaluations by different staff members. However, the development of detailed guidance takes time, and requires reflection on the types of queries or irregular cases that arise after the introduction of new requirements. With this in mind, the development process detailed in this chapter, where detailed guidance is drafted and then initially only shared internally, worked well as an approach. This allowed a period for adjustments to be made to guidelines before they are published externally.

A further lesson learned has been that English language entry requirements require regular review and updating, to keep pace with developments in the wider environment. These changes may include: the introduction or removal of English language tests; the recognition of new SELTs by UKVI; changes in UKVI published guidance; changes in test-provider or UKVI benchmarking for tests; and identification of patterns for applicant fraud. Requirements of this type are not easily changed in the middle of an annual student recruitment cycle, so conducting a detailed annual review is advisable, leaving enough time ahead of the next application cycle to make any necessary changes.

For readers who are involved in setting and presenting English language entry requirements for higher education courses, as well as those involved in making decisions on individual applicant cases, I offer several points of advice based on the developments and reflections in this chapter. The first point is that, given the inherent complexity involved in this area, minimising the number of different levels or profiles of English language test scores required for different degree programmes is desirable, from the viewpoint of presenting information that is easy to understand and work with for both university staff and applicants. This simplification of test score requirements needs to be counterbalanced against the educational and marketing value that may be derived from maintaining marginal differences in levels/scores across degree programmes, but my own experience suggests that this value is itself likely to be marginal. Simplifying overall requirements will generally require all receiving schools/departments/institutes to take a pragmatic approach to entry requirement setting that recognises the benefits of aligning with other schools/departments/institutes, rather than focusing only on their own particular preferences.

A further point of advice is that the evaluation of English language ability based on educational background has considerable scope to result in inconsistent judgements being made, unless detailed and specific guidance is put in place for staff involved in decision-making. While it is ultimately desirable to be as transparent as possible by making decision-making criteria and guidance publicly available, it may be advisable to keep some parts of the criteria/guidance for staff-only use initially, to allow for a period of refining and adjusting. After this initial trial period, edited documentation can be shared publicly for reference by applicants.

A final point of advice is that establishing a clear process for evaluating individual applicant cases will be critical to ensure smooth decision-making. This process will likely need to include more than one person, and so it is of particular importance that everyone involved is clear in advance on where final decision-making power lies, to avoid reaching an impasse when there are disagreements.

10 Conclusion

This chapter has detailed the development of English language entry requirements for prospective students at St Andrews, as well as related processes related. The newly developed requirements were successful in giving greater recognition to applicants' previous English-medium study, while still ensuring compliance with UKVI requirements. However, the new approach initially generated additional workload for staff, and some feedback was received that the online information about the requirements was confusing. These issues were addressed by creating more detailed internal guidance materials for application processing staff, and by making some improvements to the presentation of online guidance for applicants. A major lesson learned was that, when dealing with a large volume of applications, highly detailed guidance is required to reduce the number of instances where text may be interpreted divergently by decision-makers. Changes over time in the wider environment also mean that entry requirements such as this need to be reviewed on a regular basis.

For other practitioners grappling with similar challenges, several points of advice were noted. Firstly, aiming to minimise the number of different English language levels/test profiles required institutionally is desirable. Secondly, criteria and guidance to facilitate evaluation of educational background as a measure of English language ability should be detailed and specific, and should be made available to applicants to the greatest extent possible. Thirdly, a clear decision-making process is essential—in particular, all people involved in the process should be aware in advance where final decision-making power lies.

Finally, my intention has been for this chapter to highlight the complexities involved in evaluating English language ability for entry to university in a UK context. These complexities result from the interaction between multiple university-internal and university-external stakeholders, with UKVI regulations and guidance playing a particularly significant role.

References

Batty, D. (2012, August 30). Border Agency decision threatens thousands of international students. *The Guardian*. https://www.theguardian.com/education/2012/aug/30/border-agency-international-students-threat.

Carless, D. (2013). Innovation in language teaching and learning. In C. A. Chapelle (Ed.), *The encyclopedia of applied linguistics*. Blackwell Publishing Ltd. https://doi.org/10.1002/9781405198431.wbeal0540

Council of Europe. (2024). Common European framework of reference for languages (CEFR). https://www.coe.int/en/web/common-european-framework-reference-languages/home.

East, M. (2022). Mediating innovation through language teacher education. In *Mediating innovation through language teacher education*. Cambridge University Press. https://doi.org/10.1017/9781009127998

Home Office. (2024). Assessing the English language requirement. https://assets.publishing.service.gov.uk/media/65b930c04ec51d0014c9f1af/English_language_requirement.pdf

IELTS. (2024). IELTS. https://www.ielts.org/

Kachru, B. (1991). World Englishes and applied linguistics. In M. Tickoo (Ed.), *Languages and standards: Issues, attitudes and case studies* (pp. 178–205). https://files.eric.ed.gov/fulltext/ED347805.pdf

Vincent-Lancrin, S., Jacotin, G., Urgel, J., Kar, S., & González-Sancho, C. (2017). *Measuring innovation in education: A journey to the future*. OECD Publishing. www.copyright.com

Part V

Wales

Teaching Teaching: Challenges and Opportunities in the MFL Classroom

Christiane Günther and Greg Herman

For more than two decades, the documented decline in modern language uptake at KS4–5 has had a knock-on effect on the number of language students transitioning into Higher Education (Broady, 2020; Cazzoli, 2022; Watts, 2004). To try to ameliorate this decline, the authors and their colleagues across the United Kingdom engage in outreach activities to include language taster sessions, language workshops, master classes, and career talks. Such events have proved successful, at least in terms of uptake as students transition from KS4 to KS5, and subsequently to Higher Education. Over recent years, however, we have also witnessed, anecdotally at least, both a reduction in students considering a career in teaching and a higher attrition rate amongst those students going on to a PGCE. The sector-specific challenges facing Modern Languages in HE then concern both a shortage of students and a consequential shortage of teachers. In response, and within the framework set by the Welsh

---

C. Günther (✉) • G. Herman
Swansea University, Swansea, UK
e-mail: c.guenther@swansea.ac.uk; g.j.herman@swansea.ac.uk

Government's Global Futures plan (2021), in 2017 the Department of Modern Languages, Translation and Interpreting (MLTI) at Swansea University reviewed all programmes and modules that were then available to students. Arising from this review, the decision was taken to embed three pathways into our principal Modern Languages programme: these pathways would cover cultural studies, translation, and second language teaching and would offer maximum flexibility to potential students. Those with clear career aspirations would be able to specialise in a particular pathway during each year of study at Swansea University. Equally, it would be possible for the student looking for a more rounded educational experience to take modules from different pathways in different years according to their own preference.

Responsible for the teaching pathway, the authors of this reflection designed (with the aid of several colleagues) a suite of modules to cover Year One, Year Two, and Year Four (with the third year, in the case of Modern Languages students, generally being spent abroad). The outcome for a student taking one of these modules might be either an introduction to pedagogical theory or relatively isolated practical experience gained through a placement in a local school. On the other hand, if a student committed wholeheartedly to the pathway, they would gain a much more sustained grounding in both theory and practice. With an increased understanding of the realities of the modern languages classroom, and having gained significant practical experience over the course of their time with us, it was and is our hope that this grounding will have a positive effect on the high attrition rates of both PGCE students and NQTs (see, for example, Allen et al., 2016), though at the time of writing this remains to be seen.[1]

Against this backdrop, this chapter will reflect on the origins, implementation, and evaluation of the Year One (Level 4) introduction to language teaching module, over its first three years' delivery—2019–2022. As part of this reflection, it will consider the challenges we as module

---

[1] The end of the academic year 2022–2023 will mark the graduation of the first cohort of Modern Languages students who have had modules in the teaching pathway available to them in each year of their studies. Of this cohort, two students have taken every module available as part of the teaching pathway, with one student further supplementing their pedagogical knowledge with a comparative dissertation on attitudes to language learning in both the UK and France.

coordinators and teachers faced along the way, and the ways in which the module has evolved in response to both student feedback and external factors.

Prior to the launch of the teaching pathway, the department of Modern Languages, Translation and Interpreting offered a single teaching module to second year students: 'ML-250: Teaching Modern Foreign Languages to Young Learners'. This module, ever popular, sees students placed in local primary schools and serves as a key point of preparatory experience for those students expecting to teach during their year abroad. Given the success of this existing module, and in our capacity as lecturers interested and trained in the teaching and learning of MFL, we proposed that the teaching pathway should be built around this existing module. In itself, this decision caused some difficulties: whilst it would perhaps have been preferential to reverse-engineer the pathway from scratch, practical considerations of staffing and workload meant that this, regrettably, was not feasible. As such, and keeping in mind the PGCE upon which we hoped students would be enrolling at the end of their time at Swansea University, 'ML-308: Modern Languages: Classroom Practice' was designed for Year 4 (Level 6) students. Marking a progression from ML-250, this module would see students placed in local secondary schools, with emphasis placed on the soft skills required in the modern classroom (e.g. communication, classroom management, organisation). With both the Y2 and Y4 modules thus dedicated to offering practical experience in the classroom, it was clear that the missing component in our teaching pathway was a sustained engagement with pedagogical theory and an understanding of the basic mechanics of second language instruction. Simultaneously, given that this would be our students' first experience of the teaching pathway, we felt it essential that they gain at least a little experience of classroom leadership. Thus, for Year 1 (Level 4), 'ML-150: Introduction to Language Teaching' was born: a module which would allow theory to inform practice, and practice to inform reflection.

The decision to have two principal lecturers associated with the module was taken to accommodate the first challenge that was encountered after the pathway had been approved. Where the practical focus of the subsequent modules (ML-250; ML-308) and corresponding reflective assessment of those modules would allow them to be led, if necessary, by a non-speaker of the students' second language(s), the combination of theory and in-house practice-based assessment of ML-150 (a peer taught lesson aimed at absolute beginners) necessitated a teaching team capable of covering all core languages offered by the Department. A minimum of two members of staff were thus required, and given their relevant experience and the languages that they offered, the authors of this chapter were identified as the most suitable candidates on account of the range of languages that they could cover. Whilst this resolved one issue, our differing visions of what the module should entail swiftly became apparent.

Günther's vision for the module was based both on the principles underlying her own teaching philosophy as a German language teacher and on her experience of a CELTA course that she completed at Swansea University in 2014. As part of this programme, she was able to observe the teaching methodology of one particular trainer who combined the teaching of CELTA-related content by using various methods used in the MFL classroom. This resulted in a hands-on, practical, and student-centred classroom. To give two brief examples: in order to have a better understanding of reading in a second language, this teacher would combine research articles related to reading with the methods used to facilitate reading activities in the MFL classroom. Alternatively, students would learn about the effective use of speaking activities by engaging in interactive oral methods in which the skill could be simultaneously put into practice. Trainee teachers were thus simultaneously able to learn both the content and new methods for teaching, and it was this combination which sparked the idea to implement this way of teaching into ML-150.

The value of this fusion of content and method was further impressed upon Günther when working as a trainer for the Goethe-Institut London where she provided upskilling sessions and CPD courses for both primary and secondary German language teachers using the DLL (Deutsch Lehren Lernen—Learning how to teach German) series (Lundquist-Mog & Widlok, 2015 and Salomo & Mohr (2016)). These sessions, and the plethora of teaching resources—including language learning theory and methods and principles for language lessons—that she used, allowed her to develop a nuanced understanding of the needs of the contemporary second language classroom. Moreover, as the parent of two multilingual

(Welsh, English, German) primary school children, her professional understanding of primary and secondary language acquisition is supplemented with the more 'lived' perspective and experience of a parent.

In contrast, Herman's initial vision for the module was more theoretical, contextual, and historical in nature. To this end, he saw theories of learning as being a key foundation for students' learning, upon which everything else could be subsequently developed. Accordingly, he wished to develop students' awareness of theories such as behaviourism and constructivism, and their role in the twenty-first century classroom, as well as raising students' awareness of some of the more structural barriers encountered by aspiring linguists. Equally important, given the subsequent placement-based modules that students on the teaching pathway would take, was an understanding of lesson design and backwards planning, and an initial awareness of some strategies for behaviour management: two practical sets of knowledge which, in his own experience at least, challenged many trainee teachers upon their first entry into the classroom.

Despite these initial contradictory visions of the module, once planning had begun it became swiftly apparent that rather than being diametrically opposed, our knowledge, experience, and visions for ML-150 were more complimentary than antagonistic. Moreover, through a combination of our experience and interests, we would be able to provide a module that was as practical as it was theoretical, with, crucially, key classroom skills integrated throughout. Thus, the first programme of work was put together.[2]

1   Year One: 2019–2020

With 33 contact hours allocated to the module, the key aims of the authors in terms of knowledge acquisition on the part of students enrolled were as follows. First, we wanted students to have a broad awareness of primary (mother tongue) language acquisition, and how theoretical understandings of this process can inform second language acquisition

---

[2] See Appendix for details.

and pedagogy. Next, we wanted to introduce students to the four language skills (listening, reading, writing, and speaking) and both the specific challenges which these skills can pose to second language (L2) learners and the means by which they can be implemented in the classroom. Given the importance of planning in any learning and teaching environment, from a full programme of work to an individual lesson, two sessions of the module would focus on this and its importance to language teaching; facilitating this were templates used by Herman during his own PGCE in 2014. In preparation for the final piece of summative assessment—a combination of taught lesson, reflection, and mini-essay—the authors decided to ask students to deliver a brief presentation at the mid-point of the term.[3] Serving a quasi-formative purpose, this would allow us to provide feedback on some of the core skills which would subsequently be assessed as part of the summative lesson: from pitch, pace, and engagement to structure and subject matter. This feedback, we hoped, would benefit the students' final piece of summative assessment, in advance of which students were also able to take advantage of individual feedback sessions that scrutinised their lesson plans at both macro and micro levels. Perhaps most important, however, was the way in which individual classes were delivered not only to maximise student engagement and participation but also to develop their confidence and their relationships with their peers. Mindful of some previous less-than-successful attempts of asking students to take charge of their learning and direct discussion in small-group settings, increased confidence in themselves and their peers was, to our mind, essential if they were to successfully deliver a lesson after only 33 hours of instruction.

With methods, aims, and assessment thus decided, the module was advertised to the student intake who had commenced their studies in September 2019. Given our respective backgrounds and the planning which had already gone into the module, we felt confident in our ability to deliver an engaging module which would provide students with a comprehensive if introductory insight into second language acquisition. Moreover, we were pleased that the module would, as noted above,

---

[3] See Appendix for a breakdown of the 2019–2020 assessment components and their respective weightings.

provide students with both the practical and the theoretical foundations upon which they could build as they progressed through different years of study and onto the different teaching and pedagogy modules that would be subsequently available to them.

In this first year, eight students enrolled on the module. These included speakers of French, German, Spanish, and Welsh. As such, whilst the initial challenges of who would teach what and why had been relatively easily resolved, we were now presented with another challenge: how to reconcile the aim of enabling students to teach in their second (or third) language, when there was no common second language shared by all students. This was resolved by covering all topics from the perspective of a teacher of English as a second language: as such, all the core content of the module would be delivered and explored in the shared language of all students. Students would then be required to adapt and apply this knowledge to the specific circumstances of their second language—the language in which their teaching assessment would be based. Underpinning our delivery of much of this content was *The CELTA Course: Certificate in English Language Teaching to Adults [Trainer's Manual]* (Watkins et al., 2022).

The use of this book, and the decision to default to English as the lingua franca of the module despite its multilingual aims, was well-received by students. Moreover, as the module progressed from icebreakers to L2 acquisition theory, students' engagement with the content of the module was clear, as was their ever-increasing comfort in actively participating in the module.

And yet, as Robbie Burns once wrote, '[t]he best laid plans of mice and men often go awry.' Unbeknownst to us, 2020 would herald a more significant disruption to Higher Education and wider society than many could have ever predicted. On the 13th March 2020, the seventh week of the academic semester, Swansea University would announce the suspension of all face-to-face teaching until the end of the semester a few months later. Ten days later, the British Government would announce the first in a series of lockdowns and other emergency measures designed to stem the transmission of Covid-19, the ramifications of which are still being felt to this day (for a comprehensive overview of the timeline of governmental decisions taken in regards to Covid, see Institute for Government, 2022).

Whilst the impact of the pandemic on Higher Education has already been well-documented (see, for example, Austin et al., 2021; Khan, 2021), the focus of this chapter will now turn to the specific challenges that it posed for the delivery of ML-150: Introduction to Language Teaching, the means by which we responded to those challenges over the next two and a half years, and feedback received from students along the way.

In a story familiar to educators the world over, from March 2020 onwards online learning facilitated by Zoom became the "new normal": unsurprisingly, the impact on teaching was unprecedented. Given such upheaval to conventional teaching norms, and following wider consultation across the Department for Modern Languages, emergency changes were made to the assessment diet associated with the teaching module under consideration here. As such, the mini-lesson which was to be delivered by students in the final week of term, an exercise marking the culmination of the module and which would have given students the chance to showcase all they had learnt in previous weeks, was cut. Given the authors' own struggles to adapt, with no notice, to Zoom and online learning, this decision was, we felt, the least worst option: it would have been simply unfair to ask students, with so little notice, to deliver via this new medium, when even we seasoned professionals were accustomed to neither its limitations nor its potential. In its place, students would now simply submit a lesson plan, and the materials for a lesson that they would have used in more normal circumstances. A reflective task would then see them commenting on the decisions they had taken in the design of both plan and resources. In particular, this reflection would focus on objectives, scaffolding, language skills and underlying theory. The essay component of the assessment diet remained, at this stage, unchanged.

Whilst the delivery of online teaching posed a unique set of challenges, the delivery of asynchronous material via a newly acquired Virtual Learning Environment (Canvas) was also not without difficulty. From more basic functionality (e.g. how to upload work) to more sophisticated tools which would facilitate discussion and peer evaluation, the waters were deep and untested.

Despite the challenges faced by both the authors and the students during this, the pilot run of the module, the end of the semester dutifully arrived, with the majority of students passing the module.[4] It was now time for us to reflect on the successes that we had experienced during this way, as well as the challenges experienced, and what changes if any we would make to the module ahead of its next recruitment in 2020–2021.

To assist this reflection, the authors decided to contact students directly to ask their experience and perspective on the module. The reason for this approach were two-fold: first, on account of our specific needs in relation to understanding their experience of the module, we felt that the generic questions asked of students in institutionally authorised surveys tended to lack the specific focus that we sought in their appraisals. Second, we were also conscious of the flaws associated with post-module feedback in terms of gender bias (see, for example, Centra, 2000; Sirgurdardottir et al., 2023) and the limited use of metrics and quantitative data to assess the perceived performance of the teacher. Several email responses were received in response to this request, and despite the difficult circumstances which had come to define this semester, the authors were pleased to note the positive experiences attested to in these emails. As one student notes:

> Although teaching may not be my first choice career pathway in my future, I wanted to have an insight into preparing for classes as well as different approaches in the classroom […] I was fully engaged and interested and [teaching] was something I loved to learn about. There were [varied] activities which helped me [to] learn better, which enabled me to do well. This is also why I have decided to continue with [the teaching pathway] next semester.

Not dissimilarly, Student 2 writes:

> What attracted me the most to this module was the fact that teaching is the career I would like to be in after university, and by taking this module it gave me a head start in understanding and learning how to be a teacher. I did in fact learn a variety of different teaching activities. The number of

---

[4] Of eight students enrolled, we recorded 1 × 70+ mark; 1 × 60–8 mark; 2 × 50–8 mark; 1 × 40–8 mark. The three remaining students suspended their studies upon or shortly after the initial pandemic-related restrictions.

tasks and interaction was good [and] we did so much more speaking as a class and it was nice to be able to speak to my peers and to my professors instead of just listening to the professor speak for the whole [class].

Now at the end of their degree programmes, it is also interesting to note that despite the initial reservations of Student 1 with regards a career in teaching, both students cited here have successfully applied for PGCE programmes to start next academic year. That said, as educators we know that whilst it is always pleasing to receive positive appraisals of our teaching, the real value of any feedback is to be found via constructive criticism. In particular, it was an additional comment again made by Student 2 that would shape our plans for the delivery of the module the following year:

What could have been improved was perhaps the amount of work we did outside lesson. I don't remember having much to do as homework, so maybe a little more extra work would have been good, in order to recap what we did in lesson time.

Although we did not know it at this time, ineluctably this desire for additional self-study materials would be an essential component of the 2020–2021 delivery of ML-150.

2 Year Two: 2020–2021

As readers will no doubt be aware, the pandemic which had so disrupted education in the 2019–2020 academic year showed no sign of abating by the time that students were enrolling for the following academic year. The extraordinary decision was therefore taken that all teaching, for at least the first semester, would now take place online. This initial position would subsequently be extended to include the second semester.

In light of how it would now be taught, some not insignificant changes were made to the module: two hours per week of online Zoom classes would be followed by one hour of asynchronous study. Given that our contact hours were thus effectively reduced by a third, these changes included removing the Study Skills session which in the previous year had been delivered by Swansea University's Centre for Academic Success. Moreover, given that the entire module would be delivered online, the new cohort would benefit from the knowledge hastily acquired over the previous summer by the authors. This related not only to the more basic functionality of Zoom, but extended to cover all manner of online teaching tools and their application in the online classroom: from Google Sheets to JamBoard, Padlet to Mentimeter. Given that these applications would now take a central role in the online delivery of the module, not to mention wider restrictions, it followed that students would now deliver the taught lesson assessment component of the module via Zoom.

Further significant changes were also made to the module's assessment diet, given the reduction in contact hours available to us, and as a result of our experiences of the initial shift to online teaching which had first affected the module the previous year. Frustrated that students in the previous year had been unable to deliver a lesson on account of the switch to remote teaching, for 2020–2021 we decided to make the assessed lesson the central point of the module. Students would thus deliver a 20-minute introductory lesson in the language of their choice and submit a lesson plan and other resources as appropriate. This first component, and an accompanying lesson plan inclusive of all materials (worksheets, whiteboard design, visuals, PowerPoint presentations), would be worth 50% of the module as a whole. Having taught their lesson, students would then be asked to submit a written reflection on their experience: what had gone well? What had gone less well? What would they do differently in the future? This component would also be worth 50% of their overall mark. These changes, we felt, would mitigate the over-assessment that had been built into the module the previous year, whilst preventing students from being distracted from the module's key learning objectives by too many different assessment elements. Moreover, by removing both mini-essay and presentation from the assessment diet, and given the reduction in contact hours, we were able to free up additional contact time for the delivery of some of the module's core content.

To work towards this new assessment pattern and given the changes to delivery that would now last the duration of the module, significant reworkings of teaching materials were required to assuage one of our biggest concerns about this semi-permanent switch to an online environment: in particular, the effect that this switch would have on a module which was so predicated on interaction, communication, and student-led learning. Pair and small group work exercises would thus need to be delivered via Google Docs, Padlet, and Jamboard; student discussion would be facilitated by Breakout Rooms; polls, quiz questions, and brainstorming activities would be carried out by online learning tools such as Mentimeter as well as the integral functions of Zoom such as the chat function, the use of icons and poll tool. To become more acquainted with the plethora of online learning and teaching tools available and to further equip the students with the requisite experience to present and teach via Zoom, we integrated a formative pre-recorded presentation of an online tool into the curriculum. To this end, students were given a choice of various online tools such as those mentioned above and had to prepare an introduction to the chosen tool along with an analysis of its use and application in the MFL classroom. Students then uploaded their video to the learning platform and received written feedback from their peers as well as oral feedback from the authors. This activity thus served a dual purpose: (1) it improved all students' familiarity with the online tools at their disposal; (2) it allowed them to practice providing constructive criticism and feedback in a pedagogical setting. Student engagement with this exercise was of the highest order with each student submitting a comprehensive and informed review and providing feedback to their peers.

In addition to the above changes to the actively delivered module content, further revision of the module was required to facilitate the delivery of the asynchronous hour: the materials that were provided to students for this hour, though based on the original vision of the module, had to be adapted to account for the absence of on-demand teacher input. As such, pre-recorded instructional videos, combined with Canvas discussion boards and student-led peer review, became one of our principal means of enabling student interaction during this asynchronous session.

Whilst these actions featured as extraordinary responses to extraordinary circumstances, both the cohort of students who enrolled on the module that year, as well as the authors, were pleasantly surprised by the overall result. Students were engaged for the duration of the module. In both online sessions, and as they worked through the asynchronous materials provided to them, their academic progression, understanding of key concepts, and the quality of the relationships that they were building with their peers were clear to see. Of course, in part this may have been another consequence of Covid-related restrictions: for it must be remembered that at this point in time there were few opportunities for face-to-face interaction, let alone socialising, and periods of self-isolation interrupted nearly all students' studies and day-to-day routines at one point or another. As such, it is possible to read their engagement not only with the module under consideration here but with their studies more generally, as a consequence of a wider void in their lives.

3 Year Three: 2021–2022

By this point, ML-150 had known a different mode of delivery in each year that it had been live for student selection: in-person teaching transitioned at a mid-point of the semester to online teaching in 2019–2020, before moving exclusively online in 2020–2021. The academic year under consideration in this final section will iterate the changes and revisions that were made to the module for its third outing: a result of the ever-changing landscape of pandemic-affected education.

Whilst 2020–2021 was conducted exclusively online, 2021–2022 would see a partial return to the classroom and in-person teaching. To this end, all modules at Swansea University would have at least one contact hour face-to-face. This would be supplemented by one hour of online teaching and learning to be conducted via Zoom. Finally, and as per the previous year, these contact hours would be supplemented by one hour of asynchronous guided study.

If for nothing other than the mental health of students and staff alike, this partial return to a more traditional teaching set-up was welcomed warmly by all concerned. Yet, unsurprisingly, the somewhat fragmented format that one of the authors (Günther) was obliged to follow created its own set of challenges that we would need to overcome.[5] Whilst the

---

[5] Following a family bereavement, Herman was on extended leave for a significant part of the semester. Consequently, the teaching of the module in its entirety became the responsibility of

sequencing of specific activities and learning objectives could be translated with relative ease, given experience gained over previous years, to fit either an in-person or remote learning environment, there were nonetheless various new challenges that arose as a consequence of attempts to mitigate the risk of transmission arising from the ongoing pandemic.

As per previous academic years, some of the core content covered in this iteration of ML-150 included the following: the connection between primary and secondary language acquisition; the integration of the four language skills; pedagogical theory; lesson-planning. All of these were facilitated by numerous collaborative activities to enhance relationships between students and put them as much as possible at ease in each other's presence ahead of the module's summative assessment. This remained largely unchanged in the new academic year, comprising a taught lesson at the end of the module (worth 50%) and a reflection on that lesson (also worth 50%).

As intimated above, however, the partial return to in-person teaching brought with it its own unique set of challenges, many of which it would have been impossible to anticipate prior to teaching commencing, whilst others, while entirely predictable, were not within our powers to resolve. Falling into this last category was enforced social distancing, which made pair-work exercises and discussion activities particularly awkward to coordinate. This was further compounded by internal attempts to control the spread of the Coronavirus: to this end, teaching staff were not allowed to make use of or distribute paper-based resources during their in-person teaching sessions. As a result, those sessions retained much of the feel of their online counterparts, with resources shared via the overhead projector, and interactive activities similarly managed via the same tools (Padlet, Google Docs, etc.) which had been the mainstay of the previous year's online classroom. Whilst this curious blend of digital tools in the in-person classroom was somewhat difficult to reconcile with previous understandings of both in-person and remote learning, in the end it

---

Günther. Whilst these circumstances proved less than ideal for obvious reasons, they nonetheless proved that it was in fact possible for the module to be taught by a sole member of staff (supplemented with some language-specific input for assessment purposes). This lesson would be reiterated the following year (2022–2023) when staffing issues meant that Günther had to relinquish her role in the module, leaving its delivery in its entirety to Herman.

would prove fortuitous for the students' summative assessment. The first element of this, the taught lesson, was envisaged in 2021–2022 as being taught in-person (albeit with the same restrictions as detailed above). However, days before this was due to take place, one of the authors tested positive for Coronavirus. Consequently, in consultation with students, the decision was taken to move the assessment to an online format. Students would thus teach their lesson via Zoom and make use of the full array of online resources that they had been exposed to over the course of the semester and as best suited the specific content which they wished to teach. Credit to those students, the quality of those lessons was in general the highest standard that we had seen over the three years that the module had now run, and all students secured 2:1 marks or above.

Despite this relative success, during the course of the semester, it became rapidly apparent that students were suffering from 'screen fatigue'. Whilst attendance at the face-to-face sessions rarely deviated from 100%, engagement during both online classes and with the online materials provided for the asynchronous hour decreased steadily over the course of the semester. Fair to say, it would seem, that the novelty of online learning had now entirely dissipated and what students really craved was a return to 'the old normal' and in-person interaction with both their peers and their teaching staff.

In those instances where students were missing from the in-person classes, this was near exclusively due to either illness or periods of enforced self-isolation. This too, however, posed another challenge for teaching staff albeit one which had been anticipated prior to the start of the semester. Namely, how to ensure the continued learning of students who, on account of either isolation or illness, may not be able to attend in-person classes for weeks at a time. The partial if unsatisfactory solution to this quandary was the mandate that all in-person teaching would take on a hybrid format, simultaneously traversing both the real and the virtual classroom. To this end, all in-person teaching would be simultaneously disseminated via Zoom to those unable to attend. In theory, a practical solution to a very real problem and a solution which the authors struggle to improve upon. Nonetheless, the actual practicalities of this set-up proved tiring and tedious for all involved—whether teaching staff, in-person learner, or remote learner—as this solution frequently meant an effective doubling up of resources formatted for the different learning environments, and a doubling up of 'teacher talk' on account of the necessity of addressing and instructing two different audiences.

Despite the challenges experienced for the third successive year of the module being available for student selection, student feedback was once again positive:

> I have personally found this to be a very engaging and inclusive class which makes the most of the blended learning environment. Even when I have called in via zoom to an in-person class, I have felt that I was able to be an active part of the lesson, which […] is a rarity.
>
> The use of different methods such as breakout room tasks, shared google docs, jamboards, etc. have also really engaged [students] and made the classes interactive and fun.

Similar positive feedback was also obtained via the Swansea University internal peer review process, as well as from a PhD student who was auditing the module to gain experience and exposure to teaching techniques and methods as she prepared for her own career. And with 2022–2023 marking a full return to in-person teaching—no hybrid classrooms, no Zoom, no Padlets, no asynchronous teaching—this seems an appropriate point to draw this reflection to a close.

4 Discussion and Concluding Thoughts

Making its academic debut in 2019–2020, ML-150 faced no shortage of challenges over the course of its first three years. In the face of those challenges, however, it is easy to overlook the original motivation of the module and its wider innovation. At module level, this motivation was to introduce language teaching as an elective option to Y1 MFL undergraduate students. Meanwhile at programme level, the desire was to provide a pathway of modules, spanning the entire undergraduate programme, that would allow students to specialise in teaching and pedagogy and which would stand them in good stead both for their Year Abroad and for any subsequent qualification or career in education thereafter. Key to the success of this pathway (and its replication across different areas—translation and cultural studies, and as of 2024 additional languages) both in terms of marketing and student experience is its flexibility. Those who have a clear idea, at the moment of enrolment, of their future career have a dedicated suite of modules available to them. Those seeking balance and a variety of content are able to choose from all pathways as they desire.

Given the different guises under which ML-150 has run, the majority of which were not of our choosing and were instead responses to circumstances outside our control, there are also perhaps some wider lessons which may interest anyone considering a similar module. First and foremost is that an expertise in the languages of the students is not essential. Chief amongst our priorities when developing the module was the notion that its potential to recruit students from all language areas offered by the Department meant, in turn, that the teaching staff of the module should also have at the very least a moderate knowledge which would cover those languages. If nothing else, we felt this necessary to be able to comment on the accuracy of language as part of the students' taught-lesson assessment. As the module evolved, however, and as we responded to the wider circumstances, we discovered that in fact this was not necessary. The module was and is primarily concerned with teaching methods and principles and is not fundamentally seeking to test students' knowledge of their L2. As such, it is not necessary for the teaching team to be able to cover all possible languages—and indeed to do so is perhaps detrimental to the wider aims insofar as it can lead to a tendency to focus, during that final piece of assessment, on the accuracy of language over and above the methods deployed. Of course, that is not to say that accurate language is not ultimately important, particularly for those going on to a PGCE. Rather, it is simply to highlight that as a Y1 introductory module which can serve both post-A level and ab initio students, as well as students whose L1 is neither English nor any of the languages offered by the Department, it is important to keep in mind the learning outcomes desired of both the module and its students.

Related to the above point is of course the question of assessment design, and more specifically the scale and scope of assessment. In its first outing there is little doubt that we intended (had it not been for Covid) to over-assess students, keen to test their knowledge of every detail of the syllabus. Over the years, and as we gained familiarity with the content that we wished to cover and perhaps realised ourselves what the aim of the module was—to teach a module is a far different experience from planning it on paper—we realised that those smaller details of the syllabus were either not that important or could be incorporated into a much smaller range of assessment. Once again, the general lesson here, perhaps, is to focus on the bigger picture and not get caught up in the minutiae.

Key to the realisation above were our proactive requests for feedback from students. Traditional end-of-module surveys are too often either scorned or scored by students, with little qualitative input: a consequence, perhaps, of questions which are too institutionally generic. For students, this can mean a reluctance to engage with yet another survey which lacks direct relevance to the module in question. Where they do engage, the broad brushstrokes of questions linked to KPI's—feedback for the sake of feedback—are often of little use in informing teacher practice, beyond mild banalities, subjective preferences, or over-generalisations. In contrast, our decision to contact students directly with specific questions relating to module content, delivery, and assessment provided invaluable insight into their experience of the module that we were then able to incorporate into subsequent sessions, thus involving them in the creation of the curriculum at both module and pathway level.

Most significant from this feedback is the sense of purpose that students crave from their modules. Whilst there is a place for abstract and theoretical learning, what students really valued in this module was the end-goal—the lesson that they would teach at the end of the module. To reinforce this sense of putting skills into practice, the next outing of the module will see us build on our relations with local schools and provide students with authentic taster sessions as they progress through the module.

Finally, and perhaps more importantly than any pedagogical finding or innovation, was the humanistic confirmation of the strength and resilience of those students whom it has been our pleasure to teach over the last tempestuous years. Graduating later this year, 2023 will mark the culmination of studies of our first 'Covid Cohort': those who enrolled in 2019, and who knew only a few short months of 'traditional' university education. And yet, despite everything they have faced, their ability to adapt and respond to the unexpected, taking everything in our stride, and to do so with grace and good humour have reaffirmed for us the reasons that we teach.

Appendix

1. Programme of Work: 2019–2020

Week	Monday 10–12 Session #1	Session #2	Tuesday 9–10 Session #3
1	Introduction Language diagram	Mini-session in a foreign language (Welsh, German, or other) Learning styles test and analysis	How languages are learned? Second language acquisition part 1 First language acquisition
2	How languages are learned? Second language acquisition	How languages are learned? Second language acquisition	How languages are learned? Second language acquisition
3	Role of teacher and learner Pedagogical idols	Role of teacher and learner Motivating learners	Role of teacher and learner Krashen and comprehensible input, presenting vocab
4	Introduction to language skills Parts of speech	Introduction to language skills How to present grammar	How to present? Academic success training
5	Reading	Reading Mini-presentations	Listening
6	Listening Mini-presentations	Lesson planning	Writing
7	Writing Mini-presentations	Speaking	Speaking Mini-presentations
8	Lesson planning	Preparation for assignments Academic success—Writing session	Preparation for assignments
9	Individual tutoring session for planned mini-lesson	Individual tutoring session for planned mini-lesson	Individual tutoring session for planned mini-lesson
10	Mini-lessons	Mini-lessons	Mini-lessons
11–13	**EASTER BREAK**		
14	Both assignments due (01.05.2020)		

(continued)

(continued)

2. Programme of Work 2020–2021

Week	Zoom session #1	Zoom session #2	Self-study session
1	Introduction, module overview, icebreaker How are languages learned? First language acquisition.		Learning styles tests and implications for teaching languages
2	How languages are learned? Second language acquisition		Foreign language lesson—Observation task
3	Role of teacher and learner - pedagogical idols	How to present vocabulary?	Stephen Krashen: Language acquisition
4	Role of teacher and learner—motivating learners	How to teach grammar?	Workshop: How to present online Mock presentation: Teaching tools 1—Gathering information
5	Language skills: Reading A	Language skills: Reading B	Workshop—voice projection Mock presentation: Teaching tools 2—recording
6	Language skills: Listening B	Language skills: Listening A	Mock presentation: Teaching tools 3—peer feedback on videos
7	Language skills: Writing A	How to plan a lesson? Part 1 Language skills: Writing B	Workshop: How to use zoom when teaching
8	Language skills: Speaking B	Language skills: Speaking A How to plan a lesson? Part 2	Plan your lesson 1
9	Individual tutoring session for planned mini-lesson	Individual tutoring session for planned mini-lesson	Plan your lesson 2
10–12	**EASTER BREAK**		
13	Assessment—online lesson		
14	Assessment—online lesson		

3. Programme of Work 2021–2022

Week	On campus, Tuesday 12–1	Zoom Seminar Wednesday 12–1	Self-study session
1	Introduction, module overview, icebreaker	How are languages learned? First language acquisition	Learning styles tests and implications for teaching languages
2	How languages are learned? Second language acquisition	How languages are learned? Second language acquisition	Foreign language lesson—Observation task
3	Role of teacher and learner—pedagogical idols	How to present vocabulary?	Stephen Krashen: Language acquisition
4	Role of teacher and learner—motivating learners	How to teach grammar?	Presentation skills
5	Student presentations (1 minute) Language skills: Reading A	Language skills: Reading B Language skills: Listening A	Assessment preparation 1: Start to collect materials, resources for lesson
6	Language skills: Listening B	How to plan a lesson? Part 1	Assessment preparation 2: Look at suitable methods for teaching using resources from week 6
7	Study week		
8	How to plan a lesson? Part 2	Language skills: Writing A	Peer feedback on materials and methods
9	Language skills: Writing B Language skills: Speaking A	Skill-integrated lessons	Plan your lesson draft 1
10	Individual tutoring session for planned mini-lesson	Individual tutoring session for planned mini-lesson	Plan your lesson final
11	Assessment—online lesson (50%)		
12–14	**Christmas break**		
15	January assessment period Lesson plan and reflective writing task due (50%)		

References

Allen, R., et al. (2016) High costs result from four in ten trainee teachers not teaching five years later. Retrieved May 3, 2023, from https://ifs.org.uk/news/high-costs-result-four-ten-trainee-teachers-not-teaching-five-years-later

Austin, E., et al.(2021). *Journeys into higher education and employment: The impact of Covid-19 on young people*. LSE widening participation and policy briefing. Retrieved April 28, 2023, from https://www.lse.ac.uk/study-at-lse/Undergraduate/widening-participation/Assets/PDF/Journeys-into-higher-education-and-employment-the-impact-of-Covid-19-on-young-people.pdf

Broady, E. (2020). Language learning in the UK—Taking stock. *The Language Learning Journal, 48*(5), 501–507. https://doi.org/10.1080/09571736.2020.1812812

Cazzoli, M. A. (2022). Can the gap get any wider? How the new GCSE curriculum will make progression to university more challenging and less inclusive. *The Language Learning Journal, 50*(2), 268–272. https://doi.org/10.1080/09571736.2022.2046382

Centra, J. A., & Gaubatz, N. B. (2000). Is there gender bias in student evaluations of teaching? *The Journal of Higher Education, 71*(1), 17–33. https://doi.org/10.1080/00221546.2000.11780814

Institute for Government. (2022). Timeline of UK government coronavirus lockdowns and restrictions. Retrieved April 28, 2023, from https://www.instituteforgovernment.org.uk/data-visualisation/timeline-coronavirus-lockdowns

Khan, M. (2021). The impact of COVID-19 on UK higher education students: Experiences, observations and suggestions for the way forward. *Corporate Governance, 21*(6), 1172–1193. https://doi.org/10.1108/CG-09-2020-0396

Lundquist-Mog, A., & Widlok, B. (2015). *Deutsch Lehren Lernen: DaF für Kinder*. Klett (Ernst) Verlag.

Salomo, D., & Mohr, I. (2016). *Deutsch Lehren Lernen: DaF für Jugendliche*. Klett (Ernst) Verlag.

Sigurdardottir, M. S., Rafnsdottir, G. L., Jónsdóttir, A. H., & Kristofersson, D. M. (2023). Student evaluation of teaching: Gender bias in a country at the forefront of gender equality. *Higher Education Research & Development, 42*(4), 954–967. https://doi.org/10.1080/07294360.2022.2087604

Watkins, P., et al. (2022). *The CELTA Course: Certificate in English language teaching to adults. Trainer's manual* (2nd ed.). Cambridge University Press.

Watts, C. (2004). Some reasons for the decline in numbers of MFL students at degree level. *The Language Learning Journal, 29*(1), 59–67. https://doi.org/10.1080/09571730485200121

Welsh Government. (2021). Curriculum for Wales: Languages, literacy and communication. Retrieved May 10, 2023, from https://hwb.gov.wales/curriculum-for-wales/languages-literacy-and-communication/

Explicit Teaching of English Morphology and Etymology: Innovative Solutions to Developing Children's Word Decoding and Comprehension Skills in Wales

Ellen Bristow

1   Literacy Education in Wales

Since the devolution settlement in 1999, which devolved powers on education and training, Wales has had responsibility for nearly all areas of education policy. This means that to reflect its own educational needs, Wales has pursued distinct education policies from other parts of the United Kingdom (UK): its education system offers Welsh-medium, English-medium and/or bilingual (dual stream) schools; it follows its own national curriculum; and it has its own education inspectorate, Etsyn. In Wales, education is compulsory from the age of 5 to 16, but the majority of children begin their education in nursery at 4-year-old and continue beyond 16. Regardless of the medium of instruction, all

---

E. Bristow (✉)
Cardiff Metropolitan University, Cardiff, UK
e-mail: ELBristow@cardiffmet.ac.uk

© The Author(s), under exclusive license to Springer Nature Switzerland AG 2024
S. W. Chong, H. Reinders (eds.), *Innovation in Language Learning and Teaching*, New Language Learning and Teaching Environments,
https://doi.org/10.1007/978-3-031-66241-6_12

children in Wales are required to learn Welsh throughout the compulsory schooling period. The 2023 annual census of schools in Wales showed that there were 1463 local authority-maintained schools (schools funded by a local education authority), 439 of which provide Welsh-medium education (attended by 108,886 pupils, 23% of pupils; Welsh Government, 2023). The linguistic landscape of Welsh education is vast and varied and, in an attempt, to reflect its uniqueness, over in the last two decades, Wales has undergone a series of major education reforms.

In part, Wales's education reforms have occurred because of poor Programme for International Student Assessment (PISA) results. PISA measures to what extent 15-year-old pupils can apply their skills and knowledge to real-life situations and be equipped for what the Organisation for Economic Co-operation and Development (OECD) term 'full participation in society'. PISA takes place every three years and ranks countries' education systems based on a sample of 15-year-olds. For PISA 2009, the main subject assessed was literacy and results showed Welsh pupils' performances were significantly below the OECD average (16 points behind), particularly for reading (m = 480; England m = 500, Northern Ireland m = 498; and Scotland m = 506). Welsh 15-year-olds had difficulty with summarising information and, in general, performed lower on assessments of continuous text which demand age-commensurate reading attainment in reading comprehension, reading 'stamina' and an ability to infer, interpret and summarise information (Bradshaw et al., 2010). The proportion of low performers on the reading assessment was 20.6%, which was above the UK average (16.7%) and the OECD average (18%). The Assembly Minister for children, education and lifelong learning, Leighton Andrews, described these results as a 'wake up call to a complacent system' (Dauncey, 2021). Consequently, in 2011, Wales embarked upon large-scale school improvement reforms and introduced a range of policies to improve the quality and equity of its school system.

In order to try and better meet the needs of Wales's learners, a context-based approach to curriculum design was taken after the Welsh Government commissioned the OECD to conduct a review of its education system, which concluded that Wales did not have a focussed long-term vision and lacked a 'coherence and synergy' in strategies for school improvement (OECD, 2014: 116 & 108). As a response to the above findings, the Welsh Government published an education improvement plan, *Qualified for Life* (Welsh Government, 2015). Consequently, rather than subject-specific programmes, Wales transitioned to the use of six Areas of Learning and Experience (AoLEs). The AoLEs are Expressive Arts; Health and Well-being; Humanities; Languages, Literacy and Communication; Mathematics and Numeracy; and Science and Technology (see Welsh Government, 2019). The AoLEs take a more holistic approach to education, and each area is underpinned by four core purposes from which practitioners have been encouraged to develop their own school curricula that meet the specific, context-based needs of their learners. The four purposes of the new curriculum are to build:

- ambitious, capable learners, ready to learn throughout their lives;
- enterprising, creative contributors, ready to play a full part in life and work;
- ethical, informed citizens of Wales and the world;
- healthy, confident individuals, ready to lead fulfilling lives as valued members of society. (Welsh Government, 2019)

Literacy is considered one of the 'cross-cutting competencies' that should be taught and/or addressed in the classroom, regardless of which lesson a learner is in. As such, literacy and, more specifically, vocabulary skills, cut across all elements of the curriculum. However, in this research, I focussed specifically on word decoding and comprehension strategies in relation to the Languages, Literacy and Communication (LLC) AoLE. Word decoding skills have the potential to support vocabulary development and skills across the curriculum—for example, knowledge of the morphological make-up and etymology of Scientific words could support a pupils' learning in the Science and Technology AoLE. But as vocabulary skills and knowledge about language are required, addressed and tested most explicitly in the LLC AoLE, it is this area that remained the focus of the research.

2 Languages, Literacy and Communication: A New Area of Learning and Experience

The Languages, Literacy and Communication (LLC) AoLE claims to 'address the fundamental aspects of human communication [...] support learning across the whole curriculum and to enable learners to gain knowledge and skills in Welsh, English and international languages as well as in literature' (Welsh Government, 2021). The LLC guidelines continue by explaining that different languages should 'be explored in relation to one another, so too the skills of listening, speaking, reading and writing' (Welsh Government, 2021). In the previous curriculum, English language, English literature, Welsh, and other Modern Foreign languages were treated as standalone subjects. However, the new curriculum states explicitly that learners should 'transfer what they have learned about how languages work in one language to the learning and using of other languages' (Welsh Government, 2021).

One of the key 'statements of what matters' in the LLC framework is *Languages Connect Us* (Welsh Government, 2019). This statement promotes a multilingual approach to literacy education, which is intended to 'ignite learners' curiosity and enthusiasm' and provide them with a 'firm foundation for a lifelong interest in the languages of Wales and the languages of the world' (Welsh Government, 2021). The approach also aims to develop a learners' sense of their own cultural identity, as well as the cultural identities and communities of others. The aim of these approaches is to raise learners' awareness of the diversity of languages from a young age, to enable them to recognise similarities between languages, and to embrace the differences between them. In this area, learning and experience aims to support learners with developing an understanding of the 'origins, evolution, and features of a range of languages' (Welsh Government, 2021). In other words, learning about language histories and language connections is a fundamental aspect of the new curriculum.

Figure 1 (below) shows some of the morphology-based descriptions of learning included in the new curriculum. Likewise, Fig. 2 shows some of the etymology-based descriptions of learning in the new curriculum. In

Explicit Teaching of English Morphology and Etymology... 287

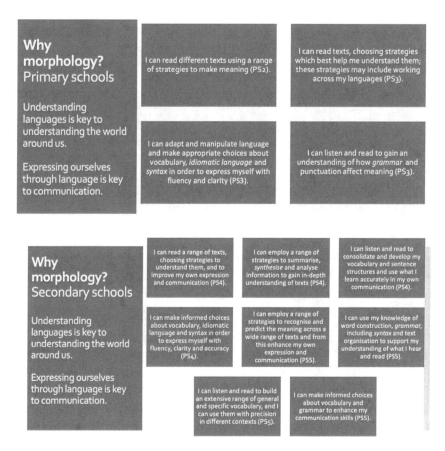

Fig. 1 Morphology-based descriptions of learning in the LLC AoLE

the figures, PS stands for progression stage and the numbers refer to primary school aims (2 and 3) or secondary school aims (4 and 5).

The LLC framework does not, however, address *how* teachers should approach instruction that supports learners with achieving the above progression steps. This is particularly problematic when considering that a recent report by Wales's Education Inspectorate, Estyn, identified that where there are shortcomings in language teaching in both Welsh-medium and English-medium schools, staff 'do not recognise the importance of learners developing their vocabulary knowledge when planning for learning or provide them with explicit opportunities to do so' (Estyn,

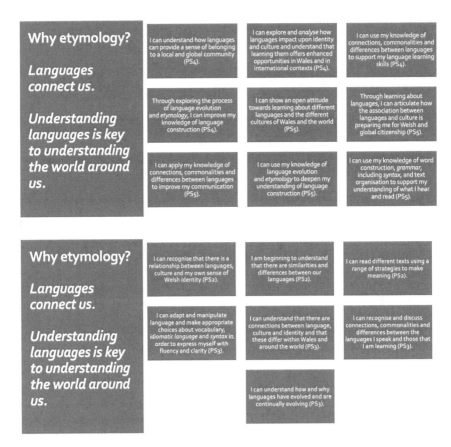

Fig. 2 Etymology-based descriptions of learning in the LLC AoLE

2021: 12). This, in turn, limits the progress that learners make. Estyn's (2021: 86) evidence suggests that in some schools, teachers feel that they do not have a 'secure enough understanding of teaching vocabulary knowledge to learners' and they find it difficult to assess the impact it has on learner progress, particularly in reading.

While the LLC guidelines provide an innovative framework from which schools can build their own context-based curriculum, exactly how they could do this is unclear. The evidence above suggests that Wales's literacy challenge is twofold: (1) understanding how to support children with developing explicit vocabulary knowledge that enables them to access the new Curriculum for Wales and the GCSE exam system which grants them access to further education and training; (2) understanding how to support practitioners with developing confidence and a 'secure understanding' (Estyn, 2021: 86) of how they can facilitate the development of learners' morphological and etymological awareness skills. Therefore, I conducted a systematic review of the literature to explore whether the explicit teaching of morphology and etymology could be integrated into literacy classroom practice in order to offer some innovative approaches to children's broader vocabulary development skills.

3 Current Approaches to Vocabulary Instruction: Issues Surrounding a Phonics-Only Approach

Generally, the link between vocabulary knowledge and reading comprehension is uncontroversial, as coefficient correlations are usually found to be very strong, falling in the 0.70 to 0.95 positive correlation range (see Biemiller, 1999; Stahl & Nagy, 2005). Although academic words occur in a variety of contexts, Corson (1997) found that they appear much more frequently in text than in speech. Thus, the ability to comprehend complex written vocabulary is key to interpreting school texts. However, the current approach to teaching children how to read in Wales may present some challenges for vocabulary comprehension. Regardless of English- or Welsh-medium status, the majority of schools in Wales use phonics-based programmes (i.e., *Jolly Phonics* in English-medium schools; see Jolly Learning, 2023) to introduce children to written words and school vocabulary. Programmes like *Jolly Phonics* teach children how to create letter-to-sound connections and blend the sounds to read words. Past word reading models, such as Perfetti's (1992) and Ehri's (1998) models, have focussed on repeated exposure of written letter combinations and sounds to ensure links become well-established and word recognition becomes more automatic. As Carlisle and Stone (2005: 431) explain, 'forging these connections involves internalising the statistical regularities in the system of mapping spellings and sounds'. Such models include mapping letter combinations like *sh* to *ship* or the *th* to *the*. Comprehensive government reviews of reading instruction (e.g., the Rose Review, 2006) also illustrate the scientific importance of phonics instruction in the initial stages of learning to read. Consequently, in Wales, both previous and current curricula encourage phonics-based instruction in early reading acquisition and children are required to demonstrate knowledge of 'grapheme-phoneme correspondences' when reading (see Welsh Government, 2016).

There is no doubt that a child needs to develop phonological knowledge about letters and sounds to read a word initially. However, Carlisle and Stone (2005: 431) suggest that such a strong focus on phonics may mean that some morphemes are 'processed as common orthographic patterns—that is, without regard for their morphemic identities and their syntactic and semantic functions'. For example, the last stage of Ehri's (1998) model is 'consolidated alphabetic phase', meaning that children are supposed to learn letters that frequently occur together (e.g., the *est* in *nest* and *pest*). Ehri (1998: 23) postulates that knowing *est* as a consolidated unit means that the letters and sounds have been analysed and 'bonded'. Ehri's (1998: 23) reasoning for this is that 'if a reader knew units such as *-est, -tion, -in,* and *-ing* as consolidated units, the task of learning longer sight words such as *question* and *interesting* would be easier'.[1] Conversely, Carlisle and Stone (2005: 431) found that 'the transparency of the structure of a word with more than one morpheme plays a role in word identification', but past word-reading models, such as Ehri's (1998), and programmes like *Jolly Phonics,* do not differentiate between letter patterns that form morphemes and those that are just sound combinations. As Castles et al. (2018: 6) argue, 'reading comprehension clearly entails more than the identification of individual words: Children are not literate if they cannot understand text'. There is very little value in a child being able to say a word if they cannot also attach some meaning to it.

Carlisle (2003) suggests that English is best characterised as a morphophonemic language—that is, a system in which emphasis should be

---

[1] Sight words are words that children recognise and can read instantly without sounding them out (for further information, see Miles et al., 2018: 715).

placed on both phonemic and morphemic elements. The ability to blend sounds to read words is important but reading sounds without meaning will come to have little value later in the education and language development process. For example, Fowler and Liberman (1995) explored second- and fourth-grade (ages seven to eight, and nine to ten) English-speaking children's ability to select the correct form of both phonologically transparent and opaque morphologically complex words. Carlisle and Stone (2005) define phonological transparency as pronunciation of a root word that is fully accessible in the derived word e.g., *warm* in *warmth* or *four* in *fourth*. On the other hand, an opaque word has a vowel/consonant shift which means the pronunciation of the root changes, i.e., *five* in *fifth* or *heal* in *health*. Fowler and Liberman's (1995: 161) participants were asked to complete sentences with the root of a derived word given to them at the beginning of the sentence, such as:

Fourth. When she counted the puppies, there were ([four])

Target words and derivations were divided by phonological transparency or opaqueness and the target items derived from six suffixes: *-ion, -ous, -y, -able, -th* and *-ation*. Fowler and Liberman's (1995) results showed that, when reading, children were more accurate at extracting root words from phonologically transparent items (m = 87%) than phonologically opaque ones (m = 74%). Carlisle and Nomanbhoy (1993) found the same root word transparency effect in kindergarten and Grade 1 children in the United States (US). Collectively, these studies suggest that instruction in phonics alone may not be enough to support children with comprehending a morphologically complex word, particularly when the word is phonologically opaque.

4 Explicit Instruction in Morphology

The LLC progression steps in the new Curriculum for Wales show that one of the key metalinguistic skills learners need to develop is morphological awareness. Morphology is the system in which the smallest units of meaning, known as morphemes (i.e., root words, prefixes and suffixes), combine to form words. Root words (sometimes referred to in the literature as 'base' or 'stem' words) carry the majority of a word's meaning. Some root words are free (i.e., they can stand alone and hold meaning e.g., *dog, go, happy,* etc.), and other root words are bound (i.e., they must be attached to other word parts to hold meaning e.g., *rupt, voc, vis,* etc.). Prefixes precede the root (e.g., *unhappy*) and suffixes follow the root (e.g., *happiness*). English frequently combines both prefixes and suffixes to form new words (e.g., *un-* + *happy* + *ness* = *unhappiness*) and the addition of some suffixes alters the spelling and sounds of the root word. Some words also add multiple prefixes (e.g., *in* + *sub* + *ordinate* = *insubordinate*) and others add multiple suffixes (e.g., *character* + *ist* + *ic*). Affixes can also be either inflectional or derivational. Inflectional affixes preserve the meaning and grammatical class of the lexeme changing only the tense or number (i.e., *dogs, going, played*), whereas derivational affixes change the grammatical class and/or meaning of the root word (i.e., *disengage, happiness, unpredictable*). English also makes use of compound words in which two root words are joined together to form a new word (e.g., *pain* + *killer* = *painkiller; note* + *book* = *notebook*). Morphemes can, therefore, have a lexical role in which new words are created from a combination of affixes and a root word, or they can be syntactical to signify the number or tense of something.

Morphology underpins both English word spellings and meaning. Resultantly, numerous researchers have investigated the role of morphology in children's language acquisition and development (e.g., Clark, 2016). Kuo and Anderson (2006: 161) propose that *morphological awareness* is 'the ability to reflect upon and manipulate morphemes and employ word formation rules in one's language'. The above definition indicates that morphological awareness is a conscious, active and explicit understanding of how words work. Given that that the new Curriculum for Wales makes clear that an explicit awareness of how language works underpins many of the named progression steps (see Fig. 1), I use the term *morphological awareness* throughout this chapter.

To explore the morphological awareness school learners require for GCSE exams in Wales, I built a corpus of past English language and literature exam papers (henceforth referred to as the GCSE word corpus). In Wales, the Welsh Joint Education Committee (WJEC) is the most frequently used examination board and GCSE syllabus provider. All GCSE papers, from 2017 onwards, are freely available for download from the WJEC website. I downloaded the available English language and English literature past papers (48 in total) which comprised question papers, excerpts of core texts, and answer booklets. I uploaded the past paper files to Sketch Engine and compiled a corpus. Overall, the corpus contained 9706 items, but this included unnecessary items such as punctuation marks, question numbers/codes and exam paper barcodes. I removed these entries resulting in a corpus of 9251 lexemes with a total of 95,942 tokens. To explore the morphological make-up of the words in the GCSE word corpus, I analysed 500 high frequency and 500 low frequency words. To do this, I tagged each of the low/frequency words by number of morphemes and morpheme types (i.e., prefix, root word, derivational suffix, etc.). Table 1 (below) shows the results of the analysis and demonstrates that 77.8% of the low frequency words were structurally complex (i.e., they were multimorphemic and comprised a number of different types of word part). Conversely, just 23.4% of the high frequency words were multimorphemic. Most of the high frequency words were just root words or root words with an inflectional suffix.

The above findings demonstrate why supporting the development of learners' morphological awareness—i.e., awareness of how words are structured and how to decode the structures— could aid word comprehension and broader metalinguistic skills. In particular, the variety of morphological structures in the low frequency GCSE word sub-corpus highlights that developing learners' awareness of derivational morphology is highly important. Investigation into morphological awareness and classroom instruction is particularly important in the UK context. As is evident through the prior and subsequent discussions of 'grades' rather than Key Stages or year groups, reviews of evidence and morphology-based studies have been, and continue to be, conducted in North America. However, the sections above make clear that awareness of how words are constructed and how their parts have meanings is crucial to accessing and understanding school-based vocabulary in Wales.

Some studies have worked to assess the impact of morphological training interventions on literacy outcomes (for full reviews, see Bowers et al., 2010 and Goodwin & Ahn, 2013) and have often found that

Table 1 Morphological analysis of high/low frequency words in the GCSE word corpus

Number of morphemes	Morphological construction of words	Percentage of word type in the high frequency GCSE words corpus	Percentage of word type in the low frequency GCSE words corpus
1 morpheme	Root word	76.6	22.2
2 morphemes	Root + root (compound)	2.2	0.4
	Root word + inflectional suffix	15.4	28.6
	Root word + derivational suffix	4.2	24.2
	Prefix + root word	0	2.2
3 morphemes	Prefix + root word + inflectional suffix	0	4.4
	Prefix + root word + derivational suffix	0.4	5.2
	Root word + derivational suffix + inflectional suffix	0.2	4
	Root word + inflectional suffix + inflectional suffix	0.2	0.2
	Root word + derivational suffix + derivational suffix	0.8	3.2
	Root word + root word + inflectional suffix	0	1.8
4 morphemes	Prefix + root word + derivational suffix + derivational suffix	0	1.6
	Prefix + root word + derivational suffix + inflectional suffix	0	1
	Root word + + derivational suffix + derivational suffix + inflectional suffix	0	0.4
	Prefix + root word + root word + inflectional suffix	0	0.4
	Prefix + prefix + root word + derivational suffix	0	0.2
	Root word + derivational suffix + derivational suffix + derivational suffix	0	0.2

morphological instruction in vocabulary, reading aloud, reading comprehension, and spelling increases children's broader literacy skills. Kirby and Bowers (2017: 439) conceptualise morphology as a 'binding agent' that 'relates [to] orthography, phonology and semantic information and thus enhances representational quality'. Children appear to acquire some morphological knowledge early in the language acquisition process (see Clark, 2016) and consequently, they develop some morphological knowledge implicitly through their experiences with language and reading. However, Tyler and Nagy (1989: 649–50) suggest that full awareness of derivational morphology includes three different aspects:

1. Relational awareness, which refers to recognising that 'words have complex internal structures and that two or more words may share a common morpheme, i.e., the ability to see morphological relations between two words that share a common morpheme base'. This means that an individual can recognise that *person* is related to *personify* and *personality*, but that *tea* is not related to *teacher*.
2. Syntactic awareness, which means knowing that 'derivational suffixes mark words for a syntactic category'. They describe syntactic awareness as 'tacit knowledge', meaning an individual understands that a word like *standardise* is a verb because of the *-ise* ending, whereas *standardisation* is a noun because of the *-ion* suffix.
3. Distributional knowledge, which requires understanding of the constraints on the connections between roots and affixes. For example, *-less* attaches to adjectives but not to verbs, so *hopeless* is an adjective, but *holdless* is not.

Tyler and Nagy (1989: 650) hypothesise that children do not acquire all three aspects of morphological awareness simultaneously. They explain that a child may understand that 'the word *regulate* exists in *regulation* without assigning any systematic part-of-speech characterisation to *-ate* or *-ion*' (Tyler & Nagy, 1989: 650). Conversely, syntactic and distributional awareness presuppose relational awareness and should, therefore, be acquired later. Condry et al.'s (1979) earlier findings support this claim, as they found that American children in second-grade (ages seven to eight) had already begun to learn the relationship between roots and derived forms with common suffixes, such as *argue* and *argument*. However, in a study of children's derivational morphology abilities, Carlisle and Nomanbhoy (1993) gave kindergarteners (ages four to six) and Grade 1 students (ages six to seven) cue words and asked them to complete the sentence i.e., *farm. My uncle is a ([farmer])*. A third of the cue words focussed on phonologically transparent derived words (e.g., *farm/farmer*), another third were phonologically opaque derived words (e.g., *explode/explosion*), and the last third were inflected words (e.g., *jacket/jackets*). The kindergarten-aged children found the tasks highly challenging. They scored an average of 37% accuracy on inflected words, 23% on phonologically transparent words, and only 2% on opaque derived words. In Grade 1, these scores increased to 61%, 41% and 11%, respectively. These findings begin to illustrate a trend: producing derived forms of phonologically opaque words takes longer and is a more complex aspect of the morphological awareness development process than other aspects, such as inflection.

Overall, the above findings suggest that the development of teaching and learning strategies that address how support learners' awareness of derivational morphology, particularly in relation to opaque word roots, could offer some innovative solutions to supporting children's broader word decoding and comprehension skills in line with progression steps in the new Curriculum for Wales. However, further research is required to understand how strategies for the explicit teaching of English derivational morphology could be integrated into current teaching and learning practices within the Welsh context.

5 Making the Case for Etymology

As discussed above, in addition to morphology, etymology now forms a key part of the LLC framework. Durkin (2009: 2) defines etymology as '[…] the application, at the level of an individual word, of methods and insights drawn from many different areas of historical linguistics, in order to produce a coherent account of that word's history'. He continues that 'a key function of etymology is that it illuminates the formal and semantic relationships between the words of a language' (Durkin, 2009: 25). As such, etymology could help learners understand patterns, structures and meanings in the modern-day vocabulary of a language (see Durkin, 2009: 27). In English, morphology and etymology are closely bound; both explore word parts and word parts meanings. Some scholars, such as Henry (1988), Abbott and Berninger (1999), and Roberts Frank (2008), suggest that instruction in word origins, such as patterns and rules regarding Latin, Ancient Greek, and Anglo-Saxon words, is another example of morphological teaching. However, in concurrence with studies by Venezky (1999) and Moats (2000), I argue that in addition to an awareness of morphology, an awareness of word origins/etymology could make the learning of words more meaningful and interesting.

I also propose that drawing a distinction between morphology and etymology is key to the development of innovative word-based teaching and learning practices because in modern-day English, we use many word parts that are rooted in various languages, namely, Latin and French and Ancient Greek. Often, these word parts are bound within a word, which means that in modern-day English, they cannot standalone, but they hold the main meaning of a whole word. For example, the word part *dict*, found in words like *dictator, dictionary* and *diction,* originates from the Latin *dictum* meaning 'said' or 'a thing said' (dictum, n. Etymology 2024). The modern-day word part *dict* holds the same meaning as its historical origin. However, it now only holds meaning when it appears in conjunction with affixes (*dict + ion*, etc.). As such, I suggest that integrating the teaching of etymology (i.e., the origins, connections and meanings of bound modern-day English words and word parts) into the LLC classroom could offer learners the opportunity to develop an awareness of how to decode and comprehend the meanings of semantically complex academic words.

Evidence from *The Latin Programme,* a Latin teaching initiative that was first piloted in London state schools in 2007, supports the above claims as evidence shows that, after three years of Latin instruction, 98% of children in Key Stage 2 (ages 8 to 10 years) reached the expected level for reading and 91% achieved the expected level for writing (Bell & Wing-Davey, 2018: 121). This data represents children from 39 different classes in 9 different schools, the majority of whom were previously considered 'underachieving'. Even after one year of instruction, 90% of pupils achieved the expected level for writing, and 80% for reading (Bell & Wing-Davey, 2018: 121). Additionally, Bell and Wing-Davey (2018: 121) argue that for pupils who have English as an additional language (EAL), particularly those who do not speak an Indo-European language at home, Latin acts as a *'tabula rasa'*. Pupils were able to spot the connections between languages and learn a new language, completely from scratch, alongside their first-language English peers. Analysis showed that this really improved EAL pupils' confidence levels, and one headteacher reported: 'We have seen a sharp increase in our literacy results as a result [of the Latin programme]. Our ethnic minority children who have English as an additional language are now taking pride in their mother tongue' (Bell & Wing-Davey, 2018: 122). The findings from this study highlight that the benefits of learning ancient languages, particularly Latin, on English literacy skills are indisputable. However, statistics demonstrate that, largely, Latin remains a subject of the privately educated or, if extended beyond that, a subject of the already highest achievers (see Swallow & Holmes-Henderson, 2021). Studying an ancient language at a state school, particularly in Wales, is still a rare opportunity.

Programmes such as *Classics for All* and the *Advocating Classics Education* association are working successfully to expand access to education in Latin, Ancient Greek and ancient history (see Swallow & Holmes-Henderson, 2021). However, after Northern Ireland, Wales has the next lowest level of engagement with these programmes. Overall, 33 centres were working with *Classics for All* at the end of 2021 (Classics for All, 2021) and only 7 centres were working with *Advocating Classics Education* in 2022 (see Advocating Classics Education, 2022). While the aforementioned programmes are working hard to widen access and participation in Classical subjects, it appears that in Wales ancient language learning opportunities are inconsistent and, therefore, so are literacy development opportunities. It seems overly ambitious that all state schools will have the capacity to engage with and/or offer their pupils a Classical languages programme. Consequently, instead, I posit that the implementation of the new Curriculum for Wales offers an opportunity to develop and embed innovative word-based teaching and learning practices into already compulsory school subjects, such as English.

Bell and Wing-Davey's (2018) suggest that ancient languages have the potential to help learners capitalise on and celebrate linguistic differences, while supporting children's literacy skills and confidence development in the English language classroom. This seems particularly important in the Welsh context when considering the bilingual nature of Wales's education system and, consequently, the linguistically diverse nature of learners. Furthermore, an analysis of the etymological make-up of the words used in past English language and literature GCSE papers strengthens the above claim. Similar to the morphology-based word analysis (Table 1), I selected 500 high frequency and 500 low frequency words and used the *Oxford English Dictionary* (*OED*) online to tag each word by the language from which the root originated. The analysis demonstrates that the historical origins of the low frequency words were both more complex and varied than those of the high frequency GCSE words. Table 2 (below) shows of the 500 low frequency words, 71.4% were rooted in a Romance language, 16.4% were rooted in a Germanic language, 4.4% were rooted in Ancient Greek, and the remaining 7.8% of words were rooted in an Other or unknown language. Conversely, 72.6% of the high frequency words were rooted in Old English. Just 23.4% were rooted in a Romance language and 3% were rooted in Ancient Greek.

The varied origins of the words that comprise the English language give reason to why past studies have recommended that etymology-based knowledge could be beneficial to children's vocabulary development (e.g., Malatesha Joshi, 2005). Yet, due to a lack of research and evidence, these authors hedge their claims about the benefits of etymology on word recognition and comprehension; all state that more research is required to fully understand what the relationship between etymology and vocabulary skills might be. Crosson et al. (2019: 690) explain that most interventions have 'focused on derivational relations (such as the role of *de* and *ion* in *detection*), leaving the potentially important role of bound roots (*tect*) unclear, despite the fact that bound roots are often the major meaning-carrying constituent in the academic lexis'. As such, it is surprising that so little is known about how an awareness of bound word parts could contribute to the development of children's vocabulary decoding and comprehension skills.

Bowers and Kirby (2010) examined whether instruction in derivational affixes, freestanding root words and bound roots supported fourth- and fifth-grade monolingual English students' abilities to infer the meanings of unfamiliar words. They found that students who received explicit instruction in the aforementioned areas were able to identify the meanings of new words more accurately than their control group

Table 2 Etymologies of high/low frequency words in the GCSE word corpus

Word family	Language of origin	Percentage of high frequency words from the language of origin	Percentage of low frequency words from the language of origin
Romance languages	Latin	19.2	28
	Latin/French	2.2	24.5
	French	2	18
	Italian	0	0.6
	Spanish	0	0.4
Germanic languages	Old English	69.6	8.2
	Germanic	1	5.8
	Old Norse	2	0.8
	Scandinavian	0	0.8
	Dutch	0	0.2
Ancient Greek		3	4.4
Other/unknown origin		1	7.8

counterparts who received no explicit instruction. As such, they conclude that teaching word analysis in this way can help students learn and decode vocabulary beyond the words taught. However, this study did not examine the effects of instruction on bound roots specifically. Nor did it offer explicit instruction in etymology itself (i.e., the origins of the word parts and how to spot etymological patterns). Additionally, all word types (i.e., free word parts and bound word parts) were analysed together. Thus, the effects of learning bound roots on word recognition and decoding skills are not disentangled from the effects of learning about productive, free-standing word parts. Consequently, the implications for instruction in bound roots, while promising, remain unclear.

Additionally, Devonshire et al. (2012) did investigate the effect of teaching children multiple levels of representation in orthography, including morphology and etymology. Children who participated in Devonshire et al.'s (2012) intervention were taught the definitions/conventions relating to prefixes, root words and suffixes; how to identify the word parts; and the rules for combining them to make new words. They were also taught some 'basic etymology', such as the fact that certain silent letters in words are etymological markers which relate to other words that share the same root, i.e., the silent <w> in *two* is an etymological marker relating to the words *twin, twice, twelve* and *twenty* (see

Devonshire et al., 2012: 89). Results showed that compared to children in the control group, who only received phonics-based instruction, the intervention group showed more knowledge of morphemes, etymology and word forms. They performed better in both reading and spelling tests, were able to understand the terms 'base word' and 'suffix' and could parse words into these constituent parts (Devonshire et al. 2012: 91). Consequently, Devonshire et al. (2012: 94) conclude that 'in addition to teaching morphology, children should be taught etymology, and rules about form, from the very beginning of their formal literacy education, from the age of five years'. However, while Devonshire et al.'s (2012) study acts as a strong foundation, I contend that further research into explicit instruction in etymology is required. As the authors acknowledge, it remains unclear how both morphology and etymology may contribute to literacy skills throughout primary school, not just in the early years. Furthermore, the focus of Devonshire et al.'s (2012) study is broader literacy skills, not vocabulary recognition and comprehension directly. This is the only study I was able to find that included etymology as one of its primary factors. Nonetheless, Henry's (1988) research makes clear that, while English includes many Latin-derived words, it also comprises morphemes that have been borrowed or derived from other languages, namely Old English, other Romance languages (i.e., French) and Ancient Greek. It seems crucial, therefore, to further investigate new approaches to explicit instruction in etymology to better understand how an awareness of English word histories, origins and meanings could support Welsh learners' broader word decoding and comprehension skills.

6   Conclusion

Overall, this chapter has demonstrated that despite extensive searches of the literature, there is still a lack of evidence and investigation into how the explicit teaching of English morphology and etymology could be integrated into the classroom and/or develop children's word awareness. The studies discussed above demonstrate that developing children's explicit morphological awareness and taking an historical approach to English word learning are not new ideas. However, very little research has been conducted in the UK context, let alone the Welsh context, and that which does exist does not offer practical teaching strategies that could be employed in the classroom. Furthermore, in relation to etymology, most of the research that exists focusses on the impact of learning Latin, not word histories and origins more broadly, and, like morphology, the majority of the research that does exist has been conducted in the United States (see Holmes-Henderson & Kelly, 2022: 4). Yet, the above findings indicate that supporting the development of learners' morphological awareness (i.e., an ability to reflect upon and manipulate morphemes and employ word formation rules in one's language) and etymological awareness (i.e., an awareness of how languages are connected, word families, etymological word patterns, etc.) could aid broader word decoding and comprehension skills. Consequently, I suggest that further research is required to understand how strategies for the explicit teaching of English etymology could be integrated into current teaching and learning practices to offer innovative solutions to children's broader literacy skills development within the Welsh context.

References

Abbott, S. P., & Berninger, V. W. (1999). It's never too late to remediate: Teaching word recognition to students with reading disabilities in grades 4–7. *Annals of Dyslexia, 49*, 221–250.

Advocating Classics Education. (2022). *Advocating classics education*. Retrieved February 1, 2024, from http://aceclassics.org.uk

Bell, B., & Wing-Davey, Z. (2018). Delivering Latin in primary schools. In A. Holmes-Henderson, S. Hunt, & M. Musié (Eds.), *Forward with classics: Classical languages in schools and communities* (pp. 111–127). Bloomsbury.

Biemiller, A. (1999). *Language and reading success*. Brookline Books.

Bowers, P. N., & Kirby, J. R. (2010). Effects of morphological instruction on vocabulary acquisition. *Reading and Writing, 23*(5), 515–537.

Bowers, P. N., Kirby, J. R., & Deacon, S. H. (2010). The effects of morphological instruction on literacy skills: A systematic review of the literature. *Review of Educational Research, 80*(2), 144–179.

Bradshaw, J., Ager, R., Burge, B., & Wheater, R. (2010). *PISA 2009: Achievement of 15-year-olds in Wales*. Retrieved February 4, 2024, from https://www.nfer.ac.uk/publications/npdz02/npdz02.pdf

Carlisle, J. F. (2003). Morphology matters in learning to read: A commentary. *Reading Psychology, 24*(3–4), 291–322. https://doi.org/10.1080/02702710390227369

Carlisle, J. F., & Nomanbhoy, D. M. (1993). Phonological and morphological awareness in first graders. *Applied PsychoLinguistics, 14*(2), 177–195.

Carlisle, J. F., & Stone, C. A. (2005). Exploring the role of morphemes in word reading. *Reading Research Quarterly, 40*(4), 428–449.

Castles, A., Rastle, K., & Nation, K. (2018). Corrigendum: Ending the reading wars: Reading acquisition from novice to expert. *Psychological science in the public interest, 19*(2), 5–51.

Clark, E. (2016). *First language acquisition* (3rd ed.). Cambridge University Press.

Classics for All. (2021). *Impact report*. Retrieved February 5, 2024, from https://classicsforall.org.uk/sites/default/files/uploads/impact%20report/CfA-Impact-Report_20102021_Digital_0.pdf

Condry, S. M., Mcmahon-Rideout, M., & Levy, A. A. (1979). A developmental investigation of selective attention to graphic, phonetic, and semantic information in words. *Perception & Psychophysics, 25*(2), 88–94.

Corson, D. (1997). The learning and use of academic English words. *Language Learning, 47*(4), 671–718.

Crosson, A. C., McKeown, M. G., Moore, D. W., & Ye, F. (2019). Extending the bounds of morphology instruction: Teaching Latin roots facilitates academic word learning for English learner adolescents. *Reading and Writing, 32*(3), 689–727.

Dauncey, M. (2021). *Improving school standards*. Retrieved February 26, 2024, from https://research.senedd.wales/2016/06/10/improving-school-standards/

Devonshire, V., Morris, P., & Fluck, M. (2012). Spelling and reading development: The effect of teaching children multiple levels of representation in their orthography. *Learning and Instruction, 25*, 85–94.

Durkin, P. (2009). *The Oxford guide to etymology*. Oxford University Press.

Ehri, L. (1998). Grapheme-phoneme knowledge is essential for learning to read words in English. In J. Metsala & L. Ehri (Eds.), *Word recognition in beginning literacy* (pp. 3–40). Erlbaum.

Estyn. (2021). *English language and literacy in settings and primary schools*. Retrieved February 5, 2024, from https://www.estyn.gov.wales/system/

files/2022-01/Estyn%20English%20language%20and%20literacy%20 E%289%29.pdf
Fowler, A., & Liberman, I. (1995). The role of phonology and orthography in morphological awareness. In L. B. Feldman (Ed.), *Morphological aspects of language processing* (pp. 157–188). Lawrence Erlbaum Associates.
Goodwin, A. P., & Ahn, S. (2013). A meta-analysis of morphological interventions in English: Effects on literacy outcomes for school-age children. *Scientific Studies of Reading, 17*(4), 257–285.
Henry, M. K. (1988). Beyond phonics: Integrated decoding and spelling instruction based on word origin and structure. *Annals of Dyslexia, 38*, 258–275.
Holmes-Henderson, A., & Kelly, K. (2022). *Ancient languages in primary schools in England: A literature review.* Retrieved February 22, 2024, from https://assets.publishing.service.gov.uk/government/uploads/system/uploads/attachment_data/file/1120024/Ancient_languages_in_primary_schools_in_England_-_A_Literature_Review.pdf
Jolly Learning. (2023). *Jolly phonics.* Retrieved February 21, 2024, from https://www.jollylearning.co.uk
Kirby, J., & Bowers, P. (2017). Morphological instruction and literacy: Binding phonological, orthographic, and semantic features of words. In K. Cain, D. L. Compton, & R. K. Parrila (Eds.), *Theories of reading development* (pp. 437–462). John Benjamins.
Kuo, L. J., & Anderson, R. C. (2006). Morphological awareness and learning to read: A cross-language perspective. *Educational Psychologist, 41*(3), 161–180.
Malatesha Joshi, R. (2005). Vocabulary: A critical component of comprehension. *Reading and Writing Quarterly, 21*(3), 209–219.
Miles, K. P., Rubin, G. B., & Gonzalez-Frey, S. (2018). Rethinking sight words. *The Reading Teacher, 71*(6), 715–726.
Moats, L. C. (2000). *Speech to print: Language exercises for teachers.* Brookes Publishing Company.
OECD. (2014). *Improving schools in Wales: An OECD perspective.* Retrieved February 3, 2024, from https://www.oecd.org/education/Improving-schools-in-Wales.pdf
Perfetti, C. A. (1992). The representation problem in reading acquisition. In P. Gough, L. Ehri, & R. Treiman (Eds.), *Reading acquisition* (pp. 145–174). Erlbaum.
Roberts Frank, A. (2008). *The effect of instruction in orthographic conventions and morphological features on the reading fluency and comprehension skills of high-school freshman.* The University of San Francisco.

Rose, J. (2006). *Independent review of the teaching of early reading*. Retrieved February 1, 2024, from https://dera.ioe.ac.uk/5551/2/report.pdf

Stahl, S. A., & Nagy, W. E. (2005). *Teaching word meanings*. Routledge.

Swallow, P., & Holmes-Henderson, A. (2021). *Working towards fairer access to classical subjects in schools:* Retrieved February 6, 2024, from https://cucdedi.wordpress.com/2021/05/24/working-towards-fairer-access-to-classical-subjects-in-schools-the-advocating-classics-education-ACE-project/

Tyler, A., & Nagy, W. (1989). The acquisition of English derivational morphology. *Journal of Memory and Language, 28*, 649–667.

Venezky, R. (1999). *The American way of spelling*. Guilford Press.

Welsh Government. (2015). *Qualified for life*. Retrieved February 6, 2024, from https://dera.ioe.ac.uk/24680/1/151021-a-curriculum-for-wales-a-curriculum-for-life-en_Redacted.pdf

Welsh Government. (2016). *Programme of study for English: Curriculum for Wales, Key Stages 2–4*. Retrieved February 8, 2024, from https://hwb.gov.wales/api/storage/71847d3a-5d5b-4103-9e1a-f6cc97b40f24/english-programme-of-study.pdf

Welsh Government. (2019). *Curriculum for Wales*. Retrieved February 9, 2024, from https://hwb.gov.wales/curriculum-for-wales/introduction/

Welsh Government. (2021). *Area of learning and experience: Languages, literacy and communication*. Retrieved February 8, 2024, from https://hwb.gov.wales/curriculum-for-wales/languages-literacy-and-communication/descriptions-of-learning/

Welsh Government. (2023). *Schools' census results: January 2023 statistics on schools, teachers and pupils including data for local authorities and Wales for January 2023*. Retrieved February 6, 2024, from https://www.gov.wales/schools-census-results-january-2023-html

Language Education for People Seeking Asylum in Wales: A Nation of Sanctuary Approach

Mike Chick and Barrie Llewelyn

1 Introduction

Being able to communicate in English is essential for newly arrived refugees and people seeking asylum. Forced migrants, who have often gone through traumatic experiences and journeys, are, understandably, desperate to build new lives, to utilise the skills and knowledge they have and to access work and education. Given their importance, there is always a huge demand for ESOL classes. For instance, in the year ending 2020/2021, nearly 5000 people enrolled on formal ESOL courses across Wales (Welsh Government ESOL review, 2023). At the same time as coping with the demands of resettlement in an unfamiliar country and through a foreign language, many sanctuary seekers are also dealing with the trauma associated with forced displacement, as well as the stress involved in navigating a hostile and complex asylum process. For these

---

M. Chick (✉) · B. Llewelyn
University of South Wales, Pontypridd, Wales
e-mail: mike.chick@southwales.ac.uk

© The Author(s), under exclusive license to Springer Nature Switzerland AG 2024
S. W. Chong, H. Reinders (eds.), *Innovation in Language Learning and Teaching*, New Language Learning and Teaching Environments,
https://doi.org/10.1007/978-3-031-66241-6_13

people, developing fluency in English is critical as they begin to find their way through health, employment, social security, housing and education systems. These challenges mean that ESOL teachers are very often seen as a vital human bridge to the new society and the ESOL classroom regarded as a prime location for getting information and for creating the bonds, bridges and links needed for building a new life in a new culture. Language teachers, in other words, are uniquely placed to positively affect the lives of people in these situations. ESOL classes provide a sense of structure to many learners' daily lives and offer both linguistic and psychological support. Indeed, the crucial role that language education might play in promoting inclusion and fostering a sense of belonging was one of the main themes to emerge during the recent review of the Welsh Government's ESOL Policy for Wales (ibid.).

At present, however, the way formal language education for migrants is organised means that teachers are often unable to maximise the potential of the ESOL classroom to ensure that recently arrived forced migrants feel respected, supported and that they are welcome in their new society (Chick, 2019). The rigorous assessment schedules that teachers are obliged to follow in order to evidence learning, along with the brokering of a mandated citizenship curriculum, frequently results in classroom time being focussed more on preparing for examinations than on exploring how ESOL classrooms can be a site for engaging in activities which validate learners' identities as citizens (Peutrell, 2019). This deficit approach to language, one which sees the newcomer as somehow lacking the prerequisites for being a full citizen until they are fluent in English, disregards the multilingual, multicultural reality of modern life, ignores the fact that linguistic diversity is a central element in learners' lives (Cooke et al., 2019) and perpetuates the ideology of one nation—one language (Blackledge, 2006). Language education for migrants, therefore, is clearly much needed, yet care must be taken that ESOL "does not reinforce the false image of monolingualism" (Cooke et al., 2019: 151).

Seen from this perspective, language education needs to be radically rethought, and this chapter looks to explore the following questions:

1. Are participatory-based pedagogies feasible in an ESOL context?
2. How do practicing ESOL teachers respond to enacting participatory-based pedagogies in the language classroom?

The chapter begins with an outline of the Welsh Government's Nation of Sanctuary ambition (2019b) and details how these aspirations align with a course of participatory pedagogy to practising teachers. A summary of the collaboration that formed this project is followed by a brief review of criticisms levelled at the present organisation of formal language education for migrants. A description of what a participatory approach to ESOL may look like and an outline of the content of the pilot course of teacher education are then provided. The final section of the chapter reports on the reflections of the teachers who participated in the project and discusses the implications for future practice.

2   Background

A Nation of Sanctuary and a Citizen's Curriculum

The UK Government has, since around 2010, been introducing policies designed to make the UK appear unattractive and unwelcoming as a destination for people seeking sanctuary with a suite of tough, unsympathetic policies that have come to be known as the hostile environment (Travis, 2013). More recently, despite widespread opposition and condemnation from faith groups, charities and even the United Nations (2022), the UK and Rwanda announced a new Migration and Economic Development Partnership, which facilitates the removal to Rwanda those asylum seekers whose claims are "inadmissible in the UK" (UK Government, 2022).

In contrast, following an extensive period of consultation with all stakeholders, including refugees and people seeking asylum, the objective of the Welsh Government is to make Wales a Nation of Sanctuary and to encourage all sectors of society to play a role in achieving this ambition (Welsh Government, 2019b). This "fosters migrants' attachment and sense of belonging to the region and strengthens the overall regional identity" and has made Wales the only country in Europe to officially engage with the sanctuary movement (Edwards & Wisthaler, 2023: 2). Although the Welsh Government has no powers over the UK's asylum policy nor over how many sanctuary seekers are dispersed across Wales, it does have complete control over matters such as health, education, housing, employment and agriculture, thus can enact policies on matters that directly affect the wellbeing of forced migrants attempting to build new lives. In recognising that much needs to be done to support their inclusion, welfare and integration, the Welsh Government drew up its Nation of Sanctuary Plan which aims to utilise the devolved powers it has to improve the welfare of sanctuary seekers (Welsh Government, 2019b). To note here is that the provision of appropriate language education is one of the central components of the Nation of Sanctuary plan and is complemented by the fact that Wales is the only country in the UK to have a language education policy for migrants (Welsh Government, 2019a).

The desire for a more inclusive and participatory approach to adult education, for all citizens in Wales, is what drives interest in the idea of a citizens' curriculum. From this perspective on adult education, learners are given a voice in the co-designing of the curriculum content thus ensuring that learning is meaningful and connected to their real-life needs. It is an approach to adult learning which organisations such as the Learning and Work Institute believe all providers should embed into syllabus design (Citizens' curriculum—Learning and Work Institute, 2023).

Participatory learning closely aligns with the philosophy underpinning a citizens' curriculum in that education seen from this perspective views co-construction of class content and direction, as well as a focus on meaningful dialogue, as central tenets of its pedagogy (e.g., see Cooke et al., 2015). For this reason, the course was included as one of a series of pilot projects that the Welsh government were funding to investigate the viability and potential of such an approach.

3 The Collaboration

Much ESOL provision takes place in informal settings, outside the funded government delivery plans (Simpson & Hunter, 2023). It is in these settings where there is evidence that grassroots initiatives are at the forefront of radical approaches to language education for migrants (Rampton & Cooke, 2021). Freed from operating under the strictures of a centralised syllabus, third sector organisations have the scope to introduce and experiment with alternative approaches to how language education may be viewed and organised. Opportunities for collaboration provide space for mutual learning and development. University academics bring their knowledge and experience to often under-resourced contexts and get frontline exposure that bridges the theory-practice gap while the third sector organisations can benefit from access to teacher education, funding for ESOL classes and better understanding of learner needs through codesigned research projects. For example, English for Action (www.efalondon.org), an educational charity which seeks to provide 'accessible, participatory, and empowering' English language classes for migrants, has a long partnership with academics from King's College London while Learning English Yorkshire and Humberside (www.learningenglish.org.uk) developed from a partnership instigated by academics from the University of Leeds. The collaboration described in this chapter stemmed from a partnership between Wales' largest third sector migrant support organisation, Oasis (Oasis Cardiff), Addysg Oedolion Cymru / Adult Learning Wales, and academics from the University of South Wales.

Oasis Cardiff

The largest of all charities providing ESOL in Wales is Oasis, based in the centre of Wales' capital city, Cardiff. Originally set up to help refugees and people seeking asylum to integrate within the local community, the team at Oasis organise and deliver a wide variety of services ranging from food clubs to trips, sports events, gardening and ESOL. The ESOL classes were initially set up to provide language learning spaces for newly arrived asylum seekers who faced the prospect of spending months on a waiting list before beginning formal ESOL classes. However, even after starting college, many students continue to access the ESOL provision at Oasis to 'top up' their formal classes and to get more opportunities to practise during vacation periods. Although there is only one full-time ESOL professional employed at the charity, there are approximately 60 volunteer teachers and teaching assistants providing informal language education.

During 2023, there were over 300 filled spaces in classes each week with new learners arriving daily, yet demand for ESOL classes often massively outstrips supply with class places allocated on a first-come, first-served basis. Drop-in Welsh classes (WSOL) are also offered, delivered by qualified Welsh language volunteer teachers.

Addysg Oedolion Cymru/Adult Learning Wales

After colleges of further education, Adult Learning Wales (ALW) is the largest provider of ESOL classes in Wales. They are the national adult community learning organisation for Wales and are committed to widening participation and promoting active citizenship. The majority of ESOL classes delivered by ALW tutors are formally assessed and follow a prescribed syllabus though they also deliver informal ESOL activities that are not tied to assessments. Given their interest in active citizenship and the curriculum team's desire to learn more about the value of introducing a citizens' curriculum, ALW were keen to participate in this project and identify ways of enhancing the language education experience of their students.

The ESOL classes delivered at Oasis and Adult Learning Wales provide crucial linguistic, psychological and emotional scaffolding for the newly arrived sanctuary seekers, enabling them to begin language learning, form friendships and access support as soon as they arrive. Language education that is freed from a prescribed syllabus allows teachers to focus on the issues most important to the lives of the learners, without the straitjacket of continually preparing class members for tests or exams. Nevertheless, this approach to language education, where themes, topics and language issues emerge from the class participants, demands a lot of teachers and there is a desperate need for continued professional development (CPD), especially for volunteers and / or teachers who are inexperienced or underqualified. For these reasons, during 2022, the Head of ESOL at Oasis, the curriculum manager at Adult Learning Wales and language education staff at the University of South Wales (USW) set about co-designing a pilot training course for the ESOL and WSOL workforce that would equip them with the tools and techniques suitable for their teaching context.

Why Is There a Need for Alternative Approaches to ESOL Classes and to ESOL Teacher Education?

Much recent research in the field of language education for migrants supports the case for fundamental changes to its organisation and delivery or, at the very least, for alternative approaches that can complement existing structures. Concerns have been documented about a variety of issues ranging from the pedagogic to the political. For instance, researchers have questioned the need for and value of a prescribed curriculum with constant assessments for migrant learners. An exam-based syllabus will, necessarily, involve preparing learners for regular tests and thus leave little time to focus on their real-life needs (Cooke, 2006; Simpson, 2015). Already dealing with the effects of forced migration, the asylum system and resettling in a new community, a regime of continuous assessment may well have detrimental effects on the motivation of migrant learners to attend classes (Sidaway, 2021; Chick & Hannagan Lewis, 2019). Moreover, policy guidelines which focus exclusively on accreditation and employability miss opportunities to develop positive 'identities of competence' (Court, 2017: 24), serve to position migrant students as 'outsiders' (Cooke, 2006) and overlook the needs of those for whom obtaining certificates and preparing for employment are not the uppermost concerns (Cox & Phipps, 2022). Aiming to get learners through a never-ending suite of assessments results in far fewer opportunities to discuss more deeply issues of citizenship or belonging, or to be more creative with the curriculum. Conventional ESOL pedagogy, in effect, stifles attempts to foster a more inclusive approach (Cooke, 2019). It has little room for projects which aim to counter the positioning of ESOL learners as outsiders and which can bring people together to break down barriers and foster friendship, tolerance and understanding amongst "diasporic locals" (Cooke & Peutrell, 2019: 229). Initiatives such as the Speak to Me Project (Speak to me... | University of South Wales), and that detailed by Goodey (2021), reveal the tremendous potential such projects have for promoting mutual understanding and learning for all in the community.

In sum, taking a human capital perspective on the organisation of ESOL provision is unfavourable to promoting inclusion and certainly falls short of offering the type of integrative experiences that may be afforded by alternative approaches (Morrice et al., 2019; Chick & Hannagan Lewis, 2019; Court, 2017).

It is also useful to note here that there is much evidence and theoretical argument from second language acquisition research about the benefit of providing language learners with opportunities to use language by talking and writing about the ideas, beliefs, hopes, etc., that they themselves hold (Long, 2015; Allwright, 2005). Furthermore, some educators argue that a prescribed syllabus, such as that enacted in conventional ESOL pedagogy, does not reflect what is now known about how languages are most efficiently acquired (e.g., see Jordan, 2019). They argue that learners' attention should be drawn to formal aspects of language as the need arises during a communicative activity—not pre-determined by the order of a coursebook or syllabus. Finally, with regard to materials used in the ESOL classroom, researchers have claimed that many coursebooks do not reflect the lived experiences of most ESOL learners and paint an artificially homogenised view of life—excluding many learners through their lack of representation of, for example, disabled people, people from minority ethnic backgrounds and members of the LGBTQ+ community (Brown & Nanguy, 2021).

The following sections describe what an alternative understanding of the ESOL classroom may entail and outline the content and approach taken on the pilot course.

4 A Participatory Approach

For ESOL teachers and researchers committed to better supporting and understanding the worlds of learners from vulnerable or marginalised backgrounds, Paulo Freire (1970) has been particularly influential. In his work on literacy education with underprivileged people in mid-twentieth-century Brazil, Freire developed the principle that knowledge is co-constructed rather than transmitted from teacher to students. This idea of co-construction in a classroom approach puts the learner very much at the centre of pedagogy, acknowledging and recognising what they bring into a class in terms of life experiences, languages and identities. For language educators, this means ensuring that a classroom atmosphere is created in which participants' existing skills, ambitions and linguistic repertoires are openly appreciated and used as tools for developing further language competency (Simpson, 2019; Cooke et al., 2019). Moreover, it entails understanding that learners are part of a community "with their own linguistic, cultural, social, affective and other resources, whose very presence reshapes the locality they live in" (Cooke & Peutrell, 2019: 229). Teaching and research viewed from this Freirean perspective is thus designed to question and challenge current practices. For the ESOL educator, it can involve a radical transformation in how the classroom is seen and understood, with the teacher trying out different approaches to organising learning—giving learners' voices far more space than conventional pedagogy allows. In this understanding of education, decisions about what is focused on in class should be 'from the students to the curriculum rather than from the curriculum to the students' (Auerbach, 1992: 19). Examples of typical issues which dominate discussions when such spaces are opened up include finding meaningful employment, the effects of trauma, culture shock, separation from family, money worries and finding accommodation. In other words, in creating activities and tasks that focus on topics and areas of need put forward by the students, class content can follow a direction emerging from the participants rather than being imposed from a prescribed curriculum.

For over three decades, language education tutors working with migrants and displaced people have been drawing on Freire's work. His underlying philosophy, that education should be dialogic, emancipatory and based on the lives of the students, resonated strongly with those teaching refugees and people seeking asylum. Teacher-researchers such as Auerbach (Auerbach, 1992, 1995), Baynham (1988), Cooke and Simpson (2008) utilised Freirean concepts in their work, motivating others to recognise the potential of participatory pedagogy, and over the last decade or so, thanks to movements such as English for Action, the approach has become more widely known and adopted across the UK, especially in community-based ESOL classes such as those delivered at Oasis.

Indeed, much research conducted in the field refers to the value of, and need for, a more participatory pedagogy in migrant language education (e.g., see Baynham, 1988; Cooke & Simpson, 2008; Brown, 2021; Cox & Phipps, 2022). The course of teacher education described here was inspired by such works in its design.

5   The Pilot Course

Content and Participants

The course consisted of 10 three-hour workshops delivered weekly from February to May 2023. Participation in the course was voluntary and non-assessed. The sessions were devised to inform the teachers of practical ways to introduce participatory learning into their classrooms and were planned around an existing resource pack on participatory approaches designed by English for Action and the Learning and Work Institute.[1] To be clear, activities described in the resource pack (pages 8–23) were presented and discussed in the workshops. The tutors then put these approaches into practice in their own teaching contexts and reflected on their outcome through answering a series of questions aimed at promoting reflection and identifying further development needs. For example, one such activity is the problem tree (p. 16). In this activity, learners might be encouraged, for instance, to list the greatest challenges they face in adjusting to life in a new society. Once any common themes have been identified, the teacher then has a greater understanding of the needs and concerns of their learners and base lessons on exploring the issues more deeply, looking at the causes of and solutions to issues raised by the class participants. Moreover, any language issues that emerge, while the learners are discussing matters relevant to their own lives, can be dealt with spontaneously by the teacher—thus meeting the learner at their linguistic point of need (i.e., what is useful and appropriate for

---

[1] Citizens' Curriculum Participatory Resource Pack—Learning and Work Institute.

them) rather than from the use of a decontextualised course book activity—which may well be inappropriate for the learners' level of fluency.

Workshops were also included on the opportunities afforded for bringing people together when a more participatory approach to syllabus design is considered. These included looking at how to introduce initiatives that foster contact between people from different backgrounds. For example, activities from the Speak to Me project (Speak to Me, 2021) were studied and their appropriacy for participants' contexts discussed. Templates were provided to facilitate cycles of action research, and recommended texts were also included as background reading on the theoretical underpinnings of the approach, on the asylum system, and on the overlap between ESOL, politics and migration. In addition to this, workshops included training on teaching basic literacy and of being creative in the ESOL classroom. For example, the basic literacy workshop drew heavily on the work of Spiegel and Sunderland (2006) in which the focus is on giving learners a voice, encouraging them to express their identities and "speak from within"; a highly significant aspect of effective practice in ESOL teaching.

Ten participants attended the workshops. Five were volunteer teachers delivering ESOL classes for Oasis and five were employed teachers, working for Addysg Oedolion Cymru/Adult Learning Wales. All participants had teaching qualifications and these ranged from a basic one-month introductory certificate such as the CELTA qualification to post-graduate qualifications such as a master's degree in TESOL. Some of the teachers were recently qualified and thus had only a few months of classroom experience, while others had been involved in language teaching for over 20 years. None of the participants had previously attended any form of training concerning participatory pedagogy.

A Note on Action Research

Action research has been described as a combination of both action and research whereby educators adopt an exploratory, investigative approach to their own professional context (Allwright & Hanks, 2009). The action, in this case, is work undertaken in the ESOL classroom and involves modifications or developments in practice aimed at bringing about greater understanding of one's teaching context and pedagogical efficacy (e.g., through trying out a participatory activity or through dealing with language issues spontaneously). The research necessitates reflecting on the successes or challenges of the modifications to teaching by bringing the experience to bear on the literature surrounding the modification and, where possible, through discussing the outcomes with peers in a community of practice (Lave & Wenger, 1991). Observation on action and subsequent reflection are key tenets of action research (Wallace, 1991). Of particular relevance to ESOL professionals, a critical and participatory approach to action research (Simpson & Chick, forthcoming) encourages the researcher not only to critique the broader social, cultural and political influences that affect education in their particular context, but also to promote more democratic and equal practices (Carr & Kemmis, 1986).

6 Discussion

The teachers' reflections included in this section are drawn from their own action research portfolio notes. The quotes below are their recorded thoughts as they observed and reflected upon their attempts to introduce participatory tasks and approaches into their classrooms. Such tasks, as contained in the Citizens' Curriculum Resource Pack (above), eschew pre-published materials and focus instead on creating an environment where learners are supported to discuss issues of interest or relevance to their lives. The observations included have been selected following a basic thematic analysis to ascertain the impact, challenges and outcomes of their attempts at organising learning along participatory lines.

Impact

The most striking observation that emerged from the action research portfolios was the radical change in beliefs and teacher identity that many of the participants articulated. This is noticeable in the way some teachers appear to have modified how they see their role and how they might organise their classrooms in future, as the following reflections demonstrate:

> *This caused a shift in my perspective as a teacher. I had previously seen English as an end unto itself. Throughout this exercise, language became more of a tool and outlet. I wasn't teaching for its own sake, I was teaching so that my learners could express themselves.* (Oasis volunteer)

> *Learners were more fluent in their speech than I had realised because they were given time to express themselves—it was a revelation.* (ALW teacher)

> *Participatory pedagogy has come as something of a minor revelation to me, and has opened up numerous lines of thought, in my mind, as to how best to approach my ESOL teaching.* (Oasis volunteer)

> *The course [on participatory pedagogy] has proved nothing short of a revelation.* (Oasis volunteer)

Considering that very few ESOL-specific language teacher qualifications exist in the UK (none of the participants had an ESOL-specific teaching qualification), it is perhaps unsurprising that a participatory approach contrasted sharply with participants' previous experience of language teacher education. The following recorded thoughts bring to light how the teachers were coming to understand that a pedagogy for ESOL had the potential to involve far more than the transmission of knowledge about language. Moreover, learning about the interconnectedness of ESOL, citizenship and politics was empowering for those teachers frustrated with having to comply with policy mandates and curriculum objectives set from above:

> *Learning the language of the country you live in should be something that the individuals concerned should have a choice in—how they do it and when they do it. Their own languages should be treated as important as English; keeping their languages alive as part of their identity and encouraging future generations to embrace this diversity.* (ALW teacher)

> *The deconstruction of hierarchy, engagement with topics relevant to learners, and eliciting both what topics are relevant, and what kind of people my learners are, were all principles that aligned with my values as an ESOL teacher and struck me as an infinitely more authentic pedagogic approach.* (Oasis volunteer)

> *I now appreciate that ESOL practitioners have a role to play in changing the ways in which people are portrayed and the lives they can lead.* (ALW teacher)

> *My lessons are more enjoyable, fun and useful. I'm connecting with learners authentically, tapping into language most valuable to them, and addressing essential concepts for the real world in a way I couldn't have come close to if teaching pre-determined content from a dusty textbook.* (Oasis volunteer)

Replacing pre-published materials with a focus on learners' lives, allowing space for learners to co-construct the direction of classes, and appreciating the linguistic repertoires of the learners also appear to have had a positive effect on the motivation of all involved, as these recollections reveal:

> *We connect with what we care about. I also hope that by co-learning and all sharing around the same subject, some sense of belonging was achieved among students.* (Oasis volunteer)

> *You can just tell when the lesson has been a success, with interaction being key to concentration and interest, and topics sparked by the importance of relevance to the learners' lived experience, being drawn out through these activities.* (Oasis volunteer)

> *I am very pleased to learn about research on linguistic diversity and multilingual cultures as I come from such a background myself… Teachers should be educated about the fact that they are teaching an additional language, not a replacement language.* (ALW teacher)

> *Levels of engagement and motivation have increased, and students have adapted to the new style of learning pretty quickly with results being seen weekly. Engagement is higher and retention appears to be more successful as it is the student that instigates the lead in what they want to learn about.* (Oasis volunteer)

Challenges

A Present-Practice-Produce (PPP) format is the predominant language instruction methodology espoused on conventional language teacher education courses. This is one in which a pre-decided language point is the focus of the lesson, so the teacher is in control of the content of the class. Conversely, with participatory learning, given its emphasis on authentic, meaningful interaction, the teacher is less able to predict which language difficulties may emerge or which learning opportunities arise. This means, in effect, that the transmissive PPP model of teaching is turned on its head as the teacher focuses on the language issues at the point of need, rather than a pre-decided language point dictated by the page of a coursebook or syllabus outline. Predictably perhaps, especially for less experienced teachers or those with less well developed language awareness, this approach to focusing on form (Long, 2015) can be challenging, as these sentiments demonstrate:

> *The sheer volume of emergent language was fantastic, but also overwhelming, and I struggled to keep notes on what to later address. Nevertheless, identifying language that the learners had used themselves provided me with an assurance that I was teaching them relevant English, within an applicable and relevant context because by the nature of participatory pedagogy, they had given me both the language and context.* (Oasis volunteer)

> *Isolating emergent language spontaneously took me out of my comfort zone of lesson planning with specific language focuses determined in advance, something I didn't feel prepared for.* (Oasis volunteer)

> *The emergent language task felt more improvised and possibly more difficult to deliver.* (Oasis volunteer)

A second major challenge in enacting a participatory pedagogy was that the shift in the power dynamic meant that classroom discussion had the potential to involve topics that could be labelled controversial or difficult (e.g., see Hepworth, 2019). Issues such as homophobia, racism, sexism are relevant to most ESOL learners' lives. While some ESOL learners may welcome the chance to articulate their experiences, beliefs or understandings, and learn about the laws, culture and attitudes prevalent in their new country, others may be uncomfortable doing so and the same is true of ESOL teachers. Conventional English language teacher education seldom touches upon this area, yet it was an issue that appeared in most of the teachers' reflections on their experience of a participatory class. The mixed responses exemplify the personal nature of this aspect of teaching, as the following thoughts show:

> *Not only have I come to better appreciate how much I can learn from my students, but I now realise that the only way I can effect positive change in their lives is to engage with the sometimes-controversial subjects that impact them.* (Oasis volunteer)

> *I would be prepared to include or discuss difficult subjects in my classes, but it requires tact, nuance, and empathy.* (Oasis volunteer)

> *[Teaching] controversial subjects does not sit naturally with my personal teaching style and may take significant further effort on my part before I can feel that I have integrated it successfully into my teaching.* (Oasis volunteer)

> *There is a moral imperative, as well as linguistic value to teaching controversial issues.* (Oasis volunteer)

Outcomes

The aim of the course was to promote reflection on an alternative way of organising the ESOL classroom and to empower the participants with the techniques, knowledge and confidence to teach from a participatory perspective. This chapter explores the first steps taken to better understand the needs of teachers who had been trained in quite different methods of classroom management. The following final reflections suggest that although further work will always be needed, this introduction to participatory pedagogy has bestowed the participants with the tools to continue their own teaching and learning journeys:

> *The improvement I saw in my own delivery over the course of my research cycles gave me hope that experience gained from the deep end will result in my growth in teaching.* (Oasis volunteer)

I appreciate the value of involving students in their learning and being flexible in my approach to teach. This helps to ensure within the short time currently allocated for such an important element of integration into British society, students dictate areas of relevance, rather than an antiquated method of traditional-style learning that may not focus on life in the UK for refugees and asylum seekers. (Oasis volunteer)

The course has given me the courage to take risks and be more flexible with my teaching. (ALW teacher)

I'm loving trying out some of these participatory approaches and targeting emergent language, the approach has really got my students communicating more organically and allowed me to address what is most important and relevant to them. (Oasis volunteer)

7 Conclusion

The thoughts of the ESOL professionals included in this chapter demonstrate the tremendous desire they hold to enact a more holistic role for their learners. Also clear is the need that exists for teachers to be supported in conceiving ESOL teaching as a vehicle for a far more emancipatory and inclusive practice. In taking an ecological view of ESOL (Cox & Phipps, 2022), that context and language use cannot be separated, classrooms become sites not merely for the assessment of language competence or the transmission of "mandated ideas of citizenship" (Cooke et al., 2023: 9) but for imparting a sense of belonging amongst learners through recognising their needs, concerns, desires and aspirations as well as the multilingual reality of their everyday lives. A reconceptualisation of ESOL would acknowledge linguistic diversity as a central element in learners' lives (Cooke et al., 2019) recognising the value of all languages and "making it clear that ESOL teachers are foregrounding just one among a range of linguistic resources that students use" (Cooke et al., 2023: 15).

Participatory learning in ESOL, as part of a citizens' curriculum approach, can play a hugely consequential role in the Welsh Government's Nation of Sanctuary aspiration and its aim to impart a meaningful sense of belonging amongst migrants to Wales. To be effective, organisations such as Oasis need to be supported in continuing to develop radical, people-based approaches to ESOL and formal providers need to be encouraged to complement their assessment-based provision with alternative forms of language education such as participatory pedagogy. Moreover, pre-service and in-service ESOL teacher development courses need to be designed that adopt a critical perspective and which provide teachers with the tools and confidence to discuss issues of social justice, inclusion and equality (Simpson & Chick, forthcoming).

Finally, we refer back to the two questions from the start of this chapter. As a reminder, the queries we posed were whether participatory approaches to ESOL were feasible and how ESOL teachers might respond to enacting a participatory approach. From the responses collated above, the answer to the former is most certainly affirmative while the latter suggests it is now crucial that ESOL-specific teacher education is revolutionised to equip our language educators with the tools and knowledge necessary to realise the potential of the ESOL classroom as a site of both belonging and transformation.

Action Research Reflection

Activity attempted: _____ .

Question	Notes
Did the learners appear to enjoy the task? If so, how do you know this? If not, why do you think they didn't?	
Did the task result in less teacher talking and more learner participation?	
What evidence did you see / hear that learners were interested and stimulated by the lesson?	
Were there any moments when you were able to react to spontaneous language needs? Were you comfortable doing so? Why / why not?	
Were there opportunities for learners to provide their own input / ideas in the lesson?	
Has doing these reflections altered how you see the ESOL classroom? If so, in what ways?	
In what ways does this approach to teaching reflect your beliefs about language and learning?	
Do you have an idea / plan / amendment for your NEXT cycle of action research? If so ... what is it?	

References

Allwright, D. (2005). From teaching points to learning opportunities and beyond. *TESOL Quarterly, 29*(1), 9–31.

Allwright, D., & Hanks, J. (2009). *The developing language learner: An introduction to exploratory practice*. Palgrave Macmillan.

Auerbach, E. R. (1992). *Making meaning, making change: Participatory curriculum development for adult ESL literacy*. Delta Publications.

Auerbach, E. R. (1995). The politics of the ESL classroom: Issues of power in pedagogical choices. In J. Tollefson (Ed.), *Power and inequality in language education* (pp. 9–33). Cambridge University Press.

Baynham, M. (1988). Action and reflection: The Freirean argument in ESL. *Language Issues, 2*(1), 6–12.

Blackledge, A. (2006). The racialisation of language in political discourse. *Critical Discourse Studies., 3*, 1.

Brown, S. (2021). The emancipation continuum: Analysing the role of ESOL in the settlement of immigrants. *British Journal of Sociology of Education*. https://doi.org/10.1080/01425692.2021.1908116

Brown, S., & Nanguy, C. (2021). Global ELT coursebooks and equalities legislation: A critical study. *New York State TESOL Journal*. 8 (2), p. 51–62, 12 p.

Carr, W., & Kemmis, S. (1986). *Becoming critical*. Deakin University Press.

Chick, M. (2019). Refugee resettlement in rural Wales: A collaborative approach. In F. Mishan (Ed.), *ESOL provision in the UK and Ireland*. Peter Lang.

Chick, M., & Hannagan Lewis, I. (2019). Language education for forced migrants: governance and approach. *Languages, 4*(3), 74.

Cooke, M. (2006). "When I wake up I dream of electricity": The lives, aspirations and 'needs' of Adult ESOL learners. *Linguistics and Education, 17*(1), 56–73.

Cooke, M. (2019). ESOL teachers as mediators of the citizenship testing regime. In M. Cooke & R. Peutrell (Eds.), *Brokering Britain, educating citizens* (pp. 63–82). Multilingual Matters.

Cooke, M., & Peutrell, R. (2019). *Brokering Britain, educating citizens: Exploring ESOL and citizenship*. Multilingual Matters.

Cooke, M., & Simpson, J. (2008). *ESOL: A critical guide*. Oxford University Press.

Cooke, M., Bryers, D., & Winstanley, B. (2015). Whose integration?: A participatory ESOL project in the UK. In J. Simpson & A. Whiteside (Eds.), *Adult education and migration: Challenging agendas in policy and practice*. Routledge. Available online: Whose Integration_0.pdf (britishcouncil.org).

Cooke, M., Bryers, D., & Winstanley, B. (2019). Our languages: Sociolinguistics in multilingual participatory ESOL. In M. Cooke & R. Peutrell (Eds.), *Brokering Britain, educating citizens*. Multilingual Matters.

Cooke, M., Rampton, B., & Simpson, J. (2023). ESOL and linguistic citizenship in England: Practical actions amid policy neglect WP308-Cooke-Rampton-Simpson-2023.-ESOL-linguistic-citizenship.pdf (wpull.org)

Court, J. (2017). 'I feel integrated when I help myself': ESOL learners' views and experiences of language learning and integration. *Language and Intercultural Communication, 17*(4), 396–421.

Cox, S., & Phipps, A. (2022). An ecological, multilingual approach to language learning with newly reunited refugee families in Scotland. *International Journal of Educational Research, 115*.

Edwards, C. W., & Wisthaler, V. (2023). The power of symbolic sanctuary: Insights from Wales on the limitations and potential of a regional approach to sanctuary. *Journal of Ethnic and Migration Studies*. https://doi.org/10.1080/1369183X.2023.2198809

Freire, P. (1970). *Pedagogy of the oppressed*. Continuum.

Goodey, C. (2021). Collaboration and learning in the community: Shifting the focus. *New York State TESOL Journal, 8*(2), 29–38.

Jordan, G. (2019). A response to Hughes. *ELT Journal, 73*(4), 456–458.

Lave, J., & Wenger, E. (1991). *Situated learning*. Cambridge University Press.

Learning and Work Institute. (2023). *Citizens' Curriculum*. Retrieved from https://learningandwork.org.uk/what-wedo/essential-life-skills/citizens-curriculum/

Long, M. H. (2015). *Second language acquisition and task-based language teaching*. Wiley-Blackwell.

Morrice, L., Tip, L., Collyer, M., & Brown, R. (2019). "You can't have a good integration when you don't have a good communication": English language learning among resettled refugees in the UK. *Journal of Refugee Studies, 34*(1), 681–699.

Peutrell, R. (2019). Thinking about citizenship and ESOL. In M. Cooke & R. Peutrell (Eds.), *Brokering Britain, educating citizens: Exploring ESOL and citizenship*. Multilingual Matters.

Rampton, B., & Cooke, M. (2021). *Collaboration between universities and third sector organisations in language education*. Working Papers in Urban Language & Literacies 281. www.wpull.or

Sidaway, K. (2021). Exploring the motivation of women studying in a multilevel ESOL class in England. *TESOL Journal, 13* (1). Exploring the motivation of women studying in a multilevel ESOL class in England—Sidaway—2022—TESOL Journal—Wiley Online Library.

Simpson, J. (2015). English for speakers of other languages (ESOL): Language education and migration. In G. Hall (Ed.), *The Routledge handbook of English language teaching*. Routledge.

Simpson, J. (2019). Policy and adult migrant language education in the UK. In M. Cooke & R. Peutrell (Eds.), *Brokering Britain, educating citizens* (pp. 25–42). Multilingual Matters.

Simpson, J., & Chick, M. (Forthcoming). Research with adult migrant language learners: Challenges and responses. In *Ethical issues in applied linguistics research*. John Benjamins.

Simpson, J., & Hunter, A. M. (2023). Policy formation for adult migrant language education in England: National neglect and its implications. *Language Policy*. https://doi.org/10.1007/s10993-023-09655-6

Speak to Me Project. (2021). https://gallery.southwales.ac.uk/past-exhibitions/speak-me/

Spiegel, M., & Sunderland, H. (2006). *Teaching basic literacy to ESOL learners*. LLU+.

Travis, A. (2013). Theresa May defends plans to create 'hostile environment'. *The Guardian*, October 10.

UK Government. (2022). Factsheet: Migration and economic development partnership—Home office in the media. https://homeofficemedia.blog.gov.uk/2022/04/14/factsheet-migrationand-economic-development-partnership

United Nations. (2022). UNHCR 'firmly' opposing UK-Rwanda offshore migration processing deal I UN News. UNHCR 'firmly' opposing UK-Rwanda offshore migration processing deal I UN News.

Wallace, M. (1991). *Training foreign language teachers*. Cambridge University Press.

Welsh Government. (2019a). English for speakers of other languages (ESOL) policy for Wales. https://gov.wales/sites/default/files/publications/2019-11/english-for-speakers-of-other-languages-esol-policy-wales.pdf

Welsh Government. (2019b). *Nation of sanctuary delivery plan*. Sanctuary I Nation of Sanctuary Plan (gov.wales).

Welsh Government. (2023). *A review of English for speakers of other languages (ESOL) policy for Wales* (gov.wales).

Part VI

Conclusion

Innovating Language Education in Partnership: The Less-Treaded Path

Sin Wang Chong and Hayo Reinders

1 Innovating vs. Innovation

We see in this book vivid examples of innovative practices by those involved in language education in the United Kingdom. Each chapter offers an in-depth review of the contexts where the innovation is situated, the process of designing, developing, and implementing the innovation, as well as the evaluation of and reflection on the innovation. We are pleased to see accounts that shed light on both the products and processes of innovation (see the introductory chapter of this book for a discussion). Chapters showcase pedagogical interventions, redesigned modules and programmes, professional development programmes for language teachers, and policy documents; equally, they document how innovations

---

S. W. Chong (✉)
University of St Andrews, St Andrews, UK
e-mail: swc5@st-andrews.ac.uk

H. Reinders
Anaheim University, Anaheim, CA, USA

© The Author(s), under exclusive license to Springer Nature Switzerland AG 2024
S. W. Chong, H. Reinders (eds.), *Innovation in Language Learning and Teaching*, New Language Learning and Teaching Environments,
https://doi.org/10.1007/978-3-031-66241-6_14

came to life and how they can be improved in the next iteration of their implementation. As mentioned in the introductory chapter of the book, we define "innovation" in this book as:

> Intentional and iterative processes to identify opportunities and creative and context-specific solutions for real-world problems or improvements on current practices.

We wish to foreground the processes of innovating, including their sources of inspiration and the challenges encountered during its implementation. In the field of language education, there needs to be a paradigm shift in understanding innovation as a verb rather than a noun. In other words, innovation should be about actions that one takes individually and collaboratively such as pondering, brainstorming, designing, tinkering, discussing, enacting, evaluating, reflecting. If innovation is only viewed as a noun, it restricts our focus to the artefacts that are the results of a complex, reflexive, and iterative process of innovating. Referring to the six-dimensional framework of innovation that we presented in the introduction chapter, we invite all who are involved in language education to view innovation holistically; including the contexts where an innovation is situated, its purposes, levels and scopes, the processes involved, its outputs, and its short-term, mid-term, and long-term impacts on those involved.

2 Partnership as the Less-Treaded Path

Although innovation takes on many different shapes and sizes, one fundamental principle towards impactful and sustainable innovation is the equitable collaboration and partnership of all stakeholders, working towards a shared goal. While our book provides an array of highly successful examples of innovation, what we find lacking are reports on innovation as a joint venture among those who play different roles in language education. We have heard again and again suggestions that pertain to two rather extreme views: on the one hand, there is the advice to "start small", implying the need for innovation to be bottom-up, for example, through teachers experimenting with new pedagogies or techniques in their classrooms. Others may argue that to have innovation produce sector-wide impact, there needs to be an overhaul in the system, pointing to the strategic roles played by government and institutional leaders. We contend that neither of these views is sufficient for solving problems or improving current practices in language education in the long term.

Let us illustrate this by drawing on Shepherd's (2014) concept of "evidence ecosystem", which exemplifies the interdependence among various stakeholders such as researchers, practitioners, and policymakers. Specifically, Shepherd presents three primary activities in an "evidence ecosystem": evidence creation, evidence translation, and evidence implementation. Evidence creation is about the generation of new knowledge and insights through conducting research, focusing on the roles of researchers. Evidence translation focuses on the roles played by the government, professional organisations, and learned societies, where they unpack and communicate complex research insights to practitioners. Evidence implementation, as the name suggests, refers to how practitioners engage with research evidence for their practice.

Since the concept of "evidence ecosystem" was originally developed for medicine and healthcare and is about research evidence, we adapt it for the discussion on innovation in language education (Fig. 1). We highlight four elements that are crucial if we want an innovation to achieve its full potential: practice, evidence, inquiry, and optics. First of all, we need practitioners who are professionals in designing and developing an innovation that would work in a specific context. Teachers are aware of the opportunities and constraints present in an educational context because of their experience in interacting with students, parents, and school leaders. Teachers are experts in the subject and in pedagogy, playing an important role in transforming an innovation from idea to implementation. Teachers need to be supported by teacher educators who are familiar with the evidence base concerning a particular area of inquiry. Teacher educators may or may not be active researchers, but they have a solid understanding of the latest developments of research because they teach on teacher education programmes in universities. Teacher educators are able to advise on the effectiveness of specific interventions based on research

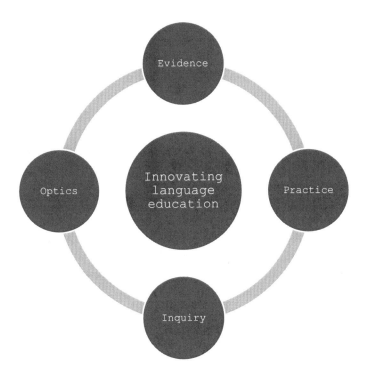

Fig. 1 An innovation ecosystem for language education

and provide recommendations on how practices are implemented internationally.

A crucial part of the innovation process is inquiry. By inquiry we mean how one collects evidence to evaluate the usefulness of an innovation or to analyse the experiences and perceptions of stakeholders. This requires knowledge and experience in research design, data collection and analysis, which may involve researchers' input. Finally, optics refers to how an innovation is perceived by members of the public and highlights that innovation can sometimes be understood as a political act to advance the agenda of the government or a particular group of people. Brokering work needs to be done to ensure the original intention of an innovation is not misunderstood or twisted and to ensure the viewpoints and concerns of various stakeholders are acknowledged and considered. People who have the relevant expertise include those who have experience in working as or for different stakeholders. For example, these can include experienced teachers who sit on advisory groups for the government, academics who serve as governors of schools. Alternatively, some educational organisations have their own marketing communications teams, with members who have worked in journalism and public relations. The input of such teams is especially valuable for complex, large-scale, and sector-wide innovations that require negotiations, communications, explanations, and lobbying to various stakeholders in the society. Such teams connect educational organisations with appropriate media outlets to disseminate news about an innovation, organise events and fora for consultations and discussions on the innovation, and informs educational organisations of public reactions about the innovation and suggests ways to respond to criticisms and scepticism.

As we hope we have demonstrated throughout this book, innovating language education is a complex endeavour, and one that brings tremendous opportunity for everyone involved. We hope this book has inspired you to initiate your own innovations.

Reference

Shepherd, J. (2014). How to achieve more effective services: The evidence ecosystem. https://orca.cardiff.ac.uk/id/eprint/69077/1/2014_JPS_What_Works.pdf

Index[1]

B
Blended learning, 30, 179–199, 274

C
CELTA, 262, 317
Child vocabulary development, 289, 299
Chinese language and culture, 157–176
Citizens' curriculum, 310, 312, 323
CLIL, *see* Content and Language Integrated Learning
Content and Language Integrated Learning (CLIL), 12, 13, 64, 65, 72–83, 85, 86, 106, 131–150
Course development, 20

COVID-19, 19, 32, 34, 179–199, 265
Culture-language nexus, 57, 58, 64, 73, 74, 168, 169
Curriculum, 9, 12, 13, 45–48, 53, 66–70, 72–74, 78, 79, 85, 104, 106, 132, 134–136, 144–146, 148, 149, 160–162, 166, 169, 171–173, 175, 247, 270, 276, 283, 285, 286, 288, 289, 291, 292, 296, 298, 308–310, 312, 313, 315, 319
Curriculum design, 45, 46, 53, 56, 59, 284

D
Doctorateness, 205–221

---

[1] Note: Page numbers followed by 'n' refer to notes.

E

EAL, *see* English as an additional language
EAP, *see* English for Academic Purposes
Ecological Systems Theory, 9
England, 3, 4, 6, 9, 13, 19–36, 43, 44, 63–86, 132, 135, 148, 149, 284
English as an additional language (EAL), 132, 234, 235, 297, 298
English for Academic Purposes (EAP), 5, 7, 13, 19–36, 215
English for Speakers of Other Languages (ESOL), 5, 13, 101–126, 307–324
ESOL, *see* English for Speakers of Other Languages
Etymology, 283–302
Explicit literacy teaching, 143

F

First-year students, 49, 51
Flipped learning, 13, 19–36, 190, 191, 194, 196
Foreign languages, 6, 7, 9, 13, 43, 68, 307

G

Global English, 42, 45, 56, 243

H

Higher education (HE), 5, 14, 23–25, 44, 58, 59, 102, 175, 179–182, 195–199, 218, 225, 229–231, 243, 244, 252, 259, 266
Holistic goals of language education, 85

I

Impact, 10, 13–14, 22–24, 45, 46, 48, 52, 53, 55, 57, 66, 69, 70, 79, 84, 102, 104, 107, 108, 116, 119, 121–125, 135, 137, 159, 174, 197, 199, 205–221, 227, 234, 266, 288, 293, 302, 318–320, 322, 332, 333
Inclusion, 181, 185, 186, 251, 308, 310, 314, 324
Innovation, 3–15, 21, 36, 41, 46, 48, 53, 64, 69, 72–74, 131–135, 138, 157, 162–165, 175, 180, 205–221, 226–227, 230, 234, 274, 276, 331–335
Innovative pedagogies, 12, 64, 85, 169
Integration, 46, 53, 104, 106, 107, 136, 146, 163, 170, 171, 207, 212, 217, 272, 310, 323
Intercultural understanding (ICU), 63–65, 67–69, 74, 77–79, 82, 85, 86
International students, 5, 6, 13, 22, 225, 227, 228, 230, 232, 233, 235
Iteration, 12, 36, 208, 272, 332

K

Key Stage 3, 66, 68, 78, 106, 133, 134, 136, 145, 146, 148

Index

L

Language, 3–15, 22, 41–59, 63–86, 102, 108–113, 119–122, 131, 135–137, 157–176, 182, 205–221, 225, 230–231, 235–237, 242–247, 250–251, 259, 285, 307–324, 331–335
Language assessment, 104, 107, 108, 111–113, 119, 120, 123, 124
Languages other than English, 43, 53, 159
Language teacher education, 319, 321, 322
Language teaching, 11, 45, 47, 55, 56, 58, 64, 67, 71, 72, 132, 160, 164, 165, 175, 214, 221, 227, 234, 260, 264, 274, 287, 317
Leadership, 12, 228, 261
Local languages, 157–176

M

Metalinguistic awareness, 291, 293
Module development, 219
Morphology, 108, 283–302
Motivation, 27, 42, 46, 64–66, 68–78, 81–83, 85, 86, 108, 134, 135, 138–140, 149, 161, 167, 169, 175, 180, 181, 189, 192, 194–196, 274, 313, 320

N

Nation of Sanctuary, 307–324
Northern Ireland, 4, 14, 22, 43, 101–126, 131–150, 284, 298

O

Online learning, 30, 35, 192–194, 198, 266, 270, 273

P

Participatory pedagogy, 13, 309, 315–317, 319, 321, 322, 324
Pedagogy, 12, 19, 28, 47, 64, 68, 72, 75–77, 103, 149, 161, 163, 168, 169, 173–176, 179, 195–198, 209, 213, 214, 264, 265, 274, 308, 310, 313–315, 319, 333
PGCE, 259–261, 264, 268, 275
Portfolio assessment, 221
Pre-sessional, 5, 19–36, 235
Primary languages, 67, 162, 164, 243, 244
Professional doctorate, 13, 205–221

R

Remote learning, 272

S

Scotland, 4, 6, 14, 22, 43, 157–161, 164, 165, 171, 182, 284
Student teaching, 29, 106, 212, 214, 259, 260n1, 261, 263, 274, 300

T

Teacher agency, 143
Teacher education, 12–14, 309, 311, 313–314, 316, 324, 333

Teaching English to Speakers of Other Languages (TESOL), 47–49, 51, 54, 55, 58, 205–206, 209–217, 220, 221, 317

Technology-enhanced learning (TEL), 179–199

W

Wales, 3, 4, 22, 43, 283–302, 307–324

Welsh education, 284

Widening participation, 13, 41–59, 312